PRAISE FOR *THE ZAPPOS EXPERIENCE*

"Often, business owners look at media darlings like Zappos with their mouths agape, full of awe but unable to take action. For those eager to do more than watch, Joseph Michelli deconstructs the Zappos story and makes it attainable."

Seth Godin
author of *Poke the Box*

"In your hands is a manifesto on how Zappos completely blew away the standard of delivering a consumer-centric experience and a revolutionary company culture. Joseph helps us all understand how to achieve a little more of that Zappos magic and happiness being crafted by one of the most influential companies of our generation."

Eric Ryan
method cofounder
person against dirty

"Zappos uses Net Promoter every day to make sure they are wowing customers and employees. In The Zappos Experience, Joseph Michelli shows how they do it. Zappos demonstrates that the best way to profitably grow a business is to build an army of promoters. Michelli shows you how Zappos builds that promoter army by making customers, employees, and investors very happy."

Fred Reichheld
Bain Fellow and author of
The Ultimate Question 2.0

THE ZAPPOS EXPERIENCE

5 PRINCIPLES *TO* INSPIRE, ENGAGE, *AND* WOW

JOSEPH A. MICHELLI

NEW YORK   CHICAGO   SAN FRANCISCO
LISBON   LONDON   MADRID   MEXICO CITY   MILAN
NEW DELHI   SAN JUAN   SEOUL   SINGAPORE
SYDNEY   TORONTO

To Fiona Katherine Michelli

You are sunshine that streams through a
window, warming every room you enter.
Never lose sight of the beauty and joy that
radiates through you, and always *believe*!
I love you. You will forever be my "little girl."

AUTHOR'S NOTE

If you would like to download a pdf file of all of the "Try These On for Size" sections of the book to be used as a group book study guide, please go to www.zappified.com/guide or point your mobile phone to the QR given here.

CONTENTS

FOREWORD

In 2010, my first book, *Delivering Happiness: A Path to Profits, Passion, and Purpose*, was published. While I was thrilled that it made the *New York Times* and *Wall Street Journal* bestseller lists, the most rewarding aspect of writing the book has been hearing on a daily basis from people who tell me how the book has inspired them to use happiness as a business model and as a guiding principle for life. We've made a lot of mistakes at Zappos, and part of my goal was to help other companies make fewer mistakes.

When Joseph Michelli approached me about *The Zappos Experience*, he said he wanted to continue the conversations that began in my book, particularly those that relate to the importance and value of a positive organizational culture, achieving work/life integration, enhancing service excellence, and facilitating personal emotional connections for delivering happiness in the workplace.

At Zappos, we've learned over the years, mostly through trial and error. A lot of what we have done has been based on instinct, and therefore it's sometimes challenging for us to explain succinctly how we do things to other organizations. I was intrigued by the prospect of a third party spending time embedded in our company and providing a comprehensive analysis of the key aspects of what makes Zappos tick. I was particularly interested in

Joseph's perspective as an organizational consultant whose specialty is creating employee engagement and customer loyalty.

At Zappos, our vision has evolved from making Zappos customers and employees happy to helping other companies and organizations make their customers and employees happy as well. In fact, Zappos Insights is a separate entity and website (www.zapposinsights.com) that we created precisely for this purpose.

So how is *The Zappos Experience* different from *Delivering Happiness*, and why should you care if you're not in the business of selling clothing and shoes online?

In all likelihood, *what* your business does will be very different from what Zappos does. My hope is that *Delivering Happiness* will help inspire the *why* of your business, while *The Zappos Experience* (along with Zappos Insights) can contribute to the *how* of your business.

I was originally asked to write a much longer foreword, but I ultimately decided to cut the length in half because (1) you're probably itching to get to the real content, (2) I personally have a disdain for reading long forewords, and (3) I'm too lazy to write any more.

Now that my part is done, I encourage you to sit back with a beverage of your choice (hydration is very important) or form a reading group so you can dive right into the ideas, tools, and discussion opportunities you'll uncover in *The Zappos Experience*.

Enjoy!

Tony Hsieh
Author of *Delivering Happiness* and
CEO of Zappos.com, Inc.

ACKNOWLEDGMENTS

How did this happen?

Don't get me wrong—I am not complaining. I'm just perplexed.

How did a guy like me, who never thought of himself as an author, complete a sixth book?

As I think about it, the answer is obvious—it is the result of a tremendous group of talented people who have worked tirelessly to move these writings along. *The Zappos Experience*, like the other books on which I have been fortunate enough to find my name, reflects the effort of a team of willing guides and adventurers.

Pulitzer Prize–winning historian and author David McCollough does a remarkable job of describing the "quest" that every book project involves: "Each book is a journey, an adventure, a hunt, a detective case, an experience, like setting foot in another continent in which you've never traveled. That's the joy of it. That's the compulsion of it. And you're fired by what we human beings are blessed with, called curiosity. It's what, among other things, distinguishes us from the cabbages. The more we know, the more we want to know; curiosity is accelerative."

Tony Hsieh, Zappos CEO, most notably facilitated this "hunt, detective case, and experience" by taking the time to evaluate this project, provide complete and open access within Zappos, review drafts, and even write the foreword. Tony has broken the mold for CEOs in America. No wonder he has sparked a Delivering Happiness Movement.

Consistent with the first value in the Zappos culture, three Zapponians were particularly instrumental in a "wow"-filled book-crafting process. Aaron Magness, Robert Richman, and Pam Cinko proved that the Zappos values are not just pretty words on paper—they are how Zapponians behave. Aaron, Robert, and Pam shared the Zappos family spirit at every turn. Their thoughtfulness, professionalism, humility, and playfulness not only made this book better, but made me better. While I am tempted to list a bevy of other Zapponians who served as guides through Zappos Headquarters and the Fulfillment Centers, I have placed those names within a special list in the Notes section in the back pages.

As for my team, I continue to be blessed by working alongside my talented, bright, and energetic research assistant, Jill Merkel. Jill put her running shoes on to chase after much of the content in this book. As always, I have benefited from the wisdom and guidance of Lloyd Rich, my publishing attorney. Tiffany Tolmen, thanks for keeping the speaking events chugging along smoothly in the midst of book madness.

My most significant companions on the Zappos journey (as they have been on three of my prior works) were Donya Dickerson, senior editor at McGraw-Hill, and Lynn Stenftenagel, my colleague at The Michelli Experience.

Donya understands what it takes to be the consummate editor. She has a keen eye for acquiring projects. She stewards and refines manuscript drafts, serves as a sounding board, and even offers needed moral support. More important, Donya is kind, compassionate, and efficient.

Lynn is simply indescribable! She is the person you want with you when your journey is difficult, when it's time to celebrate an accomplishment, and in every situation in between. She oozes "customer-centricity," and in Lynn's world, everyone is a customer. I just happen to be blessed to be the customer who derives the greatest benefit from her professional and friendship skills. Lynn, you are hugely *respected*.

At a most personal level, I wish to thank my children, Andrew and Fiona. You "inspire, engage, and wow" me. I know I don't deserve you, but I will forever be thankful for a God who has blessed me with the privilege of being your dad. Nora, my appreciation for you can never be adequately captured in an acknowledgments section. Instead, I hope to have ample opportunities to show that gratefulness in the "simple moments." May the fullness of my appreciation be abundantly clear from a deck looking at sunsets across a lake.

As with any great adventure, one must have a purpose for the quest. *You*, the readers, are that purpose! Thank *you* for taking this journey with me. I am extremely honored that you have chosen to invest your time. I hope this will truly be an experience of inspiration, engagement, and *wow*!

ZAPPOS? WHAT IS ZAPPOS?

I saw Winnie the Pooh running through the parking lot. Yes, I work at Zappos!

—@dylanbathurst (Twitter post)

Unconventional. That's one of the first words people use to describe Zappos. Even the name *Zappos* befits the unconventional character of one of the most transformational business success stories of our time.

In keeping with what you will learn about the unorthodox nature of Zappos, let's get started in a manner that's somewhat different from the beginning of your average business book. I'll quiz you! Fear not; the quiz consists of only one question, there will be no grading, and I have a hunch you'll do well. *Please choose the one response that reflects the best answer:*

Zappos is . . .

A. an Internet company that began by offering shoes online and went from virtually no sales to $1 billion in annual gross merchandise sales over a 10-year period, despite minimal advertising.

B. a purveyor of a wide array of online merchandise, including clothing accessories, home furnishings, and Halloween costumes.

C. the place where newly oriented employees are offered money to leave if they perceive themselves as not fitting the culture.

D. a company where being a little "weird" is part of the core values.

E. a work environment in which every person can offer descriptions of the company's culture that are published each year in an uncensored Culture Book.

F. one of *Fortune* magazine's top 10 best places to work.

G. the site of numerous spontaneous employee parades and other offbeat, playful activities.

H. a place where employees are offered classes on using Twitter.

I. a leader in social networking strategy and execution.

J. an obsession.

K. a standard-bearer for authentic and vibrant, albeit somewhat wacky, corporate culture.

L. a little start-up company that was sold to Amazon.com for approximately $1 billion.

M. a way of life.

N. a place where "happy hours" occur all day long and where shots of Gray Goose vodka are essential to celebration.

O. a company that helps other business leaders drive a service culture into their organizations through its Zappos Insights program.

P. a movement.

Q. the creator of more than 50,000 online product videos annually.

R. an innovator of enriched website "user" experiences.

S. actually ten companies in one, including training, fulfillment, and website divisions.

T. a business where the CEO makes $36,000 per year, wears jeans to work, sits in a centrally located cubicle, and has well over a million Twitter followers (@zappos).

U. a deliverer of happiness.

V. a company whose made-up name comes from a variation of the Spanish word for shoes: *zappatos*.

W. a place where the Headquarters and Fulfillment Centers host regular and highly sought-after tours.

X. a location where a call-center employee's longest inbound call lasted more than eight hours.

Y. a business you must study in order to achieve skyrocketing sales, an enviable culture, and a leadership position in customer service.

Z. all of the above, and so much more.

Of course the correct answer is Z, which stands for the very different and very much talked about Zappos.

Zappos is certainly different in every good sense of the word. Whether you are a customer who has been "wowed" by lightning-fast service and amazingly personal care, a social marketer who is benchmarking Zappos innovations, a business leader who wants to change a negative or sluggish workplace, or simply a student of powerful social forces, this book will offer you a chance to learn from a company that is changing the paradigm for how to deliver excellent service by embedding that service into its culture. Professor Peter Jackson, author of *Maps of Meaning: An Introduction to Cultural Geography*, wrote, "Cultures are maps of meaning through which the world is intelligible." At Zappos, leadership has offered a "map of meaning" that produces success powered by a culture of service.

BUZZ AND SUBSTANCE

It seems as if Zappos is popping up everywhere: articles in *Fast Company, Inc.*, *Harvard Business Review*, and *Psychology Today* and coverage on television programs like *CBS Sunday Morning* and *Nightline*. But is Zappos really worthy of your time and study? Are the company's lessons applicable to individuals whose businesses and lives go beyond online product sales?

Having studied, consulted with, and written about amazing businesses like Starbucks, The Ritz-Carlton Hotel Company, and the World Famous Pike Place Fish Market in Seattle, Washington, I daresay that the Zappos lessons are applicable not only to every business sector, but also to the personal and professional development of people at every level of an organization.

While the media image of Zappos often portrays an over-the-top playful culture that might not seem applicable in your industry or workplace, I challenge you to temporarily suspend your cynicism and explore the possibility that Zappos is neither too casual nor too weird. In fact, employees at Zappos demonstrate a commitment to hard work and excellence that the best companies in the most conservative of industries would envy. Style differences may exist; however, the underlying principles that drive success at Zappos will improve both your company and you. But before you accept my premise, let's make sure that we all understand how Zappos became the company it is today. Through the process of establishing a shared overview, I'll foreshadow some of the lessons any company can take away from spending time with Zappos.

JUST A SLIVER OF PERSPECTIVE

I am not here to give a comprehensive history of Zappos. In fact, no one can tell that story better than Tony Hsieh, the company's CEO. Fortunately, Tony has done a spectacular job of offering personal insights on the evolution of Zappos in his book titled *Delivering Happiness*. While I assume that many of you have picked up that book or will do so, I want to make sure that we all start with a basic understanding of several key elements that have contributed to the Zappos we are examining today. The Zappos Milestones sidebar provides a more detailed timeline of significant events in the history of Zappos.

Zappos Milestones

1999

- Founder Nick Swinmurn identifies the need for online shoe distribution and creates a site called ShoeSite.com.
- Successful entrepreneur Tony Hsieh meets Nick. Tony invests $500,000 in Swinmurn's business through a company that Tony cofounded with Alfred Lin named Venture Frogs.
- ShoeSite.com becomes Zappos.com, allowing the brand breadth for expansion beyond shoe sales.
- Negligible gross sales are reported.

2000

- Nick Swinmurn and Tony Hsieh function as co-CEOs of Zappos.
- Zappos records $1.6 million in gross sales.

2001

- Sustained effort produces $8.6 million in gross sales for Zappos.

2002

- Zappos leases the Fulfillment Centers in Shepherdsville, Kentucky.
- The brand elevates gross sales to $32 million.

2003

- Gross sales at Zappos rise to $70 million.

2004

- Sequoia Capital infuses a significant amount of cash into Zappos.
- Zappos moves its Headquarters and call-center operations to Henderson, Nevada.

2004 *(continued)*

- Zappos opens its first outlet store in Kentucky.
- Employee input is solicited for the publication of the first "Culture Book."
- Gross sales at Zappos more than double to $184 million.

2005

- Sequoia increases its investment in Zappos to a total of $35 million.
- Alfred Lin, cofounder of Venture Frogs, joins Zappos as CFO.
- A quit-now bonus of $100 is offered to new hires so that they will consider leaving the company after training if they think they aren't a fit with the culture at Zappos.
- Zappos is named E-tailer of the Year by *Footwear News*.
- Gross Zappos sales double again, to $370 million.

2006

- Nick Swinmurn leaves Zappos to follow a passion for creating other successful start-up businesses.
- Zappos expands and moves into larger Fulfillment Centers in Shepherdsville, Kentucky.
- Gross sales at Zappos climb to $597 million.

2007

- Zappos launches a Canadian site.
- Ebags.com's footwear and accessories e-tailer 6pm.com is acquired by Zappos.
- Zappos expands its product categories to include eyewear, handbags, clothing, watches, and kids' merchandise.
- Gross sales at Zappos hit $840 million.

2008

- Zappos lays off 8 percent of its workforce after investor Sequoia Capital, anticipating a sluggish economy, sends the message to its portfolio companies (including Zappos) that they need to cut expenses as much as possible and get to both profitability and positive cash flow.

Zappos Milestones

2008 *(continued)*

- Zappos Insights is launched to help leaders, managers, and employees from other businesses benchmark Zappos.
- Gross sales at Zappos hit $1 billion.

2009

- Amazon purchases Zappos for $1.2 billion.
- At age 10, Zappos debuts on *Fortune* magazine's 100 Best Companies to Work For® list at position 23, making it the highest-ranking newcomer for the year.
- Gross sales exceed $1 billion.
- Selected as Customer Service Champ by *BusinessWeek* in association with J.D. Power and Associates.
- Finalist for the Customer's Choice Awards from the National Retailer Federation.

2010

- Alfred Lin leaves Zappos to work for Sequoia Capital.
- Tony Hsieh releases his *New York Times*–bestselling book titled *Delivering Happiness.*
- Zappos moves from position 23 to position 15 on *Fortune*'s 100 Best Companies to Work For list.
- Zappos announces that to address its comprehensive business needs (including growth, seasonal workload, and attrition), it will hire 2,000 people in 2011.
- Zappos notes that it will move its corporate Headquarters from Henderson, Nevada, to the City Hall building in downtown Las Vegas.
- Zappos announces that it will open an office in San Francisco.
- Zappos overtakes L.L.Bean as the merchant delivering the best customer service according to the NRF Foundation/American Express Customers' Choice survey.

2010 (continued)
• Tony Hsieh, Jenn Lim (CEO and Chief Happiness Officer of *Delivering Happiness*) and the *Delivering Happiness* team take a 3-month, 23-city cross-country bus tour to spread happiness, share the message of the book, and talk to people inspired by it.
2011
• Zappos takes top honors in the sixth annual NRF Foundation/American Express Customers' Choice survey.
• Zappos moves from position 15 to position 6 on *Fortune*'s 100 Best Companies to Work For list.
• J.D. Power and Associates names Zappos a Customer Service Champion (one of 40 companies chosen from more than 1,000 businesses considered).
• Tony Hsieh and Jenn Lim announce the creation of the company Delivering Happiness, whose purpose is to inspire people and organizations around the world to use happiness frameworks in business and in life.

The big idea for Zappos came from little more than the observation of a frustrated consumer. Nick Swinmurn could not find a pair of size 11 Tan Airwalk Chukka boots despite a day of searching across San Francisco. This prompted Nick to wonder whether limited retail shoe selections could be expanded by an online strategy. He posed that very question to Venture Frogs, an investment company formed by college friends Tony Hsieh and Alfred Lin. But would Venture Frogs invest in Nick's idea of selling shoes online? Who would buy shoes at an Internet store without trying them on? The prevailing wisdom was that products like kitty litter (www.pets.com) would sell well online, but shoes?

Product and advertising notwithstanding, Zappos thrived, while www.pets.com became one of the premier examples of the "dot-gone" era. Despite buying a multi-million-dollar Super Bowl commercial and raising $82.5 million through an IPO in 2000, www.pets.com folded after a short run (from 1998 to 2000). Zappos remains. This just goes to show the importance of high-quality service in sustaining successful businesses.

From its inception in 1999 at the height of the dot-com boom, Zappos had a significant early history of being on the brink of extinction. Out of necessity, the company's staff members and leaders had to revolutionize a business model, craft an engaging culture, and develop unique operational features. Since I promised only to place the evolution of Zappos in perspective, I will highlight three critical, not necessarily linear, components of the Zappos survival journey. These three targeted historical pivot points offer insights regarding leadership decisions and staff efforts that kept the orders rolling in and the bankers, employees, and customers happy. Each of these pivotal transitions solidified the current Zappos culture and foreshadowed the lessons you will experience throughout the book.

1. Forging a Team with Diverse Strengths

Before Venture Frogs would agree to invest money in Nick Swinmurn's concept of an Internet shoe store, Tony Hsieh and Alfred Lin required Nick to partner with someone with expertise in the shoe business. Nick approached Fred Mossler (now known at Zappos as "just Fred"), asking him to leave a high-paying and stable job at Nordstrom. Fred recounts the unconventional way he was recruited to join the Zappos team: "Nick initially called me posing as a recruiter. He said he had something commerce-related and was looking for someone with a footwear background. I agreed to meet him at a little bar near the Nordstrom store after work one night. I went in with my suit and tie and looked around for a similarly clad person, and instead, this kid in Boardshorts and a T-shirt ran up to me, saying, 'Hi, I'm Nick. I'm not a recruiter. I've actually just got this idea.'"

Fred goes on to note that he spent approximately two hours with Nick at that initial meeting and was "peppered with questions. It was all ideas and a lot of inquiry as to what was possible and what wasn't in the shoe business. I wasn't sure what to make of our meeting, but we did communicate via e-mail for several more weeks."

Nick introduced Fred to Tony and Alfred, who had capitalized Venture Frogs through a $265 million sale of their prior business, LinkExchange, to Microsoft. Fred indicates that Tony and Alfred's prior success "gave me a little more comfort and confidence that there would be some teeth in this business." For weeks, Fred couldn't decide whether he wanted to leave Nordstrom to join Zappos, but a major shoe show was about to start, and the Zappos team would need to have a presence at the show to sign up vendors if they wanted to kick off their business and move forward. Fred recounts, "About a week before the shoe show, Nick called and said, 'Listen, if you're not going to join us, let me know now. Otherwise, I need you to take that leap of faith.' At that point, I said, 'All right. Let's do it.'"

As Zappos moved from the concept phase to an actual business, Tony, Alfred, Nick, and Fred appreciated one another's strengths and the importance of collaboration in achieving lasting business success. They merged their vastly different but important resources and set the foundation for the highly collaborative culture of Zappos today. Nick brought a great idea that identified a compelling consumer need. Fred added traditional shoe business expertise and a rich list of industry connections. Tony and Alfred contributed experience in creating entrepreneurial success, as well as adequate capital to start the company on the right trajectory. In the ensuing years, some of the faces have changed, but *the spirit of a collaborative and diverse corporate culture still offers Zappos a strong competitive advantage*.

2. The Courage to Try to Do What You Think Is "Right"

A great advantage for many Internet retailers is the low overhead they can enjoy relative to brick-and-mortar operations. By relying on their vendors to drop-ship products (send the product out directly from the vendor's warehouse), Internet retailers can focus their resources on marketing and creating easy user experiences that make their websites more attractive to customers. In this model, however, the Internet retailer loses control of service, as order fulfillment depends upon the vendors' processes.

Early on, leaders at Zappos realized that buying shoes online created considerable risk and anxiety for consumers and that this anxiety would be worsened if online shoppers had to depend upon the varied delivery practices of the company's vendors. As a result, the executive team at Zappos made the bold move to do what they felt customers needed. They leased a warehouse close to a United Parcel Service (UPS) shipping hub near Louisville, Kentucky, bought inventory from vendors, and committed to consistent and quick delivery to online purchasers. When efforts to have a third-party vendor oversee the warehouse operation faltered, Zappos took over the Fulfillment Center and, in typical Zappos fashion, used a trial-and-error approach to improve processes and maximize customer service.

The first Zappos employee to oversee the Zappos warehouse, Keith Glynn, notes, "Determining what we think is right for the customer, setting a course in that direction, diving in, making mistakes, and learning from those mistakes represents a lot of how Zappos was created. We went through the development of our own processes at the Fulfillment Center and figured things out as we went."

Among the many challenges that Keith and his team faced were the ability to code every item that came into the Fulfillment Center individually, the determination of which scanners were needed to manage inventory and locate items easily, and the selection of the best ways to stack and store merchandise so that the staff could fill orders quickly. Former COO and CFO Alfred Lin puts it this way: "The one thing that I think Zappos has done really well is to have a culture where you try new things, make mistakes, minimize the costs of those mistakes, but learn from them so that you don't make the same mistakes again." Keith and his team pioneered many breakthroughs as a result of their resilient approach, and today others frequently benchmark the processes of the Zappos Fulfillment Centers.

The Zappos story is rich with examples of its leaders thinking beyond the short-term profits of the company and targeting what they believe is right for their customers now and into the future. Once the customer's need is identified, leaders at Zappos demonstrate a consistent track record of assuming growth-oriented risks and making costly investments in areas like inventory management and customer service delivery. In the chapters ahead, you will be provided opportunities to learn from the customer-centric practices at Zappos to *deliver products or services as efficiently as possible*. You will experience a nimble company that is not afraid to set lofty service goals and learn from its miscalculations.

3. Passion, Determination, and Humility

During the most arduous and desperate times in the early evolution of Zappos, Tony Hsieh became increasingly more involved with and committed to the company. From what started as a fairly hands-off approach to Zappos operations, Tony became more instrumental in the daily affairs of the business. Through his passionate increase in effort, and ever-dwindling financial resources, the brand averted one near-death experience after another.

Whether it was moving a fledgling Zappos into the Venture Frogs office space or extending extra personal money so that Zappos could make payroll, Tony led by example. Rhonda Ford, one of the first employees hired at the Zappos Fulfillment Center, notes, "It was tough going early on. When I pulled into the parking lot for the first time, I wasn't sure if I was in the right place because there wasn't even a sign. The leaders handed me a scanner and said my job was to verify the orders that came down the line. That was my training. But the care and compassion I have experienced ever since has been amazing. In those early days, Zappos leaders helped our small team of about 20 people set up the Fulfillment Center. From the beginning, those leaders demonstrated concern about us, seeking to know us personally. Tony was right there. He expressed genuine interest in our kids and our hobbies. Tony and the other leaders have always treated us as equals. We are all Zappos. Leaders have never been too self-important to pick orders or to run across the warehouse so that a customer's item makes it on the delivery truck. We follow the leadership's example of dedicated effort. Zappos used to operate on very tight resources, but something about our leaders' humility and persistence gave me comfort that we would make it."

Zappos would not be around today were it not for the presence, dedication, and humility of the company's early leaders. Additionally, Zappos would not be worthy of study if it weren't for its rich culture of determination and emotional investment demonstrated daily by all staff members (Zapponians). In many ways, individuals and companies facing early adversity that thrive against the odds often learn *it pays to be humble, impassioned, and persistent.*

ZAPPOS UNIQUE VALUE PROPOSITION—MORE THAN WORDS: ACTION AND PEOPLE

The leaders at Zappos have the all-too-rare distinction of practicing what they preach. This is particularly true when it comes to service, values, and culture. For all the leadership hype about service being a priority across the business landscape, Sherrie Mersdorf, senior database marketing analyst at Cvent, notes, "The quality of customer service has been on a serious decline for years. Research from TARP Worldwide and the American Customer Satisfaction Index both agree." By contrast, at Zappos, where the tagline is "powered by service," the strength of service behaviors is resulting in customer engagement scores that continue to rise and customer loyalty that has fueled the company's steep sales escalation.

When it comes to culture and values, CEO Tony Hsieh might sound somewhat like other leaders by referring to his company's values as being "synonymous" with the Zappos brand. However, Tony also understands that it takes far more than words to produce a values-based culture; "The best way to know the Zappos culture is to take a tour or interact with our people.

Values are not what we put on paper; they're what people do and how they feel doing it."

From the inception of the company, Zappos leadership understood the importance of feelings in determining behavior. For example, the leaders continually seek to translate values into feelings of "trust" for all stakeholders (vendors, employees, and customers). Trust at the customer level takes the form of free returns, sending out a new order to replace a yet-to-be-returned item long before that item is received back at Zappos, and honoring returns up to 365 days from date of purchase. While many traditional business leaders might view these Zappos "trusting" policies as unnecessary expense, Zappos has structured its approach in a well-designed cost strategy.

According to Alicia ("AJ") Jackson, a Customer Loyalty Team (CLT) member, the trust experienced by customers is also reflected in the faith extended to staff, "Our leaders put such a great level of trust in us to do the right thing without hemming us in through scripts or unnecessary rules. They also encourage us to grow and have fun with our peers. Because of the way we are treated, Zappos gets the best from us, and so do our customers. Obviously, some people will violate trust, and you can manage that when it happens, but that doesn't justify distrusting. You get so much in return when trust is extended—you get wow."

By making consistent choices to trust staff members and customers in often small but unexpected ways, the leadership at Zappos has essentially created customer wows, a loving family environment, and an enriched customer experience. Some Zappos customer communiqués even sign off, "With love, The Zappos Customer Loyalty Team." For some, "love" may seem like an odd concept in the context of business, but in the words of Peter

Senge, author of the classic business book *The Fifth Discipline*, love is nothing more nor less than "a commitment to someone else's growth and development." Zappos lives that commitment to staff members, customers, and vendors alike.

How far will Zappos go to earn trust and love? What measures will it take to live up to a core value of "delivering wow through service"? One need only look to how the company's leaders handled a major pricing error. The situation is best described in the words of Aaron Magness, senior director, Brand Marketing & Business Development, in a blog post on the Zappos Family blog site immediately after the error occurred:

> Hey everyone—As many of you may know (and I'm sure a lot of you do not), 6pm.com is our sister site. 6pm.com is where brandaholics go for their guilt free daily fix of the brands they crave. Every day, the site highlights discounts on products ranging up to 70% off. Well, this morning, we made a big mistake in our pricing engine that capped everything on the site at $49.95. The mistake started at midnight and went until around 6:00 am PST. When we figured out the mistake was happening, we had to shut down the site for a bit until we got the pricing problem fixed.
>
> While we're sure this was a great deal for customers, it was inadvertent, and we took a big loss (over $1.6 million— ouch) selling so many items so far under cost. However, it was our mistake. We will be honoring all purchases that took place on 6pm.com during our mess up. We apologize to anyone that was confused and/or frustrated during

our little hiccup and thank you all for being such great customers. We hope you continue to Shop. Save. Smile. at 6pm.com.

Cheers!
Aaron Magness

Something tells me that, unlike Zappos, many other companies purporting to have customer- and employee-centric values would not have shown this much "love." Those businesses would probably have found a way to invalidate the errant purchases (possibly offering a token coupon to offset the blow of the canceled sale), and they certainly would have dismissed or reprimanded the responsible employee (as opposed to seeing it as an opportunity for that employee's growth and development). To be trusted, one must trust. To become a beloved brand, business leaders must demonstrate their genuine interest in the well-being of their staff members and customers. Whether for business or in one's personal life, Zappos demonstrates that love and trust can't be commanded or demanded and that they must be offered if they are to be received.

Because leaders at Zappos demonstrate a commitment to the growth and development ("love") of their company's employees and their customers, consumers and staff return their love for Zappos through consistent referrals, positive social media chatter, and repeat business. This loyalty, resulting in 75 percent of orders each day being placed by returning customers, allows Zappos to spend less on marketing and advertising and instead invest more in truly delivering wow through service.

Building a vibrant culture, living in accordance with one's values, and translating service directly into loyal return business are but a few of the many differentiators between Zappos and other well-intentioned companies. I have come to call the totality of these differences the "Zappos Experience."

A comprehensive expression of insider views can be found each year in the Zappos Culture Book, which is available free of charge to anyone who wants one. Go to http://culturebook.org or if you have QR reader software installed on your mobile phone camera, point the camera at the box provided here and head directly to the site.

WHAT IS THE ZAPPOS EXPERIENCE?

There is no shortage of opinions from both inside and outside Zappos as to what constitutes the Zappos Experience. For our purposes, I will offer just a few voices of Zapponians on the Zappos Experience.

CEO Tony Hsieh shares, "If you want to know the Zappos Experience, look to our 10 core values." Former COO and CFO Alfred Lin comments that the Zappos Experience is "about getting the culture right so we can treat the customer right. If we do the right thing for the customer and improve the customer experience, everything else follows." Fred Mossler, "just Fred," suggests, "From a merchandising perspective, the Zappos Experience is a great opportunity, a blank slate to hopefully set up the utopia and create a world where it's win/win. It's also about putting people's passion in a place where they have the greatest likelihood to deliver excellent results." Chris Nielsen, the current CFO at Zappos, who joined the company from Amazon after Alfred's departure, describes the Zappos Experience as the reaction he gets when he mentions that he works for Zappos: "It's an emotional connection. When I talk to people about working here, they don't mention our products as much as they say, 'I love Zappos.'"

A sampling of Zappos employees produced the following descriptions of the Zappos Experience:

> It's not about selling merchandise. I don't even think of us as a retailer. To be honest, the Zappos Experience is about wanting to change the world and the way people are treated in business.
> Rachael Brown, Pipeline Team

> It is working hard but also taking mini-play breaks. It is leadership understanding that fun helps to get things done and that happy employees give so much more. It is a family. My husband is disabled. I lost my father recently. I lost a brother

*at Christmas. The fact that I can come to work and
have fun is central to the quality of my life. The
Zappos Experience is something I thank God for
every day.*

Mary Johnson, Zappos Fulfillment Centers

*Put simply, it's the freedom and the expectation
that you will do the right thing for people.*

Jeff Lewis, Customer Loyalty Team (CLT) member

Maybe the best way to appreciate the Zappos Experience
is through an example of the way Zappos staff members do the
right thing for people—customers and noncustomers alike. Jesse
Cabaniss, CLT member, notes, "A customer called and shared
that her neighbor's house had just burned down. In an instant,
our entire CLT voluntarily went into action. We took up a collection for our customer's neighbor. We looked for items that could
help them or make their day. It wasn't so much about money;
it was about compassion and encouragement. So we put cards,
heartfelt messages, Zappos T-shirts, etc., into a big care package.
I know a lot of people would think it odd to do something like
that for a stranger or someone who isn't likely to produce a profit
for you in return, but that's just the way we do things here at Zappos. The company takes care of us. We take care of one another
and even care for the people we happen upon." Although the
staff expected nothing from their efforts, Jesse happily reports,
"We received a thank-you e-mail and even a video from our customer and the family whose home had burned down. I think everyone in the company saw that video. It was playing all the time,
and it was a reminder of why we are here and what it means to
work at Zappos."

I have often suggested the measure of you as a person is what people say about you when you are not around. This is equally true for brands. Many customer voices are included throughout the book, but it seems only fitting, given the innovative use of Twitter at Zappos, to share how some customers "tweet" their take on the Zappos Experience in 140 characters or less:

> @ptubach
> Went to an Indian restaurant that gave me a free beer for showing up too early to get my food. This place is like the Zappos of Indian food!

> @kaydtastic
> Ordered boots from zappos last night at midnight, and they've already shipped. It happens that way every time, but it still amazes me!

> @stevemcstud
> **Me:** We should get an Au Pair
> **Her:** What if I don't like her
> **Me:** We send her back to where she came from
> **Her:** This isn't Zappos!

While not everything can be returned as easily as Zappos products, one thing is certain: customers keep returning to the Zappos website to place orders, and they encourage their friends and colleagues to do the same.

From my perspective, the Zappos Experience reflects a culture that is committed to impassioned service delivery, transparent communication, acceptance of differences, and weirdness—a highly playful, highly productive, and innovative business where staff members and customers become fully engaged and emotionally connected.

YOUR UNIQUE OPPORTUNITY TO GET ZAPPED

Since the company acts from its values to "build open and honest relationships with communication" and to "pursue growth and learning," I have been given the opportunity to guide you through one of the wackiest winners in business history. To that end, I have identified five core business principles that I will use as a map for your behind-the-scenes exploration of the company. This inside look reveals how you can elevate service excellence in your business and your personal life. While these principles may seem fairly easy to grasp, applying them consistently may prove challenging. Typically it is consistent execution that differentiates a Zappos from other well-meaning yet average businesses or mediocre individual service providers.

From my perspective, the Zappos Experience can best be described as adherence to the following business precepts:

1. Serve a perfect fit.

2. Make it effortlessly swift.

3. Step into the personal.

4. S T R E T C H.

5. Play to win.

With the expedited velocity of an order being processed from the Zappos website immediately to your door, let's dive into each of these concepts and together learn how Zappos can help you zap your leadership, your culture, and your service, be it professional or personal, to the next level!

Serve a Perfect Fit

Coming together is a beginning.
Keeping together is progress.
Working together is success.
—HENRY FORD

Let's assume you have a job opening. Your final decision comes down to a choice between two equally qualified candidates; both applicants present well and have impressive work histories in addition to glowing references. How do you decide which will be the better fit for your organization? Just as customers seek an ideal fit from your products or services (in the case of Zappos, maybe a pair of shoes or a jacket), you must seek staff members who suit your culture. As you will soon see, one of the key elements in Zappos success has been its leadership's uncanny ability to bring together a team of like-minded employees who are dedicated to common goals and objectives. Zappos has, in essence, made a priority of ways to "serve a perfect fit" between its purpose and its people.

By "serving a perfect fit," I am referring to the importance of identifying your core values and selecting individuals who share those values. The principle also entails the use of your company values to inform your business decisions and to defend your culture against internal and external threats. Few businesses define culture, communicate values, or serve a better culture fit than Zappos.

Like all the principles in this book, "Serve a Perfect Fit" is unpacked across two chapters. Chapter 2, "It All Comes Back to Culture," focuses on how the leaders at Zappos chose and uncovered the core values that underpin their company. It explores the all-inclusive process the leaders use to articulate the Zappos values, and it examines how your company can either create your first set of values or reexamine your existing ones. "It All Comes Back to Culture" concludes with approaches used by Zappos leaders and staff to hire people with whom they want to spend time.

Chapter 3, "Culture Should Be a Verb," takes you through the Zappos revolutionary approach to new hire orientation and onboarding. In fact, the Zappos enculturation process is so different from ordinary paradigms that it will make you think twice about the way you bring your new hires into your business. "Culture Should Be a Verb" also offers a view of the one-of-a-kind strategies that supercharge the Zappos culture. Without further ado, it's time to use Zappos as a benchmark for your corporate culture and values.

2

IT ALL COMES BACK TO CULTURE

While the Zappos culture is enviably strong today, the journey to its well-defined values was not exactly linear. The way the leaders at Zappos developed their culture and defined their values should offer hope, insight, and encouragement to those who lack a written set of values or feel there is a gap between their purported corporate values and the actual culture of their business.

Most businesses already have a set of written values that sound as if they could apply at any and every business. In many cases, employees are not able to recite those values, let alone act in accordance with them, and have no idea where the guiding principles came from. Staff members may not see the values as being relevant to their day-to-day lives and may even view them as being out of step with current business conditions. And in cases where the corporate values do capture the core qualities of a business, the actions of employees may not demonstrate the values in a way that allows consumers to differentiate the business from its competition. Ultimately, many company leaders just don't know what makes them different from rival businesses or what is at the core of their identity. They are "doing" business, but internal guiding or defining principles do not drive them.

"Serving a perfect fit" implies that you fully understand your business so that you can determine such things as whether a new hire will blend in well or even whether the signage throughout your building fits with the essence of your brand. We will examine how Zappos came to know who it is and how it determined what cultural characteristics were needed for success. This exploration will offer a valuable template that will let you identify, evolve, and gain input into the relevance and uniqueness of your corporate values. You will also see how the leaders at Zappos take their core values and use them to select employees who fit their unique culture. This should serve to guide your processes for creating multiple filters to ensure that you select those who truly will "serve a perfect fit" for you.

SOME VALUES ARE KNOWN AT THE START; OTHERS ARE DISCOVERED ON THE JOURNEY

While a positive corporate culture was always on the radar of the leaders at Zappos (given their prior experiences in less-than-positive work environments), as in so many other start-ups, these leaders did not *explicitly* define their core values when they launched their business. However, even without writing their values down, the Zappos leaders *implicitly* demonstrated what they believed by the actions they took in establishing the business. For example, from the beginning, the Zappos leadership aspired to create a work environment that was fun and communal. These leaders understood that people who play together stay together and that a team and family spirit was essential for their brand's survival. To give their company the best chance of success with the limited human and early financial capital they had at their disposal, the Zappos leadership believed members of their small team would be heavily reliant on one another and would be spending an inordinate number of hours together. If the work wasn't fun and the team wasn't tightly connected, the heavy lifting required at start-up would not have been possible.

While concepts like "fun" or creating a "family spirit" were considerations from the outset, the Zappos current value to "deliver wow through service" was not a significant consideration at the company's launch. Originally, the leaders at Zappos merely sought to develop a user-friendly website with a vast shoe selection that would attract the $2 billion market of people who buy shoes from catalogs. Specifically, Zappos was envisioned to be the "premier destination for online shoes."

As the Zappos juggernaut began to pick up speed and as its online inventory expanded, its leaders began to clearly see that product selection alone would not be sufficient to sustain long-term success. As a result, those leaders began to widen their strategic focus and appreciate the importance of delivering service excellence. Former COO and CFO Alfred Lin comments, "When we launched, we weren't as aware of the importance of service delivery to the success of Zappos. That's why we started with a drop-ship model—letting vendors send out shoes from their warehouses to the Zappos customers. Early on, when we heard from customers or potential customers or sought their input directly, it became very obvious that to buy any product online, particularly a pair of shoes, customers had to have faith that the shoes would show up as promised in a timely fashion after their credit card payment was processed." In essence, the customers valued not only selection and ease of use, but also service reliability.

When the leaders at Zappos identified service excellence as being central to the future of their business, the young company was functionally, albeit not formally, making a commitment to adopt the same value that its customers were placing on service delivery. Actions like the discontinuance of drop shipping demonstrated that Zappos was beginning to see service as a priority. When CEO Tony Hsieh stated, "We want to be the best in customer service," in essence, he formally declared that Zappos would place a high value on service and that its leaders would act accordingly. As a result, decisions were required to support that declared value. The actions that followed, many of which involved extensive capitalization and disruptions for the young company, were completely consistent with Tony's declaration. These challenges included the leasing of the Zappos Fulfillment Center operation in Kentucky, technological solutions to help vendors see exactly how their products were selling on the Zappos .com website, and a move of the Zappos corporate Headquarters and call center from San Francisco to Las Vegas. The latter move, for example, was predicated on leaders appreciating that Las Vegas had a rich service-based workforce that was accustomed to working around the clock and that such a talent pool would be essential to meet the needs of a growing call center.

While the company still lacked a formal statement of values, the Zappos cultural identity was evolving in the direction of service. It's been said that if you want to know what someone values, watch where he places his feet and what he does with his wallet. Customers vote their values with their wallets. Leaders demonstrate their values through their decisions about priorities and resources. For example, when companies talk about corporate social responsibility but act solely for profits and short-term gains, it is the implicit value (the unstated one) of seeking money that trumps the explicit value (the formally expressed one) of social good. At Zappos, values were becoming clearer based on both what was beginning to be stated and what leaders were actually doing.

TRY THESE ON FOR SIZE

1. Do you have explicit corporate values? If so, do those values reflect a blend of your founding principles and the evolving demands of the marketplace? Or are they static and immutable?

2. What do your customers value? How do your corporate values match up with the wants, needs, and desires of your customers?

3. Since values can be both explicit (stated) and implicit (unstated), do your corporate actions align with your stated values? If not, what do the major decisions of your business suggest about your company's real values?

4. How willing are you to consider revising your stated values to match your demonstrated actions or revising your actions to match your stated values? What might those revisions look like?

THE VALUE OF WRITTEN VALUES

Early on, although some aspects of the Zappos key business values were being articulated publicly, none had been codified into a "core values" document. Like many entrepreneurs, the early leaders at Zappos were doers. They saw opportunity and seized it. By nature, they sought to be nimble and adaptive and did not wish to be encumbered by policies and practices associated with corporate behemoths. In fact, the Zappos leadership resisted producing a set of written company values because they viewed the document production process as a fundamentally "corporate" exercise. However, in the end, scalability and the unsettling nature of growth pushed the company to translate its unique culture into words.

When Zappos was in its early start-up phase, the small band of Zapponians shared many common traits, including a strong willingness to embrace change, a determined work ethic, and the capacity to develop tight social bonds from fun activities that emerged in the midst of long hours dedicated to the business. In those days, when the company needed talent in a given area, this group often turned to friends or friends of friends to fill the demands of the growing business. As a result of these informal hiring processes, new hires tended to be fairly similar to the individuals who were already on board at Zappos. Layoffs and lean economic times also helped trim out those who were least committed to the Zappos concept. So the Zappos zealots rolled on!

For a considerable portion of Zappos history, Tony and Fred were a part of all hiring decisions to make sure that new hires would "fit" into Zappos unique culture. As the business grew, leaders at Zappos increasingly began to rely on outside firms to recruit and select talent. However, it became alarmingly clear that this outsourced talent selection process was threatening the Zappos culture and the brand's future.

Rachael Brown, manager of Pipeline, the Zappos department that is responsible for training and development, notes, "When we were hiring straight from employment agencies, we weren't serving a good fit, let alone a perfect Zappos fit. We'd hold orientation classes for 30 new hires and immediately realize that few of these individuals were likely to be successful here. These people weren't going to be happy in our environment, and I was concerned about their impact on a culture I loved. I didn't like seeing people get hired by agencies who didn't understand us." Loren Becker, supervisor of Pipeline, adds, "While we had a strong culture when we started training, we didn't have our values articulated. Fortunately, Tony stepped up by simply sending out an e-mail asking, 'Who in our company do you think is really successful and what do they do? What are their attributes?' Tony got all those attributes compiled and asked us to look at a list of about 37 descriptors. In essence, he was surveying us on what we thought our culture was and what it should be." Tony started a process to put into words what had previously been a strong but unstated culture. It was hoped that those words would essentially describe Zappos, so that the right people could find their way to the company and be selected.

Where else but Zappos does the CEO uncover the values of the organization by starting with a companywide e-mail? There is no way that could work. It's absurd! Right?

Wrong! Rather than taking the more traditional approach of bringing senior leaders to a facilitated off-site retreat and generating a list of values that sound more like platitudes and less like cultural descriptors or realistic road maps for action, Tony Hsieh turned directly to the Zappos family. In keeping with the spirit of collaboration discussed in Chapter 1, Tony sought the diverse strengths of the entire employee base. His inquiry went to the heart of what key factors had been fueling and directing Zappos all along. By asking for and listening to the input of his staff, Tony received broad and unusual descriptors that weren't limited to the insights of only a few senior leaders.

What an odd yet refreshing way to define the essence of a culture—by listening to the collective voices of those who live and create it every day. By drawing upon the insights of the entire employee base, Tony gained instant ownership of and buy-in for the final written set of values. Tony and other Zappos leaders did not need to create a communication plan to educate and "sell" the values internally. Moreover, as shown in the table on page 35, Tony's approach resulted in values unlike those that typically emerge from leadership retreats.

TRY THESE ON FOR SIZE

1. What are your personal values? Have you taken the time to examine your values lately? If you asked people who know you well, what values would they ascribe to you? Would those values align with your self-perception?

2. From a business perspective, are you willing to ask your entire company to weigh in on your current and aspirational values? What percentage of your company's employees would say that your current values meet the CRUD test of being credible, relevant, unique, and durable?

3. How would you describe the values that currently define your company?

4. What values can you credibly aspire to in your business? What would it take to move those values from aspiration to reality?

Comparative List of Traditional Corporate Values vs. the Zappos 10 Core Values	
TRADITIONAL	**ZAPPOS CORE VALUES**
Honesty	1. Deliver wow through service
Respect	2. Embrace and drive change
Responsibility	3. Create fun and a little weirdness
Fairness	4. Be adventurous, creative, and open-minded
Excellence	5. Pursue growth and learning
Professionalism	6. Build open and honest relationships with communication
Diversity	7. Build a positive team and family spirit
Efficiency	8. Do more with less
Flexibility	9. Be passionate and determined
Innovation	10. Be humble

TO FIT, IT MUST BE TANGIBLE

Given the challenges that came to Zappos with growth and relocation, articulating and preserving its culture rose to and remains a
substantial business priority. By extending the process of defining
core values to the entire organization, Zappos leaders signified that
culture is everyone's domain and responsibility. The core values
that emerged from enterprisewide involvement essentially differ-
entiated Zappos from any other e-commerce competitor.

The Zappos process of defining values provides tools that
all of us can use to clarify our personal and corporate values.
To fully capture the unique dynamic forces that are at play in
a given culture, all stakeholders must participate in answering

questions like: Who are we? What brings us together? What do we collectively value? Leaders need to listen to the consensus of their people and weave their teams' voices into a defining document that serves the overall well-being and sustainability of the business. If this values identification process is handled well, as was the case at Zappos, the resulting values will be credible, relevant, unique, and durable (easily and lovingly remembered by the acronym CRUD).

MAYBE FOR A START-UP LIKE ZAPPOS, BUT NOT FOR ME

Some business owners with long-standing written values might accept the lessons of the Zappos core value creation but feel incapable of changing their existing values structure. Those leaders might even concede that some of their values are a little stale, are a bit out of sync with reality, or lack demonstrated acceptance by their people. But those executives may liken values to children: you can't send them back for new ones. While change simply for the sake of change is a flawed business approach, so too is an unwillingness to reevaluate or change aspects of your business when those components lack relevance or ring hollow. Refining values is a big deal, but not refining them may be a deal breaker.

Realizing that his business might benefit from an injection of new ideas, Dave Brautigan, COO of Atlanta Refrigeration, a commercial HVAC, refrigeration, and cooking equipment sales and service company in Atlanta, Georgia, took part in an initial Zappos Insights group training. Dave was one of 10 people selected from a group who applied on the Zappos website to participate in this new project, which became the launch pad for a corporate training arm of Zappos formally referred to as Zappos Insights (much more on Zappos Insights in Chapter 9). Dave and other group members traveled to the Zappos Headquarters in Nevada and spent two days engaging in sessions about the culture at Zappos and participating in conversations with members of the Zappos staff, including considerable time with senior leadership.

Dave reported that his interest in Zappos was sparked by what he had researched about the company. Approximately nine years before participating in the Zappos Insights group, Dave and his brother had assumed management of his father's company. According to Dave, "When my father ran the business, he had 8 employees and about $800,000 in annual revenue during those 30 years of business operation. When my brother and I took over, we grew the business to more than 100 employees and $15 million in annual revenue. But we were having problems from a culture standpoint, and I couldn't figure out why. I knew that Zappos was operating in a very different industry, as our workforce was composed of fairly introverted people doing highly technical work in the field, but we still wanted to deliver the same customer service for which Zappos is known."

Among the many practical tips Dave took away from that first extended encounter with Zappos was a realization that the leverage point for elevating service execution was a reconsideration of the "habits" or "values" that had long since been defined at Atlanta Refrigeration. Dave notes, "The Zappos customer service agents are like our technicians. Those jobs can attract less than fully motivated, 'let's go take over the world'–type people. Worse yet, people are often selected primarily based on their technical skills, not on how they will serve others or whether their values will allow them to fit in with others on the team. In a nutshell, we realized we had work to do to better clarify who we really were and what we really valued. That was a huge launching point for us."

No matter what developmental stage your business is in, it is not too late to recheck and reset your culture. If your business is not operating maximally, it is probably time for you to rethink the types of people you will need to select to make the journey ahead. If your culture is functional, it may be time to determine its essence and start making selection choices that are consistent with the values that drive your uniqueness. A willingness to take a hard stand in the selection process and hold out for people who align with your values represents a quintessential discipline needed to "serve a perfect fit."

ZAPPIFIED BRAIN BREAK

Did you know? While shoes have a long history, the decomposition of their source material has left a short archaeological record. The oldest physical evidence of shoes dates back about 10,000 years. Those shoe remnants were found at dig sites in (drum roll please) . . . you guessed it—Oregon and California. Does that mean that both Zappos and shoes can be traced back to California?

VALUES AWARENESS—THE TICKET FOR ADMISSION

If you have *any* contact with Zappos, you are likely to be exposed to the company's 10 core values. When you visit the zappos.com website, you will see one of the 10 core values on a revolving banner prominently located on the landing page. Customers will also see the values printed on the delivery boxes. If you are seeking employment at Zappos, you better have a keen awareness of the company's values. Frankly, it would be difficult for applicants to miss the core values, even as they begin to contemplate employment. For example, as you click to the Zappos job listing page, you will see a message in a Zappos playful voice emphasizing the importance of checking out the Zappos core values before you consider employment. Here is an example of a typical Zappos job page:

> The Zappos Family currently has career opportunities in 2 fabulous locations. One location is in the "City of Sin." Yep, Las Vegas, Nevada. Our other location is home to the Jim Beam Distillery and the Zappos Fulfillment Centers. You got it, Shepherdsville, Kentucky. We do not currently have any work-from-home opportunities. (Sorry!)

> Please check out the Zappos Family's 10 Core Values before applying! They are the heart and soul of our culture and central to how we do business. If you are "fun and a little weird"—and think the other 9 Core Values fit you too—please take a look at our openings, and find the one or two that best fit your skills, experience, and interest!

> Why consider opportunities with us? In February 2011, Zappos.com, Inc. and its affiliates were named #6 on the 2010 Fortune: 100 Best Companies to Work For List.

> And . . . we're hiring like crazy right now and looking for smart, forward-thinking problem solvers to join our world-class and fairly wacky team.

Zappos unashamedly puts its values right up front. The employment page, with its written emphasis on values, is enriched by videos showing what it's like to work at Zappos and other videos made by Zapponians who talk about and, yes, sing about the relationship of values to the Zappos Experience. It takes extra clicks to get to pages where a list of jobs is posted and where the technical requirements of a job can be found.

In the spirit of being a little weird and embracing change, Zappos also encourages applicants to break the mold of ordinary applications by noting, "Cover letters are soooo old-fashioned, don't you think? Show us who you are with a cover letter VIDEO! You will be able to upload one when applying for a position."

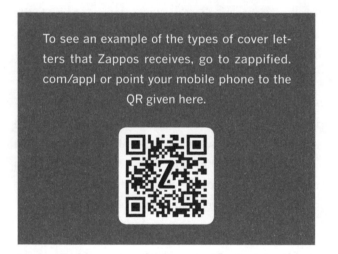

To see an example of the types of cover letters that Zappos receives, go to zappified. com/appl or point your mobile phone to the QR given here.

Social media messages from prospective applicants speak to the energy invested in these videos, with people tweeting about spending the better part of a week shooting the video that will accompany their application. Hmmm, I wonder which form of cover letter would give an employer a better sense of how passionate, determined, adventurous, creative, open-minded, and humble an applicant is—a typed narrative or a free-form video submission.

> ### TRY THESE ON FOR SIZE
>
> 1. How prominent are your values in the prospective applicant's journey to your job posting?
>
> 2. Do you specifically direct applicants to review your core values?
>
> 3. Have you involved your employees in videos, or other creative vehicles that fit your business, to give a flavor for the role of values in your organization?
>
> 4. Do you give applicants options on how they present their application or cover letter so that you can get a richer sense of them even before you look at their qualifications?

SELECT ONLY THOSE WITH WHOM YOU WOULD WANT TO SPEND TIME

Let's assume a prospective employee sends her application and video cover letter to Zappos, believing she is a culture fit. Let's further assume this applicant may or may not have the technical skills that are optimal for a listed job. What happens next? According to Rebecca Henry Ratner, HR director at Zappos, "That's when the fun begins for us. Because we are lucky enough to have a distinct and desirable brand, we get huge volumes of applicants. After an initial screening with unusual questions that are specifically crafted to gauge an applicant's alignment with our values, those who appear to fit best with our culture will go through an involved process of 'getting to know you.' We want to make sure those applicants really are right for us and, equally important, that we are right for them." (For more specific information on culture fit questions asked at Zappos, a downloadable "Zappos Family Core Values Interview Assessment Guide" is available to Zappos Insights members.)

Rebecca makes it clear that Zappos is *not* right for everyone and that a lot of people who visit the corporate Headquarters near Las Vegas conclude that they will *not* be happy in a playful, energized environment. Rebecca shares, "Zappos would drive some people nuts. Being here would cause them to feel that they've entered an overgrown fraternity house. To thrive here, whether as a shoe buyer or as an accountant, you have to be able to switch gears in and out of work and play. One minute you may be focused on your work; the next you may be participating in or supporting colleagues in a Ping-Pong challenge." Rebecca notes, "The one thing that's essential for every employee at Zappos is to be a defender of our culture. I see my job in HR not as a regulator or a policing agent, which is the role I was asked to play when I worked in the gaming industry, but instead, I am both a facilitator and a protector of culture." To achieve the goal of serving a perfect fit that preserves the Zappos culture, recruiters in the HR department are given the task of providing the first major test of culture fit.

Brandis Paden, recruiting supervisor at Zappos, describes her cultural vigilance duties by noting, "It really starts from the first interaction with a prospect. You'd be surprised how much you can tell about the likelihood of fit from the start of a phone conversation or by the nature of e-mail correspondence. Since we know our values and our culture, it becomes even clearer as the process progresses. Does the journey suggest a person who is high maintenance? Are they more about what the company can do for them versus achieving a good partnership for everyone?"

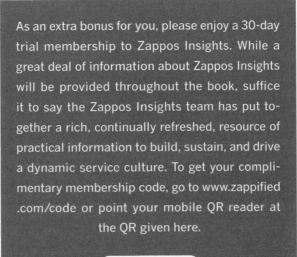

As an extra bonus for you, please enjoy a 30-day trial membership to Zappos Insights. While a great deal of information about Zappos Insights will be provided throughout the book, suffice it to say the Zappos Insights team has put together a rich, continually refreshed, resource of practical information to build, sustain, and drive a dynamic service culture. To get your complimentary membership code, go to www.zappified .com/code or point your mobile QR reader at the QR given here.

Brandis suggests that a simple telephone conversation between promising candidates and a recruiter can assess such things as whether the applicant is just trying to find any job or possibly hoping to leave an unpleasant job rather than being genuinely drawn to what makes Zappos unique. Brandis relates, "An important question at Zappos is how the applicant feels about socializing with people they work with outside of the office. That's especially huge for managerial positions, since managers are asked to spend at least 10 to 20 percent of their time outside the office with their employees. You'd be surprised how many people make it clear that they don't socialize with subordinates.

While that works elsewhere, it's not going to fly in an environment where humility and family spirit reign supreme. You may be a great person, but you aren't going to fit here."

Zappos understands that not all managerial candidates feel comfortable forging friendship relationships with their team. As a result, Zappos has created questions to determine whether those applicants will be able to handle the unique aspects of the Zappos culture. It behooves every business leader to clearly delineate the idiosyncrasies of working in that culture, so applicants can be assessed in relation to those company-specific needs. It is worthwhile to think about how you do business differently from your competitors. What separates the people who thrive in your environment from those who flounder? What might be new or unusual about the things you value when compared to the environments your new hires typically leave?

Once recruiters identify individuals who are likely to fit the Zappos culture, those individuals are sent to the next level of screening with a hiring manager. That hiring manager is tasked with making certain the applicant can meet the technical demands of a job (for example, that an HR benefits coordinator candidate has experience working with specific payroll and human resource information systems used at Zappos) and also makes additional assessments of the applicant's all-important alignment with the Zappos values. This is way too important to be missed:

> Zappos seeks culture fit before skills fit.

Falling in love with an applicant's skills can predispose some companies to settle for a less-than-desirable or even toxic personality. That hiring manager must also consider how likely the applicant would be to fit with the specific characteristics and dynamics of the team with which he would be working.

Jeanne Markel, director of casual lifestyle at Zappos, is actively involved in hiring employees for her team and notes, "Depending upon the position, I'll bring in an applicant to meet the team even if the applicant has no predetermined skill set. I know Zappos has a well-defined technical education curriculum, and if the person fits our values regarding learning and growth, we can teach the technical aspects of the job. For some positions, I'd obviously be looking for a specific set of skills. But in both cases, I am building on the recruiter's assessment and looking for someone who has a great attitude and passion. Both of those characteristics can't be taught, and they are necessary to fit with the Zappos culture and to get that person to the next levels of our organization." (The "well-defined technical education curriculum" that Jeanne refers to, known at Zappos as "Pipeline," is discussed in detail in Chapter 8.)

As if the HR and leadership screening for applicant values and personality are not enough, the screening, like the Energizer bunny, keeps going and going. After the hiring manager narrows the field of applicants, members of the prospective Zappos teams further assess the remaining candidates for "fit." Galen Hardy, who carries the Zappos title of "clothing czar," shares, "My team consists of about 20 people. It would be impractical for the applicant and the entire team to engage in an interview during an eight-hour day, so we rotate 4 members of our team to do the culture fit/team fit interviews. But those team members have to do more than interview; they have to really get to know that applicant on behalf of the team."

Galen notes that applicants often fly to Las Vegas for their full-day interviews and are picked up at the airport by Zappos shuttle drivers. Those drivers are asked for input as to whether the applicants demonstrated Zappos-like values during their rides to the interviews. Galen continues, "Most applicants are here for an evening, and we will go off-site to enjoy cocktails and appetizers with the applicant. That way, our entire team can come and get to know the applicant. You can learn a lot more about a person at a happy hour than you can learn in an interview room." After applicants visit, Zappos teams typically engage in a series of discussions to determine which applicant will provide the most perfect culture fit.

So how does all this relate to you and your business? Zappos offers a panoply of ideas that you can use to uncover your core values or to help you select the applicants who match your values. But what tools will you apply to increase the likelihood you will select staff members who are a culture fit? Will you create questions that explore whether your applicants align with your core values? (For example, at Zappos, interviewees might be asked to rate themselves on a scale of 1 to 10 as to how weird they are. This is followed by a more important question: Why did you give yourself the rating you did? Augusta Scott, Zappos coach, remembers being asked to draw a pig. "I was somewhat shocked, but I made him rainbow-colored. He still sits next to me on the wall of my cubicle.") Maybe it's off to happy hour with your team and your job finalists? Whatever it is, great leaders define, screen, and select for culture.

In spite of all this evaluation of fit, Tony Hsieh believes that bad hiring has cost Zappos more than $100 million. He notes, "This cost is a result of not only the bad hires we've made, but the decisions those people have made and how they have contributed to additional poor selections." Ultimately, Tony views errant choices as the biggest of the company's leadership mistakes. Chapter 3 will help you understand why Tony would make such a statement. It will also help you appreciate how an invitation for employment at Zappos is just the beginning of a very involved process of further exploring whether a new hire truly belongs at Zappos.

- The course of business is not static and seldom is fully defined at launch.

- Many corporate values are present in the actions of the early leaders of a business; others emerge in response to what customers value.

- Values are both explicitly stated and implicitly present in action.

- Explicit values can be codified or simply articulated by the leadership.

- As social units mature, capturing values in written form is essential to alignment and growth.

- Values creation should not be relegated to a "special few."

- The more you involve people in giving input, the less you have to sell them on the product of that input.

- Define your core values now or refresh your already defined values.

- Measure your values against the CRUD test.

- Let applicants know about your values before they can find your job postings.

- Create interview questions that get at the applicant's core values.

- Build multiple levels of values screening.

- Assess applicants in both formal and casual settings.

- Maximize the number of people who can give input on applicant selection.

CULTURE SHOULD
BE A VERB

Up to this point in our exploration of Zappos, we have analyzed the way the company highlights the importance of its corporate values to prospective applicants, how it creates multiple levels of screening to sift not only for technical skill but for culture fit, and ways leaders design informal and formal aspects of the selection process to assess the likelihood that a prospective employee will thrive at Zappos. But what happens once it is determined that an applicant either fits or does *not* fit with the Zappos culture? This chapter demonstrates important next steps in what is a continuing gauntlet of new hire orientation and values education. It then shows how this critical piece fits into the big picture, by outlining the constant care and feeding of the Zappos culture that occurs daily at all levels of the organization. By focusing on the Zappos onboarding process at the

Nevada location, you will be given an opportunity to examine your own new hire orientation strategies and compare them to one of the most involved, novel, and effective enculturation programs in business today.

I DON'T FIT—WHAT SIZE DO I NEED TO BE?

Many great and talented people seek employment at Zappos, but few are selected. Christa Foley, Zappos recruiting manager, reports that the actual applicant-to-job ratio for positions in Nevada hovers at around 30,000 applications annually for about 450 filled positions. In essence, 1.5 percent of all applicants make it through the rigorous cultural and technical hurdles. At many businesses, applicants have to conclude that they weren't selected simply because the "offer letter" never arrives in their mailbox. However, consistent with the Zappos values, leadership makes a point of letting unsuccessful applicants know the results of the application process. This may seem like a small courtesy, but it speaks to the company's willingness to act in a way that is consistent with values such as "build open and honest relationships with communication" and "deliver wow through service."

Andrew Kovacs, sourcing specialist, shares, "We aren't just here to serve customers who are in a transaction buying our products. We serve all stakeholders, including all applicants, some of whom may even be our actual customers. Communicating with applicants to let them know their status is simply a way of being respectful and serving them. Therefore, we provide applicants an automatic reply that we received their résumé, and we follow up again to let them know whether or not we are moving forward with their application. That takes time. But, come on; we're Zappos." Christa Foley suggests that closing the communication loop with unsuccessful applicants also gives those individuals an opportunity to grow. She notes, "If we've talked to someone, interviewed them and ended up not moving forward, we will be as direct as we can concerning why they weren't chosen. We could just say thanks for your time, but we try to highlight what was missing on the technical side or things they can do to improve the way they interview."

It is easy to get so busy with the people who "fit" your organization that your HR department fails to provide respectful and helpful communication to those who were not chosen. However, at Zappos, values matter, and they are of the utmost importance when people might otherwise accept shortcuts. For Zappos leaders, it's critical that values be adhered to in both pleasant and less-than-pleasant business circumstances, including the way Zappos handles unsuccessful applicants.

I'M IN—ZAPPOS CHOSE ME

After everything applicants go through to be offered a job at Zappos, and given the small percentage that are actually chosen, you would think that an invitation to employment would be the end of the "culture fit" process. In truth, it is the first leg of a rather long trek.

To give you a feel for the challenges and the significance of the journey, let me offer a real-life example of a highly skilled professional who was hired to lead a non-customer-facing business division at Zappos. Because of the technical and leadership nature of the position, Zappos executives had left the job unfilled for over a year, waiting for the "right person" to be selected. Thinking they had found that person, Zappos relocated the successful applicant to Nevada. In most businesses, a leadership-level new hire might experience an expedited orientation, with minimal to moderate focus on cultural values, so that the person can immediately jump into departmental leadership responsibilities. Not so at Zappos. This leader, like all other new hires, was required to go through *four weeks* of customer service training (referred to as new hire/CLT training) originally designed for Customer Loyalty Team members (Zapponians who answer calls when people place an order by phone, have a product question, need to process a return, etc.). Zappos does not exempt leaders from this training because the training is viewed as an opportunity to create a common experience around a core customer-facing function. Leaders are also expected to encounter the joys and challenges of serving customers in the call center environment.

As suggested in Chapter 2, the screening process at Zappos is designed to select employees who will be eager to dive into a culture and service orientation process. However, in the case of our unnamed executive, the individual participated in the new hire/CLT class only reluctantly and somewhat marginally. After several attempts to encourage him to embrace the process, the new hire was deemed to not truly fit the Zappos culture and was terminated. After a year of waiting, extensive recruiting costs, a significant investment of time and money in the interview process, and substantial relocation expenses, Zappos leaders determined that this highly sought-after executive was not right for their culture.

BREAKING DOWN THE ZAPPOS
ONBOARDING PROCESS

From my perspective, onboarding at Zappos achieves a wide range of beneficial outcomes. For example, it clearly communicates and demonstrates the core values while highlighting the importance of service at Zappos. In addition, it extends the opportunity to assess the fit of employees, and it establishes interdepartmental collaboration and empathy. Let's take a look at how these types of benefits emerge from what many might see as an unnecessarily costly process of orientation.

Déjà Vu—Culture, Values, and Service

Can you really imagine employees throughout your organization going through a month of training that would typically be offered for an entry-level service job? Can you see an accountant, an IT professional, and the new CFO all actively participating alongside a new hire who may be entering the workforce for the first time? All of these individuals would be learning about the company's history, philosophy, and values. They would gain insights into the importance of customer service, understand the company's long-term vision, and even spend two weeks taking real calls from real customers. How humbling would that be? What would that suggest about the importance of service or your expectation that everyone is responsible for your company's culture?

Rather than squeezing orientation into a single day and trying to pack that day full of information on policies and procedures, a discussion of key elements of the employee handbook, a mini-version of corporate history, and a cursory review of the company's mission, vision, and values, the Nevada Zappos month-long process represents a well-designed cultural immersion. In their book *Onboarding: How to Get Your New Employees up to Speed in Half the Time*, George Bradt and Mary Vonnegut define onboarding as "the process of *acquiring, accommodating, assimilating* and *accelerating* new team members, whether they come from outside or inside the organization." Zappos fully demonstrates enculturation, as defined by Bradt and Vonnegut. The authors write that the leadership at Zappos has developed a process that takes "new hires they *acquired* through a well-crafted selection process and *accommodates* them with tools they will need to be successful at Zappos. Additionally the onboarding month *assimilates* new hires into the Zappos culture and *accelerates* their readiness to step into their formal job responsibilities."

The extended onboarding process at Zappos includes, but is not limited to, an overview of the 10 core values, the history behind each value, and presentations from 10 managerial-level representatives from different departments, each of whom shares what a specific value means personally and to the business overall. Technical training and customer service information provided during the course culminates with hours of direct phone contact between the new hires and actual Zappos customers. As you might imagine, this wealth of real-life experience creates an added advantage when the company needs the entire Nevada workforce to pitch in during periods of extremely high call volumes.

Christina Colligan, CLT manager, reflects, "I don't know another business that has every employee go through such an involved orientation process. It costs Zappos a great deal when it comes to productivity and salaries, but it is worth it in terms of grounding all of us on the importance of the Zappos values.

The process really is an immersion in culture. Everyone at Zappos gets the same rich introduction to values and to customer service. We are all in orientation together, and we are all Zappos together." David Hinden, a merchandising assistant at Zappos, notes, "Of all the things I learned in that initial four weeks of training, the piece that was of the utmost importance to me was how Zappos expects us all to do business. I had to switch gears from prior experiences, where I'd learned to be suspicious of customers or strive to protect the company at all costs. Instead, I started thinking about the value of doing the right thing for customers and for my peers so they can do the right thing for our customers as well. The CLT training helps you let go of the old ways and align with the Zappos way." Cognitive psychologists talk about a concept they refer to as "proactive interference," which refers to the difficulty people have in letting go of information they previously learned in order to acquire new skills. Effective onboarding often helps new hires "unlearn" behaviors that may interfere with the way things are or need to be done in your culture.

Brandis Paden, recruiting supervisor, notes, "During that four weeks of training, the new team members realize we do a lot of work here. We expect them to understand customer service, culture, and the core values and contribute to all of those things. I think it does catch people off guard. They realize how serious we are about our culture." As values are slowly presented through weeks of orientation, staff members develop deeper connections to the company and more seriously internalize those values through their own experience.

When talking about the protracted orientation process, individuals throughout Zappos, particularly those who are working as members of the CLT, often share how the onboarding validates the importance of service and the role of the CLT. Derek Carder, CLT supervisor, notes, "In a lot of businesses, call center staff are not held in esteem. We are often more of a cost center than a revenue center in the minds of many leaders. Even at Zappos, only a small portion of the company's sales comes through the CLT; the rest is through online purchases. Despite the fact that we are not driving the money, everyone in the company has to experience our job. That really tells you how important personal service is here."

ZAPPIFIED BRAIN BREAK

"**P**aul is dead." Well, that is supposedly what you hear when you play a specific Beatles song backward. The Beatles, known for backmasking, or deliberately embedding backward hidden messages, in their 1966 album *Revolver*, added to a swirl of rumors concerning Paul McCartney's possible death when they purportedly placed the "Paul is dead" message in the song "Getting Better" on their 1967 *Sgt. Pepper's Lonely Hearts Club Band* album. Hidden messages didn't go away with the 1960s. Just as we have been using QR mobile technology throughout this book, Zappos has embedded hidden messages on bar codes on its delivery boxes and packages. Zappos buyers can use their mobile phones to find a special message. Once they scan the bar code and share their "happy" experiences by forwarding photos to Zappos, they are provided with a "special treat."

Having every new hire handle customer calls sends a clear message that service is everyone's business. It is the common objective of all Zapponians. In the end, everyone in the company must be equipped to make connections with customers across all Zappos contact channels. For many companies, there are two cultures: the one that affects the executives, and the one in which the rest of the organization operates. Despite the obvious cost of the Zappos orientation process, the all-inclusive nature of the training contributes to a single and unified Zappos culture. In and of itself, this is a significant return on investment.

In the spirit of the Zappos special bar codes, feel free to use your mobile QR reader to access the bonus stories and lessons of Zappos culture and service that are embedded in this code:

Of course, you are also welcome to access these stories by pointing your browser to zappified.com/bonus.

Screening and Teaming

By offering a monthlong training course for all Nevada employees, Zappos has essentially extended the opportunity to screen for the culture fit of new hires. While a candidate may interview well over a series of calls and even during a day of onsite formal and informal contacts, it is difficult to sustain a façade of openness, creativity, passion, or humility for a solid month.

Sourcing specialist Andrew Kovacs shares the screening power of new hire/CLT training: "We hired a manager from an industry that is often contentious, although we thought we had hired a guy who was more collaborative than the industry norm. Maybe he would have been if he actually got into the job, but we never found out because he didn't make it through the call center training program." Andrew explains, "Throughout recruitment and selection, all applicants are told that they will be involved in the call center training class from 7 a.m. to 4 p.m. Monday through Friday. No ifs, ands, or buts. People who ultimately go on to work in the call center, of necessity, are relied upon to show up as scheduled and be on time, so we set that expectation in the training class. Even those who won't later be CLT members are held to these standards during training, and we tell people you cannot be a minute late. Depending on the case, we might ask a person to come back to the next class if they were late, or we will simply let them go." In the case of the newly hired manager, Andrew notes, "He showed up late on more than one occasion. It is such a basic requirement for employment, and he didn't deliver. In addition, he became indignant when the issue was raised, as if the training were beneath him. Fortunately, he was let go before he could contaminate our culture. As recruiters, we look at those situations to see if there was anything we could have done to screen the person out during the selection process, but it's great to have the CLT training there as a continuation of the culture fit evaluation."

While the new hire/CLT training process reduces the number of people who slip through and "contaminate" the Zappos culture, it also helps to forge interdepartmental relationships and build positive team spirit. Ashley Perry, newly hired CLT member, gives a sense of how training sets the stage for fun and family spirit. "When I went through the training, I'd update my social media pages with everything we did, and my friends would say, 'I can't believe they call that work and you are getting paid!' We had a maple syrup chugging contest as part of an obstacle course activity. We did a variation of rock-paper-scissors that we called wizards-warlocks-monsters, and we even sang karaoke. Don't get me wrong; we worked a lot. But the fun brought new people from across the entire company into what I can best call a family environment." At the end of the new hire training, the class participants work together on a project that is associated with the Zappos core values. An example of one such project, "you got faced," will be outlined in detail in Chapter 10. Suffice it to say that these projects further engage participants in culture-related team building and set the tone that culture is the responsibility of every employee. The activities further suggest that culture is not an abstract or amorphous phenomenon. Rather, it is the foundation of successful business and can be enhanced by the efforts of dedicated individuals working collaboratively.

In addition to encouraging camaraderie and teamwork, the Zappos orientation journey helps individuals throughout the organization hear the "voice of the customer" and understand what it takes to meet or exceed the customer's wants, needs, and desires. In essence, it helps even non-customer-facing staff understand what is required to "deliver wow through service." Many organizations struggle to address customer needs effectively because of rigid organizational boundaries or limited trust across departments. The process of bringing new employees on board can send the message that "we are all working together for a common purpose." Furthermore, it can place new hires in a setting with individuals from across the organization to learn and serve the transcendent needs of the customer.

Mark Madej, software engineer, articulates the team and customer experience benefits of new hire/CLT onboarding: "From day one, it's such a great vibe. In CLT training, they get you so excited about everything. It's different from anywhere else. They allow us to take that time. Any other company would think it's such a waste, but it really isn't. As developers, we were able to see all the software tools from the customer's perspective and the CLT rep's point of view. As a result of being in CLT training and having to answer customer calls, developers like me saw the complexity of the software involved in a process that the CLTs were using. So, we created a tool to automate the whole mess and make the process easier on the CLT member and the customer. We wouldn't have come up with that fix if we

TRY THESE ON FOR SIZE

1. Is your onboarding process the same for front-line workers and for executives? If separate tracks exist, what does that suggest about your culture?

2. How many hours of your orientation process address policy, procedures, and other such matters? How many hours are dedicated to culture?

3. Does your onboarding process immerse participants in your culture, or does it simply preview that culture?

4. How effectively does your orientation process build empathy for the customer experience and create interdepartmental connections?

hadn't been on the phone with customers and seen the problem for ourselves. That's how you invest money in training and see real-time results."

How can employees truly embrace a culture unless they are immersed in it? Have the "let's make orientation quick" approaches really proved to be less costly in the end? For Zappos, a lengthy and involved orientation is a "pay now or pay later" proposition, where the leaders at Zappos view culture and service as too valuable to neglect at the front end. How about you?

CLT TRAINING IS ENDING—NOW WHAT?

Let's assume you have successfully completed the Zappos new hire/CLT training. What's next for you? Well, first and foremost, you have a decision to make. At this point, you will be asked to decide whether you want to take a sizable payout (something on the order of $4,000) and leave Zappos or head to your job area. *Let me restate that so you don't think you misread it. You've completed the orientation class, and you are asked to decide whether you think you are a culture fit.* If you decide the Zappos culture is *not* for you, Zappos will give you a substantial amount of walking money to move on and seek employment elsewhere.

How revolutionary! Zappos offers new hires an incentive to engage in a thoughtful self-assessment of their "goodness of fit" with the company. When Jack Welch was the head of General Electric, he championed the practice of differentiation, in which the "bottom 10 percent" of the organization was routinely asked to leave. He noted that "one of the best things about differentiation is that people in the bottom 10 percent . . . very often go on to successful careers at companies and in pursuits where they truly belong and where they can excel." By contrast, Zappos prompts, encourages, and supports new hires as they decide whether they are likely to thrive at Zappos or are better suited to excel elsewhere.

But why would you offer someone so much money to leave? Leadership at Zappos wants to provide an amount that enables prospective candidates to make the right decision and not feel they need to stay in a culture that does not fit them just to avert a lengthy period of unemployment. The amount of money attached to the offer has increased over time and is likely to vary with the economy. Similarly, the amount of time new hires have to take the buyout has also changed. In the early days, an employee had to take the offer before leaving the orientation class. Now new employees have up to three weeks after being in their actual jobs. Essentially, this gives new hires an opportunity to decide whether they are a fit based on their collective experiences in the orientation training and in their specific work area. According to Rebecca Henry Ratner, director of HR, approximately 2 percent of all new hires ultimately take the money and seek employment elsewhere.

The novel nature of the Zappos approach in paying employees to leave has received widespread attention in established business publications like *The Economist* and *Harvard Business Review*, as well as in countless blog posts. A number of blog articles on sites like The Consumerist and VisionWiz focus exclusively on the buyout. Without sufficient detail, the notion of paying your employees to leave after orientation can sound like a bad management practice. In fact, it's difficult to appreciate the full genius of the offer unless one places it in the context of everything that Zappos does to screen for fit. With the perspective you have gained from these two chapters, the $4,000 walking money can easily be seen as a well-positioned last step in a very involved process of protecting the Zappos culture.

It is hard to imagine that even 2 percent of new hires—those who have experienced the richness of the Zappos culture and passed all of the screening hurdles—would walk away within the first couple of months of employment. However, those who do would *not* have "served a perfect fit."

TRY THESE ON FOR SIZE

1. What do you think of Zappos paying new hires to leave?

2. What is your guess as to the percentage of new hires who would leave your business if they were given a similar offer?

3. Would you ever consider paying people to leave your company if those individuals sensed that they were not a culture fit? Why, or why not?

4. If you were to give a similar offer after orientation, would your enculturation process allow new hires to make a realistic assessment of their fit?

KEEPING THE CULTURE ALIVE

After all this culture screening, Zappos employees head to their respective departments, and, for many, additional education is provided to help them address the specific technical aspects of their jobs. But how do these new hires, and, for that matter, all

Zapponians, maintain the cultural romance long after the orientation honeymoon has ended? The remainder of this chapter will examine just a few of the key ways in which culture is constantly nurtured at Zappos. For the purposes of this exploration, I will focus on three key aspects of cultural care at Zappos:

1. Incorporating values into regular progress conversations

2. Budgeting money for cultural activities

3. Encouraging open expression of opinions about culture

Incorporating Values into Regular Progress Conversations

Leadership trainer John E. Jones once said, "What gets measured gets done; what gets measured and fed back gets done well; what gets rewarded gets repeated." Using that quote as a guideline, culture at Zappos gets done, done well, and repeated.

Zappos has always placed "living the core values" at the center of conversations between employees and managers. For many years, Zappos engaged in a process of annual performance reviews. During the time of those reviews, 50 percent of an employee's evaluation was based on the Zappos 10 core values. That evaluation process emphasized how much an employee contributed to each of the key drivers of the Zappos culture. From the beginning of their employment, Zapponians were informed that the embodiment of the Zappos values would be a key indicator of success in the company. In preparation for the annual performance reviews, staff members were asked to evaluate themselves on the performance review form depicted here. The employee's supervisor

We evaluated the performance review process and decided it was time for a change! Whoo-hoo, we love change :) During this evaluation period, we decided to move away from the 1–5 rating scale and use the ratings listed below. We also believe it is important to find out how employees feel they are performing in comparison to how the manager/supervisor feels the employee is performing. So in addition to the rating scale change, we are asking everyone to have employees complete a self-review as an official part of the review process. It is our hope that this new process will initiate more open dialogue between the employee and the manager/supervisor and allow everyone to dive deeper into the great, the good, and the so-so.

Please evaluate expectations in the following areas. Ratings and definitions are as follows:

Outstanding (O) = exceeds expectations, **Satisfactory (S)** = meets expectations consistently, **Needs Improvement (N)** = did not meet expectations.

Please note: The rating cells will accept only **O, S, or N**.

CORE VALUES (Please rate how the employee embodies the Core Values.)	RATING		
FACTOR	MANAGER	EMPLOYEE	FINAL
You understand and exhibit great customer service to internal and/or external customers.			
You view your job as more than 9–5 and more than your job description, and are eager to go above and beyond.			
You suggest alternatives for accomplishing tasks and/or process improvements. In addition, if your suggestions are not implemented, you accept the reason in a positive manner and are able to move forward with the decision that is made.			

FACTOR	MANAGER	EMPLOYEE	FINAL
You thrive in the Zappos environment. You accept changes to policies, procedures, and processes as part of the growth of the company. You do not complain about the changes but rather accept and embrace such changes enthusiastically.			
You take an active interest in creating fun (and a little weirdness) in the workplace.			
You encourage the different backgrounds, lifestyles, and personalities of your coworkers. Diversity is both understood and embraced.			
You are willing to take risks and step outside of your comfort zone to achieve success.			
You display creativity.			
You challenge yourself to grow and learn, both personally and professionally.			
You understand your department and the company's vision.			
You are open and honest in your communications.			
You understand that good communication also includes good listening as displayed in your interactions.			
You work well with your coworkers and foster teamwork within your department or area.			
You encourage a positive team spirit and do not display negativity in the workplace.			

CORE VALUES *(continued)*	RATING		
FACTOR	MANAGER	EMPLOYEE	FINAL
You work to improve efficiency at the office.			
You can get the job done and work with the resources at hand or come up with a work-around if resources are missing.			
You have passion, drive, and perseverance.			
You show respect to others, no matter what position you hold within the company.			
You understand that every opinion is valuable and that great ideas can come from anyone.			
Overall rating (average of above ratings)			

Comments:

PERFORMANCE	RATING		
FACTOR	MANAGER	EMPLOYEE	FINAL
You demonstrate competence in required job skills and knowledge.			
You demonstrate accuracy, clarity, consistency, and thoroughness of work.			
Productivity standards are met.			
Work assignments are planned, organized, and analyzed for optimum results.			
You meet job expectations.			

FACTOR	MANAGER	EMPLOYEE	FINAL
You accomplished previously established goals and objectives.			
You arrive to work as scheduled each day, on time.			
Overall rating (average of above ratings)			
Comments:			

LEADERSHIP	RATING		
FACTOR	MANAGER	EMPLOYEE	FINAL
You set clear goals and direction for accomplishing team objectives.			
You regularly attend leadership meetings and communicate the information to your direct reports.			
You use feedback from surveys and/ or focus groups to help maintain a successful team environment.			
You inspire others to live and breathe our core values.			
You participate in helping the team learn and grow professionally and personally.			
Overall rating (average of above ratings)			
Comments:			

GROWTH POTENTIAL	RATING		
FACTOR	MANAGER	EMPLOYEE	FINAL
You seek opportunities to learn and further your understanding of the business.			
You show leadership in relationships and discussions with peers.			
You participate in group discussions and contribute constructively in meetings.			
You seek responsibilities and assignments outside of your usual job description.			
You share knowledge and experience with others in a constructive, helpful way.			
Overall growth potential rating			
Comments:			

OVERALL SCORE

Please list below, the percentage that each section graded should apply to the employee's overall evaluation rating. Please ensure that all four areas equal 100%. *Note:* You should work with your departmental manager to determine what weighting values should be used.

Core values % weighting	50%	
Performance % weighting	30%	
Leadership % weighting	10%	
Growth potential % weighting	10%	
Overall rating for this evaluation period	100%	

also completed that form. During the evaluation process, employees and supervisors would discuss the evaluations, with an emphasis on the employee's strengths and opportunities for growth. Over my tenure as an organizational consultant, I have seen very few organizations weigh "culture contribution" or "embodiment of values" as heavily in the overall assessment of employee performance. Nor have I seen many businesses orient employees to the notion that participation in the culture would be a key metric of employment success.

Of late, Zappos has moved away from this formalized annual performance review process. Despite that change, the leaders have maintained the significance of embodying values for overall employment success. In fact, Zappos has evolved to an employee growth conversation called "cultural assessments." HR director Rebecca Henry Ratner notes that the change was made to facilitate conversations between managers and employees that were more in keeping with a culture of growth and learning. "For us, the 'once a year, sit down and tell you how you're doing review' became a crutch for managers who did not have to make sure that they consistently knew if and how their people were living our values and otherwise performing. So our company took a risk and did away with an annual performance review, and we certainly don't know whether that will be ideal for us, but we think so. For now, managers will be expected to regularly give feedback on the same dimensions they would have covered in the review process, but now they won't be doing it in a formal, annual, score-generating way." Rebecca went on to add that Zappos is constantly looking for ways to encourage consistent conversations about values-based behavior. This shift away from "annual scores" to "regular discussions" reflects the leadership's forward-thinking approach.

As with most business processes, it is important for companies to regularly evaluate and improve the way performance reviews are conducted. For many, a good starting place for that improvement process can be assessing employees' behavior associated with the company's core values. According to a study by the business publication *Workforce Management*, most major companies have *not* joined Zappos in eliminating the annual performance review altogether; however, a number of businesses (like Zappos) are shifting from a performance approach to a growth and development model. Independent of the issue of whether or not to formally evaluate, most companies could benefit from increasing the degree to which "culture contribution" or "living the company values" is discussed and held out as a part of employee responsibility. Speaking before a group of senior marketing executives, Tony Hsieh went so far as to say that he feels more comfortable "firing someone for not contributing to an innovative work culture than for poor work performance." He has also suggested that Zappos has lost $100 million from having people in the company who did not contribute to the culture. How many conversations are taking place in your business about how well each individual is personifying the organization's core values and enhancing the work environment?

Budgeting Money for Cultural Activities

Given all the time and money that Zappos invests in selecting and training employees and communicating with them about culture, you might be wondering how Zappos makes a profit or has the resources available to pay for ongoing activities to keep its culture alive. In a nutshell, Zappos tends to pay employees near the median level of competitive salaries, whereas its parent company, Amazon, pays around the 75th percentile. According to Donavan Roberson, Zappos Insights culture evangelist, "We invest that 25 percent difference into activities that build our culture. Some might say that we are taking a hit in salary, but we are building a culture dedicated to the happiness of our people. When a person's life comes to an end, that person doesn't look back and think, 'Okay, how much money did I make per year?' The person is thinking, 'How was my life; how was my every day; how much did I enjoy my job; what did I accomplish; what did I learn?' These are the things that are much more important to people than salary." Tony Hsieh suggests that culture does not need to be a costly investment: "Clearly, we are spending a lot more than most companies on benefits such as our medical and dental insurance. While we pay at or slightly above market rates for entry-level staff, we also live our values to 'do more with less' and 'be humble' by managing leadership salaries such that the higher you are in the organization, the more likely you are to be paid below the market range."

In essence, Zappos builds an infrastructure of activities and support systems for each of its core values. From a benefits perspective, Zappos offers employees free meals, adds free sodas and snacks, and tops all that off with one of the most comprehensive health plans around. One can't interview a Zappos employee about the way the company "delivers wow through service" without the staff member referring to the company's generosity. Mary Johnson of the Zappos Fulfillment Center typifies the sentiment: "It's amazing what they do for us here, from the best insurance package to free food every single day. We have huge fall, spring, and summer festivals. There seems to always be a get-together going on. The pay is competitive, but when you add in all the free stuff and the insurance, it's just phenomenal."

Keeping employees healthy and having fun events is one thing, but why does Zappos feel that free food, which is a major expense, is key to its culture? According to Craig Adkins, vice president of Fulfillment Operations, "The idea of feeding staff really didn't emerge as a compensation or retention strategy; instead, the main idea was socialization. We wanted to have staff members all sit down and eat with one another and have conversations. It's worked out well for us. Managers and leaders engage with their teams. Managers get to know about the families and kids of their team members, and they better understand what motivates and interests them. It's not a free meal as much as it is a time for us to sit down together in community."

In addition to employee benefits, values are brought to life at Zappos, in part, because managers in Nevada are encouraged to spend 10 to 20 percent of their time outside of work with their employees, and coworkers are expected to spend the same amount of time with one another and with their managers. Budgets are provided for supervisors to facilitate off-work activities, including such things as holding barbecues at managers' homes, engaging in "happy hours" at Zappos, or taking the team to a local bowling alley. As you will see in Chapter 11, these connections are also forged through impromptu celebrations, many of which are anchored in making performance goals. Jamie Naughton, Zappos speaker of the house, notes, "It's not as much about the money we have available to spend on our people as it is making a point of bringing people together. Since one of our values includes doing more with less, we stretch our budget at every opportunity. For example, we had a cookie-eating competition that was hugely successful and cost us all of $20. We do carnivals with homemade games. Often it's nothing fancy because it's not what you do—it's that you take the time to do something to create fun and connection. Our people just enjoy the spirit of play and the quirky unpredictability that comes with keeping values like fun, adventure, and change continually front and center." Chapter 10, "Play Well," examines how Zappos consistently creates an energized and fun workplace, which in turn strengthens the Zappos family and drives key business objectives.

Encouraging Open Expression of Opinions about Culture

These fun, family spirit, and wow elements of the Zappos culture are liberally splashed across the Internet, shared with callers during customer service interactions, reflected on the Zappos website, and enjoyed by visitors during the frequent tours that pass through Headquarters. While elements of the onboarding process at the Fulfillment Centers in Kentucky differ from those in Nevada because of varied job demands, that playful culture can be experienced through the increasing numbers of tours moving through the Kentucky facility and fun daily warm-up meetings. Ultimately, leaders at Zappos are such zealots about the power of a positive business culture that they feel compelled to share that passion.

As part of that zealotry, Zapponians regularly share their unique culture via Twitter posts, blogs, and even YouTube videos. Many businesses dissuade their employees from talking about work in social networks, but the Zappos leaders encourage it, thus ensuring that the culture is experienced both within and beyond the walls of the Zappos facilities. Zappos staff members are even provided with training on setting up and using Twitter accounts, and a corporate communication policy of "be real and use good judgment" signals to employees that they may speak freely and wisely.

Further reflection on the Zappos culture is promoted by the annual publication of the Zappos Culture Book. All Zapponians are thus offered the chance to talk about their company. This uncensored book is then made available to anyone who is interested in the company's culture. In keeping with the Zappos value "build open and honest relationships with communication," the book represents a transparent view of Zappos. After scouring all entries in all editions of the Culture Book, I am hard-pressed to find anything worse than the following:

> Life at Zappos is constantly in motion. The ongoing changes, growth, and challenges are tremendous. It's full of both happiness and pain.

But even that entry ends with,

> Outsiders simply talk about how great their company may be, but Zapponians live and rave about the awesome culture here.

More typically, the input is something like

> I truly believe that we are at the forefront of a new movement, where people treat each other as family. . . . I no longer accept bad customer service from other people and other companies. I challenge them to do and be better, to try to WOW me. Most of the time it works! WOW!

or

> Zappos culture means to live, have fun, and love. We work
> very hard at Zappos, but we are shown that our hard
> work and dedication are appreciated. This appreciation
> enables me to give 100 percent. I enjoy coming to work
> with my family at Zappos.

Please see Appendix B for more examples of Culture Book comments.

By asking staff members to write their thoughts about Zappos and by turning those written comments into a bound volume that is received by all employees, the company's leaders essentially help Zapponians redefine and personalize the evolving Zappos culture. Aaron Magness, senior director, Brand Marketing & Business Development, notes, "When you read through the book, you can feel the richness of this culture. We see the Culture Book as a crucial way for every person at Zappos to put their Zappos Experience into words." In essence, Zappos leaders have enabled all employees to literally "write the book" on their company.

Jenn Lim, CEO and chief happiness officer of Delivering Happiness (the company and movement that has evolved from the book of the same name), has created every annual Zappos Culture Book since its inception and identifies a broad range of benefits that result from its publication. "It's a testament to Zappos real commitment to transparency," according to Jenn. "Since we print everything—good and bad—the Culture Book has become a snapshot of Zappos values in action and lets us compare our strengths and weaknesses, year to year. Over time, we expanded it to include the voice of business partners, vendors, and customers, since we believe happiness can be delivered to every person Zappos comes in contact with."

It's Tony Hsieh's belief that "brand is a lagging indicator of culture." Because the Culture Book is sent to anyone in the world that requests one, it has essentially become a "brand book" that extends awareness of what Zappos represents, while creating an emotional connection to Zappos in places even outside of the areas they ship to and service. They regularly hear from avid fans worldwide, for example, those in Japan and Brazil.

The idea of publishing a book that reflects a company's commitment to culture has become a compelling concept, and companies ranging from the M Resort in Las Vegas (of the MGM Mirage family) to Amazon.com have asked how they can create one of their own. As a result, Delivering Happiness is providing a service to help other organizations put together culture books customized to their unique values, employees, and culture.

Jenn Lim adds, "As we've seen in books like Jim Collins' *Good to Great*, the most important part of a company's culture is not that it merely has values, but that the employees actually commit to them. The Culture Book started as an off-the-cuff idea, but it has evolved into something that has helped Zappos identify whether or not we're putting our money *and* values where our mouth is." (More information on Delivering Happiness—the company and the movement—can be found in Chapter 9.)

We have come full circle with Zappos through selection, onboarding, and a few aspects of culture elevation. You will see the completion of the circle when you appreciate that applicants often request the Zappos Culture Book as they contemplate employment. In essence, the Culture Book is a by-product of the culture, which also helps prospective applicants decide whether they can "serve a perfect fit" at Zappos. Such was the case for a person who essentially tweeted that he could not survive in the Zappos culture of extroversion but appreciated that for those who enjoyed such an environment, it would be a dream to work there.

If staff members were asked to write an unedited book on your culture, what would it say? How would it affect new hires who are deciding whether they would "serve a perfect fit" for you? Take the chance and publish a Culture Book. At its worst, it will be a road map for culture change!

Delivering Happiness can be a resource if you need assistance in creating a culture book for your own organization. You can find this organization at www.deliveringhappiness.com, facebook.com/deliveringhappiness, and @DHMovement and @DHMovementCEO on Twitter. Or simply point the QR reader on your mobile device here.

Chapter 3 *Ideas to Run With*

- Communicating with those who have been passed over for employment essentially defines applicants as customers of your brand.

- Onboarding involves acquiring, accommodating, assimilating, and accelerating.

- Orientation is an opportunity to set equal expectations for leaders and nonleaders and to signal a unified culture.

- New hires need an opportunity to be immersed in, not just made aware of, your culture.

- Culture is a two-way street; both the applicant and the existing staff can and should be called upon to evaluate an applicant or new hire's "goodness of fit."

- That which gets measured gets done. Are you measuring values-based behavior for everyone in your organization?

- Culture happens by default or by design. Great leaders design their culture, set values in motion, and stir up the culture regularly.

Make It Effortlessly Swift

The more effort customers must put forth in a service interaction, the less likely they are to be loyal.

—JEFFREY HENNING

In the discussion of Principle 1, "Serve a Perfect Fit," you saw how Zappos selects and orients for a service culture. The leadership at Zappos views culture strength as the foundation for employee engagement and, ultimately, for customer loyalty. Zappos leaders understand that a cohesive culture and a highly involved workforce contribute to a wide range of robust business outcomes. In fact, research consistently demonstrates the connection between employee engagement and productivity, employee retention, improved safety, and overall business profitability. By building a tight employee community, Zappos has developed a platform for outstanding service. But correlations between workforce engagement and customer loyalty are nothing more than, well, correlations. What else must be added to the mix to ensure high-quality service delivery?

The next two chapters, which make up Principle 2, look at how Zappos masters the fundamentals of customer service. Chapter 4, "Less Effort, More Customers," focuses on how Zappos makes all aspects of the customer experience as effortless as possible. You will get a glimpse of the Zappos obsession with customer ease, smooth-running customer/user experiences, and process accuracy. Chapter 5, "The Ticket to the Big Service Dance: Velocity, Knowledge, Recovery, and Surprise," offers insights into how Zappos instills a sense of urgency into service delivery. It will also take you through Zappos leading-edge approaches to driving product expertise and forward-thinking service recovery.

What are we waiting for? It's time to "make it effortlessly swift."

LESS EFFORT,
MORE CUSTOMERS

I've never encountered a business owner or leader who said, "I wish fewer of my customers were raving fans." We all want to maximize that special group of high-value customers who not only support our business through steady repeat purchases, but also eagerly refer new customers to us. While a great deal is known about the factors that drive customers away from a business, the attributes that lead to customer evangelism are the subject of considerable debate. That exact debate played out very clearly in two vastly different articles in a single issue of the *Harvard Business Review*. The titles of the two articles were "Stop Trying to Delight Your Customers" and "How I Did It: Zappos' CEO on Going to Extremes for Customers."

The authors of "Stop Trying to Delight Your Customers," Matthew Dixon, Karen Freeman, and Nicholas Toman, reported, "Conventional wisdom holds that to increase loyalty, companies must 'delight' customers by exceeding service expectations.

A large-scale study of contact-center and self-service interactions, however, finds that what customers really want (but rarely get) is just a satisfactory solution to their service issue." "How I Did It: Zappos' CEO on Going to Extremes for Customers," written by Zappos CEO Tony Hsieh, suggested that service excellence requires dedicated commitment to such Zappos service values as "deliver wow through service."

So when it comes to customer loyalty, which is it—to wow or not to wow? The answer is actually simple. It's *both*!

Consistent with Tony Hsieh's perspective, "wow" is an important dimension of customer loyalty and should be pursued. The first step in that pursuit is achieved by making sure you are simply "getting it right" (delivering exactly what customers want the first time you serve them) and "making it easy" (reducing the overall effort required for customers to get their needs met). Once accurate and easy service delivery occurs consistently, customers can be "wowed" if the business exceeds their expectations and/or offers personalized care. The importance of accurate and easy service delivery is well demonstrated by Dixon, Freeman, and Toman's research, which, in a nutshell, shows the following:

- Delighting customers should not be the first priority in building customer loyalty.

- Reducing your customers' effort to get their problems solved is the low-hanging fruit in the loyalty journey.

- Acting to reduce your customers' effort can actually reduce your service costs.

Given the importance of effortless customer service and the Zappos commitment to delivering wow through service, let's examine what Zappos does to increase customer ease.

EASE OF SERVICE COMES IN MANY FORMS

Overall, 95 percent of all Zappos sales happen on the company's website! Thus, despite the emphasis placed on handling customer calls, most customers connect with Zappos through the Internet. For a brand that is known for personal service, it is striking that so much of the "service experience" has to be translated through the company's website.

The online service world in which Zappos thrives is itself an outgrowth of making life easier for the customer. Remember Nick Swinmurn walking around San Francisco looking for his size 11 Tan Airwalk Chukka boots? Zappos was created so that consumers could, at their convenience, search from an available inventory of 5 million or more items. That inventory eclipses what customers could find by going down to their local brick-and-mortar stores. Better yet, consumers do not need to conform their shopping to a store's hours; there are no transportation costs or parking challenges, and customers don't need to check their hair or make themselves otherwise more presentable before they shop.

Rafael Mojica, senior user experience architect at Zappos, explained how he and other members of the user experience team view their jobs. "It is an obsession to make our website—and ultimately all Zappos touch points—more user-friendly. We spend the bulk of our time focused on our website's ease of navigation. Although our customers are very satisfied with our navigation, we will never be content. We want to think through everything that the customers might want and how they can get their needs met with the least effort. The design and development process is not as intuitive as you might think because it's not simply about providing information. Too much information can be overwhelming. Our goal is to provide what customers need exactly when they need it." At the heart of all well-designed customer experiences is a dedicated commitment to understanding the customer's wants and desires. With that understanding, processes are crafted to ensure that the customers get what they want, when they want it, with the least effort possible.

Rafael goes on to add, "Zappos often has to track and execute against customer needs, even when some of those needs pose sizable logistic or technical challenges. We have to nail every part of the customer journey, from the moment a customer gets to the website to the moment when that customer finishes the order. Every aspect must be a pleasant experience." Rafael's comments highlight the concentrated effort that excellent service providers expend. Namely, they map out the entire customer journey and seek to meet and anticipate customers' needs flawlessly at every significant contact point.

In designing and improving the user experience, the Zappos user experience (UX) team relies on a combination of active listening, user research, intuition, and trial-and-error approaches. Specifically, the team utilizes quantitative and qualitative analysts as well as designers and quality improvement experts, all of whom are working to infer what customers want. Collectively, this expertise is deployed to examine the user's on-site behavior at both a macro and a granular level. The team members also talk with and listen to customers' input for desired changes and for the viability of new features or redesigns.

From the standpoint of direct listening, Zappos has a link prominently displayed on its landing page that asks, "HOW DO YOU LIKE OUR WEBSITE? We'd like to get your feedback." That link enables users to complete an online survey in which they are able to compare the Zappos website to others, give an overall assessment of their experience, and specifically provide ratings on a scale of 1 to 7 concerning things like overall ease of website use, ability to find products, the effort needed to use a gift card, or the ease of checkout. Qualitative questions ask customers to provide "suggestions or ideas to improve the Zappos website" and say that, if "you had difficulties using the website today, please feel free to share your experience."

Lianna Shen of the UX team notes that the feedback provided by users has proved very helpful in reducing the effort that other customers have to exert throughout the experience. She notes, "The best ideas come from customers. They help us see things we would have never seen. We might have thought we had the shopping experience well mapped out until a customer writes, 'Hey, what if you did this?' or 'If you organized your category this way, it would make more sense for me to shop it.' In the end, it's our job to ensure that the site makes sense and works easily for users." As with most surveys of this type, only a small percentage of users take the time to offer suggestions. A customer's purpose for being on the site is principally to have a positive shopping experience, *not* to help design the website. So to gain more comprehensive information on what customers want, UX team members have to collect data based on visitor use patterns.

Zappos Web analyst Christina Kim notes, "If you are our customer, I'm watching you. Actually, I am watching you only as part of aggregate data collected from everything that is happening on the site. From a trend perspective, we are attempting to understand what is and isn't working across the site. I use tools to look at how many people cumulatively visit the site and how the traffic generally moves from page to page. If we introduce a new graphic design image to help users get from one place to the next, I'll be measuring data on all the clicks around the image and working with the visual design team and maybe even copywriters to ensure that we are doing the best we can to help customers easily get where they want to go. It's like making sure that signage in a building is actually helping customers get to their destinations."

On a less macro and more detailed level, individual UX team members look at the actual site visits of selected unidentified guests. That analysis examines such things as where those visitors spend their time. It gets to questions like, what is the user's specific page-to-page journey? Which pages didn't seem to interest the customer? By combining aggregate and individualized analyses, designers can identify programming glitches or confusing language that leads to "shopping cart abandonment"—situations in which people place items in their shopping cart, but leave the site without purchasing that merchandise. Once breakdowns are identified, the UX team designers fix them so other shoppers don't encounter them and so shoppers who do not complete their transactions can receive cart recovery e-mails.

In addition to inferring customer wants and needs based on the users' behavior, Zappos involves customers in the specifics of the website design through a process of user testing. Rafael Mojica notes, "We incorporate what we learn from analytic data into the way we design a new feature or redesign an old one. We then show our customers the new product, ask them to use the feature, track data on their use, and ask them to give us their feedback about it." Rafael adds, "The users' participation, our tracking software, and a willingness to listen help us understand when the customers can't find what they are looking for, or that they don't know what's happening when they are on a given page. In essence, it allows us to adjust our design completely around our users' needs."

Certainly online customer tracking tools are extremely sophisticated. For example, they allow user experience experts to literally see the cursor movement of visitors as those visitors navigate through a website, thus allowing access to valuable information on customer behavior patterns. While user experience tools are particularly refined, every business in both the online and the brick-and-mortar world should strive to understand where customers encounter resistance when they are trying to get their stated and unstated needs met.

As the Zappos user experience team demonstrates, aggregate and individualized data paint a picture of the customer journey from which quality improvement inferences can be drawn. Improvements based on those inferences must then be measured through additional customer research and assessed through active listening to customer reactions.

The difference between good and great service begins with watching customers' behavior—not to be intrusive, but to be

TRY THESE ON FOR SIZE

1. How much do you know about your customers' wants, needs, and desires?

2. What have you done to design a customer experience that not only responds to customer needs but also anticipates them?

3. Have you mapped your customer journey across all contact points, and do you understand the sequence of events that your customers encounter as they seek to have their needs met?

4. What qualitative and quantitative methods are you using to track your customers' journey with your business?

5. How are you using the voice of your customers to refine your processes in order to make your customers' time with you as effortless as possible?

helpful. From that observation, improvements can be attempted in areas where customers are struggling to get their needs met. Additionally, customer observation ensures that the attempted improvements have the desired effects on the overall customer experience.

GIVE ME WHAT I NEED TO MAKE A SOUND DECISION

The word *service* not only implies that someone else is going to put out effort on your behalf, but also suggests that an individual or business will help you make a product selection that meets your needs. Much as when they are buying from a printed catalog, Zappos customers face the challenge of choosing an item without the benefit of being able to touch it or try it on. To compensate for this significant disadvantage, Zappos has been a leader in online product presentation.

Fred Mossler, "just Fred" at Zappos, notes, "At the time we got started, people who sold footwear online were scanning images directly out of a paper catalog. The pictures were usually really grainy, and the sellers would scan in only one color. The catalog would say that the product was also available in other colors. So the customer had to guess what kind of 'red' the shoe would be. It made the shopping experience really difficult for the customer. At Zappos, we knew from the very start that we wanted to make shopping pleasant, so we made a commitment to show the customers what they were going to receive by taking our own pictures of every product in every single color from multiple angles. We started with three or four photo angles, and we are now up to eight angles plus video. In the beginning, it was very expensive to do it this way, but we felt it was the best and the only viable option."

Zappos has since set standards for written and pictorial Web-based product presentation and in the process has improved the quality and efficiency with which content is generated. From a visual perspective, Dan Campbell, Zappos photo supervisor, explains that Zappos needs to shoot a lot of images quickly, while also making sure that the images accurately assist the website user in making the best possible purchase. To that end, Dan notes, "When the first-of-its-kind item comes into the Fulfillment Centers, every size and color of that item is diverted directly to us. The product comes to us via conveyors, and then the prep team takes the item for the photo shoot. Once the item is shot, we immediately upload our images. Our quality control team looks at the images and makes sure that each image matches the description. The photographs are then sent to our imaging team, which cleans them up, crops them, resizes them, and gets them ready to go onto the Web. On average, there are at least 800 images taken per photographer per day. Let's say that, on average, we have 20 photographers working; that means we are shooting around 16,000 images daily. Those images help our customers to richly experience our products and make their choices in well-informed ways." Sixteen thousand images a day is the tangible and substantial manifestation of a commitment to give customers an abundant source of pictorial data to guide their purchases.

There definitely can be significant initial costs and logistical challenges involved in helping customers make better-informed choices, but, over time, improved efficiency typically drives down expense and generates great customer service benefits. When considering what it takes to help customers make knowledgeable decisions, leaders should think about offering guidance as a long-term investment. The more you assist your customers in getting what they want, the more those customers will turn to you as a trusted advisor for future products and services. As technology costs recede with time and as you improve your efficiencies, those initial investments often reap substantial returns.

As Zappos demonstrates, service excellence is a complex matter of disciplined investment, a commitment to customer ease, and attentiveness to all aspects of the customer journey. It also requires a willingness to remove the barriers that create customer resistance and a desire to earn customers' trust by guiding them to solutions and products that meet their needs.

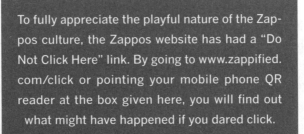

To fully appreciate the playful nature of the Zappos culture, the Zappos website has had a "Do Not Click Here" link. By going to www.zappified. com/click or pointing your mobile phone QR reader at the box given here, you will find out what might have happened if you dared click.

GETTING IT RIGHT

At its most fundamental level, customer satisfaction is a measure of whether your business is perceived as being competent at delivering in a way that meets the customers' expectations. While customers' expectations will vary depending on what is normal for your industry and what you specifically promise through your marketing efforts, customers universally become dissatisfied

ZAPPIFIED BRAIN BREAK

Please identify the nurse depicted here:

If you guessed Dr. Meredith Grey from *Grey's Anatomy* or Major Margaret "Hot Lips" Houlihan from *M*A*S*H*, you were close. Tony Hsieh's debut as a nurse— at least it is thought that it was his debut—occurred in a video describing Zappos benefits that is presented to all employees.

When Tony and then CFO Alfred Lin were asked if they would participate in the video by dressing up as nurses, they both agreed without even asking about the video's purpose. If you want your team to "embrace and drive change," "be adventurous, creative, and open-minded," and "create fun and a little weirdness"; it doesn't get much better than this. Would your CEO do the same? If you are the CEO, you might think about expanding your wardrobe for the next companywide meeting. Zappos has ample items in inventory to meet your needs.

when their expectations are not met. At Zappos, customers typically expect they are ordering a product that (1) is accurately described and depicted on the website, (2) has a price at checkout that matches the price listed for the product, (3) will be delivered within the time frame promised, (4) when opened, will match what was ordered, and (5) will meet the customers' intended use.

To deliver on all five of these expectations, Zappos creates many checks and rechecks, so let's look at a couple of these key areas of quality assurance. Specifically, we will explore how Zappos makes sure customers see accurate product descriptions on the website, receive what they ordered, and ultimately get products that work for them.

What You See Is What You Get

Have you ever noticed how ads for weight-loss products often depict "before" and "after" results using photos that not only demonstrate the weight-loss power of the advertised product but also show the transformation of a depressed, sweatsuit-wearing couch potato into a well-dressed, enlivened fashion model? The camera angles and posture of the so-called actual customer also go a long way to enhance the visual significance of the product's effectiveness. Better yet, how many of us own a product that looked so good on the infomercial that we couldn't resist buying it, only to discover that we wouldn't wish ownership on our worst enemy? Thanks to this type of advertising hype, customers have become skeptical about the authenticity of product representations.

When customers place an order on the Zappos website, they expect that what they see is what they'll get. Thus, to deliver on this customer expectation, Zappos makes a herculean effort to cut the hype and accurately inform the consumer of the precise details of the product. We learned earlier in the chapter how product quality teams make sure the photos of the Zappos products meet image and presentation standards and how they also check that those pictures match the item descriptions prior to the pictures' being placed on the website. Those two processes, however, are only part of an extensive set of quality reviews that begin with copywriters verifying product specifications prior to writing narrative descriptions and include such things as pains-taking effort to depict the color of the item accurately on the website. Christina Mulholland, Zappos senior image coordina-tor, notes, "We do everything in our power to capture the true color of a product. We constantly calibrate the monitors that we view our pictures on to make sure our screens represent true color. We physically compare the actual item to the color of the image on our screens. When people call the Zappos Customer Loyalty Team for a return, the CLT members code the reason for the return. When products are returned because of a wrong color, we will grab the product from our inventory, bring it to our desk, and reevaluate the color match." To meet customer ex-pectations, Zappos focuses on product presentation accuracy at every turn.

In addition to the reliability of product descriptions and de-pictions, customers expect that the item in their Zappos box will be the one they ordered. Fortunately or unfortunately for Zap-pos, errant service delivery has become a huge source of pain for many consumers today. It's fortunate in the sense that customers have come to expect so little when it comes to order fulfillment and unfortunate given that past bad experiences with online ful-fillment have left some customers wanting to physically place the items they want in real shopping carts.

In the drive-through restaurant sector, for example, the greatest factor in achieving customer satisfaction (considerably more significant than product quality) is order accuracy. Despite the significance of this customer expectation, MAX Interna-tional, a company that provides solutions for recording customer transactions, reports that drive-through orders are wrong 10 to 15 percent of the time. Given that 70 percent of restaurant vis-its are processed through the drive-through lane, MAX Interna-tional calculates industrywide losses from inaccurate orders and customer dissatisfaction as amounting to more than $8 billion. That's a lot of missing french fries!

By comparison to a drive-through restaurant order, imagine the challenge Zappos faces in order fulfillment accuracy. Let's assume you click the "submit my order" button on the Zappos website: What must happen for that product to arrive at your door (often the next day)? That click initiates a cascade of redundant processes and inventory management strategies involving the Zappos Fulfillment Centers in Shepherdsville, Kentucky. The Shepherdsville complex consists of two warehouses with a total of more than 1 million square feet of space. The facility contains roughly 5 million items and would hold approximately 744 average U.S. homes or 17 football fields.

Each day, vendor trucks deliver items to the Fulfillment Centers' inbound loading docks, and tens of thousands of items are processed into those buildings. Your item has to make it from the vendor truck to a location in the Fulfillment Centers where, through a combination of human and automated "pickers," it can be quickly selected (along with approximately 65,000 other items on any given day). Your item then needs to make it from the picker to the packaging area. Finally, it needs to be placed in your box with your correct address label affixed and then be processed out of the building to the local UPS distribution center. Voilà, it's at your door. That makes getting the french fries in the bag seem a much easier task, doesn't it?

Zappos innovations in inventory management offer great insights into the lengths to which service businesses must go to get the order right and not let the customer down. If you were to visit the storage racks at Zappos, you would see what looks like a cluttered closet. Items are not stored in tidy matching boxes. For example, you will not find all the size 7, medium width, chestnut Ugg kids' classic boots next to the same boot in a wider width. In fact, you will not even see all the size 7, medium width, chestnut Ugg kids' classic boots in the same storage space or even in the same aisle. Instead, you will see a mishmash of products and brands, all sharing shelf space. This "disorganized organization" results from Zappos leadership's decision that every product entering the warehouse must be given its own unique "license plate number" (LPN). In essence, Zappos can have 20 exactly identical items, but each will have its own LPN. Once the LPN is generated and placed on the item, the item is placed in the next available spot in the warehouse, and a central computer tracks the item's LPN and its location.

When you click that "submit my order" button, the computer looks for an LPN associated with the product you are purchasing. Pickers located strategically throughout the warehouse are instructed via handheld scanners as to which nearby rack holds your item. These individuals find your product, scan the LPN to verify it with the computer, visually inspect your item, and place it on an easily accessible conveyor. Craig Adkins, vice president of Zappos Fulfillment Operations, explains more about the accuracy checks that take place from picking to shipping: "We don't tell our people to pick a Nike, Adidas, or Reebok; we tell them to pick LPN 7705. This makes it a lot easier and more accurate to pick the item. It's not based on the criteria of size, width, color, fabric, or brand. All they're looking for is 7705. When they pick 7705, the box also has a bar code on it, and they have a scanner in their hands, so they scan that item. The scanner will tell the picker whether he has picked the correct target. That information plus a visual inspection of the product represents a first-level accuracy check. When our picker puts the item on the conveyor, it goes downstream through a number of additional scan points to make sure that this is the correct selection. When the item gets put into a shipping container to go to a customer, the product is scanned once again to verify that it is in fact part of the customer's order. Once that is verified, a shipping label is printed along with the order ID. The item is scanned yet again to make sure it matches what is supposed to be put in the shipping box and matches the packing slip." Check, recheck, and check again at every step of the way. When customer expectations and order fulfillment really matter, brands like Zappos leave little to chance.

TRY THESE ON FOR SIZE

1. Are you commited to helping customers make well-informed choices? Is the accuracy of your order processing important to your service value proposition?

2. How do you help customers make objective, accurate purchase decisions?

3. If order fulfillment is important to your brand, how well are you executing?

4. Losses caused by fulfillment error rates of 10 to 15 percent in the drive-through quick-service restaurant sector are estimated at $8 billion. How much do you think your company could gain, in terms of revenue and customer satisfaction, if you improved the accuracy of your order fulfillment?

5. What opportunities exist in your company to innovate inventory strategies or to build redundant systems of accuracy checking?

WHAT? WE GOT IT RIGHT, BUT YOU DON'T LIKE IT?

Despite all the meticulousness about the accurate depiction of items on the Zappos website, the creation of innovative product license plates, and repeated product checks, the customer might open the Zappos box and determine that the item ordered just doesn't work for him. Through no fault of Zappos, customers may have purchased items that don't look as good on them as they had hoped or don't fit as well as they had expected. Zappos does everything to get the right product to their customers, but sometimes the product fails to meet a customer's expectation. Now what?

This "moment of truth" is probably the clearest differentiator between minor-league and major-league service brands. In fact, many service brands take a "you chose it, we delivered it, and now it's going to be difficult to return it" approach. By contrast, Zappos stands behind a return policy written in plain English:

FREE Shipping:

Unlike many other websites that have special rules and lots of fine print, Zappos.com offers free shipping on all domestic orders placed on our website, with no minimum order sizes or special exceptions.

Just because shipping is free doesn't mean it should take a long time. Zappos.com understands that getting your items quickly is important to you, so we make every effort to process your order quickly. When you order from our website, you can expect to receive your order within 4-5 business days.

FREE Returns:

If you are not 100% satisfied with your purchase, you can return your order to the warehouse for a full refund. We believe that in order to have the best possible online shopping experience, our customers should not have to pay for domestic return shipping. So if for whatever reason you're not happy with your purchase, just go through our easy self-service return process to print out a free return label—your domestic shipping costs are prepaid.

With Zappos Retail, Inc.'s 365-day return policy, there are no special catches or exceptions. All we ask is that you send the items back to us in the original packaging and make sure that the merchandise is in the same condition.

Free returns for 365 days go a long way to making sure the business "gets it right" for its customers and ultimately that customers "get what is exactly right for them." When the customers know that they will get what they want, that the company will help them make the best choice, and that the entire process will be as effortless as possible, they often feel "wowed." That "wow" experience is reflected in exemplary customer reviews about operational excellence at Zappos found on social media sites that essentially say things like:

Zappos.com is a fantastic place to buy shoes online. Historically, when it comes to buying a pair of shoes I would only go to a store so I could make sure they fit. . . . But, Zappos makes it so easy to return the shoes that I have changed my shoe shopping behavior. If my shoes don't fit, I just pack 'em back up and Zappos pays the postage.

Zappos you rock!! I ordered over $600 worth of shoes just to determine which ones would be perfect for my wedding. I loved that shipping was free, and that they arrived the next day. In the comfort of my home and without time pressure, I tried all the shoes on, picked my favorite, and returned the rest with your free returns! It could not have been easier!

Let's face it; we live in a world of crappy customer service. By contrast, Zappos is a ray of sunshine. It's time corporate America takes note of Zappos great business model. I buy merchandise there all the time. I love their selection and. . . returns are a breeze.

Or, regularly on Twitter.com where, with brevity, customers offer comments like:

The *Zappos shopping experience* is frighteningly easy.

The tireless focus of Zappos leadership toward getting it right and making it easy serves as the foundation for delivering wow through service. In the next chapter, we will examine how Zappos focuses on velocity, builds staff members' passion as well as their product and service knowledge, manages breakdowns, and does little things to exceed customers' expectations. Then, we will look at how those actions work together to create customers who are unwaveringly loyal!

Chapter 4 *Ideas to Run With*

- Reducing customer effort increases customer loyalty.

- It is difficult to wow customers unless you execute on the basics of service.

- Service implies that a service provider will make a customer's life easier.

- Customer ease does *not* just happen. It has to be designed into the customer experience.

- In order to meet the wants, needs, and desires of your customers, you should invest in qualitative and quantitative approaches that help you understand customer preferences.

- Customer surveys are helpful but limited when it comes to collecting the "voice of the customer." Aggregate and granular customer behavior data fuel informed inferences about customer preferences. Those inferences need to be checked by making further observations and by asking customers for their feedback.

- In order to deliver customer satisfaction, you must study and execute on your service promises.

- The process of delivering to your customers' expectations often involves considerable expense, process innovation, and redundancy in delivery systems.

- When you help customers get their needs met easily and assist them to buy what they want, and you deliver those items reliably, customers not only are satisfied but are often wowed and loyal!

THE TICKET TO THE BIG SERVICE DANCE: VELOCITY, KNOWLEDGE, RECOVERY, AND SURPRISE

It doesn't seem like such a big deal, does it? Zappos consistently provides service that is easy and accurate, it helps customers make informed choices, and it gives consumers generous and painless returns. Then again, take a moment to think about how many companies actually execute that complete service package.

I'll even assume your business is like Zappos and you currently demonstrate *all* the service behaviors outlined in Chapter 4. In that case, you're looking to take your service up a level. So what's next? According to international studies like those done by Convergys, when a company masters ease and accuracy, its customers are looking for expedited service, knowledgeable staff, and other aspects of the experience that add value. Interestingly enough, many research studies show that personalized service (which occurs when service is modified to meet the specific needs of a customer or when an emotional connection is forged with a specific customer) is a long way down on customers' wish lists. Given this hierarchy of customer wants, I will reserve the Zappos approach for creating personalized care for Principle 3, "Step into the Personal." For now, we will look at what Zappos does to add value through service, including

1. Emphasizing velocity

2. Increasing staff members' knowledge of products and service delivery

3. Elevating service recovery

4. Delivering surprise beyond the predicted and normative

To set the tone for several of the topics covered in this chapter, Alfred Lin, former COO and CEO at Zappos, notes, "In 1999, when the company started, we didn't have the notion of customer service that we have today. Our service improvements were the result of very small incremental changes, whether they were to our return policy or the speed of our shipping processes. Often the difference between okay service and great service is a matter of executing on the basics and offering a slight extra that makes the customer go 'wow.' From our point of view, the cost difference between a 'wow experience' and an average experience is not much, while the benefit to the customer is huge." Similarly, Alfred adds, "We were fortunate to understand that, from a customer's perspective, loyalty is less about delivering to your word and more about what you do when you don't deliver. It's what we do that 0.1 to 1 percent of the time when we screw up that really matters." Few leaders fully understand the tremendous opportunity employee knowledge, operational excellence, and swift service recovery offer for enhancing customer loyalty. Let's zip toward some of the service wows that begin with rapid execution.

EMPHASIZING VELOCITY

It's been said that most of us have about as much time as we have money, and often we have too little of both. In a world where my children stand at a microwave exhorting, "Come on, come on; I don't have all minute," it's clear that consumers have become accustomed to instant everything. Many sectors of our economy are the direct result of service speed innovations. Whether it's quick service restaurants driven by companies like McDonald's, where orders are to be completed in two minutes or less, airport ticket kiosks, ATM machines, or drive-through liquor stores, speed is an important service proposition for most businesses. The ultimate challenge of all this "need for speed" is the ability to manage both the quickness of service and the effect of that quickness on overall service quality. Service that is executed too rapidly can be fraught with errors and may lead to customers feeling rushed.

As an alternative to the word *speed*, I suggest the term *service velocity*. As you may recall from physics class, "velocity" is the measurement of the rate and direction of change in an object's position. So when I refer to service velocity, I am talking about service speed coupled with an accurate and well-positioned customer experience. By that definition, Zappos has resoundingly mastered pinpoint service velocity.

At the time of Amazon's acquisition of Zappos, Jason Busch of Spend Matters talked about the core delivery competencies of both companies by noting, "Zappos customer experience is seamless and integrated. Amazon would never upgrade shipping to overnight, for example, as Zappos does, except through the Amazon Prime program. Amazon's warehouse is very innovative, but Amazon is focused on warehousing and lowering costs. Zappos has learned it's about more than just cost. It's about user experience, and people are willing to pay for that."

The relationship between Zappos delivery strength and the velocity of product delivery is well articulated by Marshall Kirkpatrick, vice president of content development at ReadWriteWeb. Marshall notes, "Amazon is a master of the supply chain. It's got so much capacity, . . . and Zappos is no slouch at rushing goods to your house. Just last week the Zappos elves delivered a new pair of shoes to my home the morning after I ordered them late at night!"

In my view, the magic of service velocity at Zappos might be the "elves," but it definitely is linked to consistent leadership decisions giving priority to rapid service, the inculcation of a sense of service urgency, and a commitment to deliver beyond industry standards and customer expectations.

When leadership decided to open the Zappos Fulfillment Center in 2002, the "where" of that warehouse decision came down to issues of delivery speed. By selecting Fulfillment Center locations near Worldport, the worldwide air hub for UPS (United Parcel Service), located at the Louisville International Airport in Kentucky, Zappos was immediately able to provide one-, two-, or three-day conventional transit time to a larger percentage of the U.S. population than from any other shipping point. According to Justin Williams, project manager at Zappos, the Kentucky location set the stage for a service velocity mindset: "We understood that leadership's choice of location for the Fulfillment Centers came from leaders stepping into the place of customers waiting to get their merchandise. That mindset carries over to all of us. No one likes to wait, particularly for something they are excited about. The way we develop our delivery system shocks people, even those inside of our company. We've actually had our own customer service reps cancel orders and reenter new ones because they didn't believe that an order placed at 12:30 a.m. was actually going to get delivered that same day. Our reps thought there was an error in the system, and they'd try to alert us at the Fulfillment Centers. Nothing was wrong; the order was fulfilled at 1:00 a.m., to be delivered by 1:00 p.m. the same day."

This service velocity mindset starts at the top of the organization and is held in areas well beyond the Fulfillment Centers in Kentucky. Anthony Vicars, director of fulfillment, notes, "When Tony Hsieh received an unexpected $75,000 to $100,000 credit from UPS, he demonstrated how important speed and service are by telling UPS to just exhaust the credit by giving next-day delivery upgrades for upcoming customer shipments. You know your leadership is serious about service speed when your CEO says, 'No thanks. I don't want our money back; we will just give customers complimentary upgrades. Give the credit back to the customer in the form of more expedited deliveries.'"

Employees notice when leaders make choices on behalf of service velocity, and so do customers. Rapid order fulfillment is one of the most commonly mentioned aspects of Zappos service excellence, according to online reviews. The following examples are very typical of tweets and customer posts about how the Zappos service velocity captures the attention and gratitude of their consumers:

> **@MorphMpls**
> Completely blown away by @zappos delivery time. Ordered Thurs noon, shoes on doorstep noon Friday. And standard shipping! Wow. :)

> My daughter's birthday shoes came so quickly. I am amazed. How could I have ordered them Monday evening and received them in the early afternoon Tuesday. You have exceeded my expectations and more importantly you have made for a very happy birthday girl. Thank you Zappos!

> I'll admit it, your delivery speed has spoiled me, but please don't stop! Why is it when I order online from other websites, it takes so long to get my merchandise? It's about time for other online retailers to step up to the Zappos Experience!!!

Service velocity happens at every contact point between the customer and Zappos. While customers overtly appreciate the "lightning fast" delivery, some of the rapidness of Zappos would probably be noticed only if it were missing. César Ritz, founder of The Ritz-Carlton Hotel Company, once said, "People like to be served, but invisibly." Two areas where invisible but important service takes place at Zappos are the load speed of pages on the Zappos website and the urgency with which Customer Loyalty Team (CLT) members answer calls.

As evidenced by the work of the user experience team in Chapter 4, Zappos invests heavily in making the website user experience as easy as possible. In addition, the company spends a considerable amount of money to make the website experience fast. In fact, according to Joseph Yi, who writes a social commerce blog entitled Viralogy, "If an eCommerce site is slow in loading a page, they are risking losing a potential sale. In an age where consumers have more and more options when it comes to shopping online, making sure that your site is optimized to bring a user the best experience possible includes making sure that your site has fast load times. If you take a look at some of the top eCommerce sites, page load times are in and around 3.5 seconds max." According to Joseph, the load times for these top sites have been assessed as follows: Dell.com at 3.3 seconds, BlueNile. com at 2.8 seconds, Overstock.com at 2.6 seconds, and the winner, Zappos, at 1.9 seconds.

From the standpoint of response urgency at the Zappos call center, the company sets performance goals of answering 80 percent of incoming calls within 20 seconds. Since Zappos is concerned about the customer experience, not simply service speed, call response urgency is targeted, but the length of a call is not. The goal is not to rush customers off the phone, but instead to be readily available to take calls as they are received. Mary Teitsma, a member of the CLT, notes, "While some of our customer calls last for hours, we focus on being quick to answer. From there, the call will commence at the customer's pace. With some customers, it becomes clear that they want to get on and off the call.

In those cases, we need to address the customer's issue quickly. I've had customers where I've literally placed an order within a minute's time because they're in a rush." Zappos has found a way to manage the logistic challenge of staffing its call center to answer quickly, but then pace those inbound calls to match the customers' needs. In fact, Zappos not only is able to hit its call-answering speed goal, but typically well exceeds it. Pam Cinko, Zappos Insights logistical ninja, demonstrates the significance of this answering speed by noting, "I was giving a tour of our facilities and mentioned our phone response standards. A little bit later, I thought one of the people on my tour was lagging behind, only to find that he was on his cell phone. He said, 'Hey, I just dialed the call center, and you were right; they picked up within five rings.' The man then told the CLT member who had answered his call, 'Hey, I'm here on the tour; I wanted to say hi to you! Where are you sitting?' The CLT member stood up and waved, and they finished their conversation face to face." Where else would this happen?

Most customers notice only if a company fails to respond swiftly to their needs, but because of the Zappos reputation for response time, sometimes people, like the caller on the tour, are actually testing the service velocity at Zappos. The magnitude of these experiments is reflected in online reviews like the following:

> Zappos zaps the customer experience at every turn . . . It starts with fast servers and an easy quick online check out process. It follows through to swift, clear order tracking communication and amazing product delivery. I had heard the hype and decided I would conduct a test to see if Zappos could match the claims I had been hearing. So I ordered merchandise from Zappos and comparable goods

from a competitor. The results—Zappos delivery within 36 hours; the competitor—well it's been three weeks and I am still waiting.

While most of us notice slow-loading Web pages or long delivery times, can you imagine your customers consciously clocking your service velocity, assessing your server page load speed, or shopping you and your competitors simultaneously? As business leaders, we would be wise to assume that service velocity is something our customers are always either consciously or unconsciously assessing.

TRY THESE ON FOR SIZE

1. Are you focused only on the speed of your service?

2. What actions by the leadership demonstrate a corporate commitment to service velocity?

3. What is the Internet chatter about your service speed and effectiveness?

4. Do service standards exist for service urgency across all channels of contact (phone, chat, Web, face to face) with customers? Is your service being delivered consistently against those standards?

5. Are your customers aware of your service velocity standards? How would customers test your service against your standards or against your competition? What would they find?

INCREASING STAFF MEMBERS' KNOWLEDGE OF PRODUCTS AND SERVICE DELIVERY

A significant source of customer distress and frustration comes from dealing with ill-informed or completely clueless staff members. In fact, studies of customer dissatisfaction consistently show how important it is to have employees who can address the customer's need during the customer's first contact. That research also suggests that the prime reason customers stop dealing with a business is poor service interactions, not faulty products. According to Tony Hsieh, "While most contact with Zappos happens on our website without human interaction, on average, every customer contacts us at least once at some point during his lifetime."

Given that most Zappos customers will have limited direct contact with Zapponians, the impact of those infrequent telephone or chat contacts takes on greater significance. In the buzz lingo of customer experience design, these types of important interactions are referred to as "moments of truth," a phrase coined by Jan Carlzon when he was the president and CEO of Scandinavian Airlines System.

While the personal aspects of these contacts will be addressed in the upcoming principle, let's take a look at how Zappos makes sure that knowledgeable Zapponians are ready to represent the brand during these human-to-human moments of truth. In large measure, knowledge readiness at Zappos is a direct result of the company's disciplined commitment to being a learning organization. In 1990, Peter Senge wrote the revolutionary book *The Fifth Discipline*, in which he urged business leaders to practice a consistent approach to knowledge acquisition. Senge specifically defined learning organizations as places "where people continually expand their capacity to create the results they truly desire, where new and expansive patterns of thinking are nurtured, where collective aspiration is set free, and where people are continually learning to see the whole together."

Consistent with this approach, the leadership at Zappos has supported continuous training that results in engaged customers and that nurtures the personal and professional aspirations of Zappos employees. This disciplined approach to knowledge transfer differs from the more situational commitments seen in other businesses. Unlike other companies, Zappos views training as an essential investment that needs to remain constant and not be subject to economic factors. In essence, Zappos sees learning as being essential to its mission. At a tactical level, Zappos often must train or retrain employees on how to deliver customer service that drives the Zappos Experience.

Zappos leadership supports a training model that focuses not only on the "satisfaction" of customers, but on their "happiness" as well. Upon completing the CLT orientation outlined in Chapter 3, Zappos staff members throughout the organization receive core classes in skills that are essential to knowledgeable service delivery. Aaron Magness, senior director, Brand Marketing & Business Development, notes, "A lot of companies will hire applicants largely based on their education level. They'll hire MBAs because of the skills those individuals probably acquired during their education. We, on the other hand, will hire primarily based on the passions of the individuals, and then we will teach them to do what we need them to do. Of course, our approach has positives and negatives. Sometimes we'll get incredibly passionate people without the true skill set for their role, and that's where our well-developed training comes into play." While the comprehensive Zappos training curriculum, Pipeline, will be examined in Chapter 8, "Zappos University," an example of this core skill development occurs for CLT members as they enter the "incubation phase" of their training.

According to Ashley Perry, a newly hired Zappos CLT member, "Incubation lasts a little over three weeks. It furthers your learning through classes in things like how to write high-quality e-mails, which gets a new hire e-mail certified. Additionally, the new employees receive training on how to be excellent at all aspects of their job, like handling customer returns. They will have been taking calls from their third week of orientation training, and that continues all the way through incubation." Laura Miller, a CLT member who is an ambassador for the incubation program, talks about her role as a mentor to new hires who are going through incubation: "As an ambassador, I will take my 'incubabies' around and just talk with them. I'll ask how their calls are going and informally be available with insight, tips, and tools." Laura's comments not only suggest a balance between on-the-job and classroom training at Zappos, but also show how experienced staff members are encouraged to be responsible for advancing the training and development of their peers.

An example of what Laura alludes to as tools is the Zappos informational wiki. As Chris Peake, director of performance, merchandising, describes it, "The wiki is a resource where CLT members can find additional information by brand and category and get additional answers for frequently asked questions. You want to make sure you are giving the customers the right information. So, CLT members have that information right at their fingertips, in addition to all the other resources that are already online." Having the right information just a click away when the customer needs it most—what a great goal for any business.

Suffice it to say the incubation period of CLT members is just a small part of ongoing processes to elevate the quality of service that occurs during CLT calls or online chat sessions. Since many of the additional knowledge development tools (supervisor involvement, customer feedback, and the "Sharing Great Calls" program) also affect the emotional connection between Zappos staff members and customers, those tools will be discussed in Chapter 7. For now, it's important to simply appreciate that service skills training and product knowledge acquisition are continual processes at Zappos. Leaders throughout the organization appreciate the benefit of ongoing skills development both for those receiving the training and for peers who serve as trainers and mentors. Learning benefits both the teacher and the student!

ZAPPIFIED BRAIN BREAK

*T*ony Hsieh officially announced the following on his blog:

Zappos.com, Inc. has filed a class action lawsuit against the Walt Disney Company over false advertising. Tony Hsieh, CEO of Zappos, says it's just one battle in his efforts to prevent companies from making misleading claims.

The lawsuit alleges that Disneyland's tagline of being "The Happiest Place on Earth" is "clearly false, deceptive, and confusing to the marketplace," and it cites internal Net Promoter Score (NPS) metrics that suggest that the designation should be given to Zappos.com, Inc.

Of course, the post was issued on April 1, April Fools' Day, but it had its intended satirical effect and was widely circulated on the Internet.

ELEVATING SERVICE RECOVERY

How can I put this gently? Sometimes, despite its knowledgeable staff, operational redundancies, and extreme effort to deliver products easily, quickly, and accurately, Zappos gets it wrong! In the course of millions of site visits and tens of thousands of calls and purchases each day, Zappos makes mistakes. But Zappos doesn't categorize those errors as failures; instead, each of those mistakes serves as an outstanding opportunity for both its business and its customers.

The work of researchers like Amy Smith and Ruth Bolton, published in the *Journal of Service Research*, shows that a company's recovery from mistakes has substantial impact on customer perceptions and on the future purchases of those consumers. Research indicates that customers who experience a service breakdown and receive a swift, helpful resolution are more likely to recommend that business to a friend or colleague than customers who experienced no service issues at all. Like that of many great service brands, the leadership at Zappos clearly sends the message that some of the most challenging and important service moments occur in response to Zappos errors. Former CFO Alfred Lin shares the lengths to which Zappos will go when the company is the source of a customer's inconvenience: "If we screw up, we will absolutely make it right for the customer. There was a situation where a lady contacted me and said, 'All I wanted was this pair of shoes that I ordered.'" According to Alfred, that customer had gotten black shoes instead of blue ones. She brought that to the attention of the CLT staff members, but in their efforts to expedite a fix for the problem, they twice sent more black shoes, not blue ones.

Alfred continues, "When this customer contacted me, she kindly said, 'You guys look like you are a reputable company, but I'm not going to do business with you anymore." In addition to refunding her money, offering his apologies, and giving the customer a coupon for an additional pair of shoes at Zappos, Alfred and other Zapponians kept searching for the genesis of the problem and for complete resolution. Alfred shared, "We found the source of our error, which involved moving into a new distribution building. But that shouldn't be relevant to our customer; we were totally wrong. To make matters worse, the blue shoes were no longer being produced and couldn't be reordered. That did not stop us. We contacted our Clarks representative (the manufacturer of her desired shoe), and thanks to incessant calling on his part, we were finally able to find her blue shoes in a Clarks retail store. A few weeks later, we were able to send the blue ones to her." Alfred's "blue shoe" story is an example of the tone for service recovery set from the top at Zappos. Clearly, apologies, refunds, and a free pair of shoes were not enough, given the circumstances. Even though the customer had clearly stated that she was not going to do business with Zappos again, that didn't stop the Zappos team (and its vendor partner Clarks) from hunting down those blue shoes.

Great service organizations won't end their service recovery processes until they make their customer whole again (*integrity* derives from the root for the word *integer,* which denotes wholeness). This commitment to wholeness is maintained even when the customer has vowed never to do business with that company again. Companies like Zappos act swiftly, take responsibility (often even when the fault is beyond their control), enable staff discretion to fix problems, compensate fairly, do a little something extra to acknowledge inconveniences, and follow up until the issue is brought to satisfactory closure.

It is leadership tenacity, passion, and follow-through that inspire empowered Zappos staff members to produce customer service recovery stories like one shared by customer Karen Batchelor in a Social Media for Small Business blog post aptly entitled "My Un-complaint against Zappos." Karen explains:

> Last week I ordered 2 pairs of black cargo shorts by Jag for the summer that's finally coming to Michigan. I've ordered from Zappos before, . . . and in the past whatever I ordered was available in my size and arrived as promised—end of story. But when my Zappos package arrived today, I was disappointed. There were 2 pairs of black shorts inside but in 2 different sizes—one not mine. . . . I picked up the phone 1) to complain and 2) to see if that second pair of shorts was still available. This is where the story gets good. My call was connected to a very cordial Zappos customer service rep. . . . When I explained my dilemma, she went into action. . . . She checked to see if the other pair of shorts was still available. The bad news was they weren't. Darn it but I'll live. Then the nice young customer service rep apologized profusely and offered the following solution to the Zappos mistake in filling my order. . . . She e-mailed me a return label for the UPS package AND a return form completely filled in with all the details of my wrong size black shorts. No need to fill out the form while trying to find an SKU number somewhere on the garment. She enrolled me in the Zappos VIP program which gets me an upgrade of 1-day shipping on any future orders. When I decided to order another item for $7 more than the shorts, she told me she wouldn't charge me for the difference. And finally, she gave me a $10 coupon

I can use for future purchases. I'm still picking myself up
off the floor.

In many ways, the Zappos approach to service recovery, as
evidenced in Karen's post, is an amplification of all aspects of
the Zappos service platform. Because Zappos draws people to

TRY THESE ON FOR SIZE

1. From the standpoint of being a learning organization,
   is your business a place where people continually
   expand their capacity to create results that are truly
   desired?

2. Would your company be described as nurturing new
   and expansive patterns of thinking, and is it a place
   where collective aspirations are set free and where
   people are continually learning to see the whole
   together?

3. What processes and training do you have in place
   to drive product and service knowledge? Is support
   for this training consistent, or does it fluctuate with
   economic factors?

4. How effective is your service recovery? What are your
   customers saying about the effectiveness of your
   response to product or service breakdowns?

5. Does your leadership set the tone for the importance
   of service recovery efforts?

purchase from it based on the company's service reputation, staff members have to be able to turn negative interactions into happy endings. Dissatisfied or disappointed customers can quickly become vocal detractors unless breakdowns are seen as opportunities for "delivering wow through service." A knowledgeable Zappos employee living the company values apologized to Karen about a Zappos error. In the process, that employee swiftly eased Karen's effort and went to the trouble of making sure that Karen was not just satisfied but happy, albeit "floored" by the experience. In many ways, Karen's service recovery story also captures the last element in Zappos basic service template: the power of surprise!

DELIVERING SURPRISE BEYOND THE PREDICTED AND NORMATIVE

I am convinced that customers will say "wow" in response to service in two basic circumstances:

1. When you exceed their expectations

2. When you make a personal emotional connection with them

Since Chapter 6 will focus on creating personal emotional connections, let's examine how Zappos delivers service that addresses the first of these two conditions: exceeding expectations.

While many people talk about exceeding customer expectations, very few of them discuss the nature of those expectations in the first place. From my perspective, customer expectations are easily evaluated in terms of those that are predicted and those that are normative. By *predicted*, I am talking about realistic, practical, or anticipated outcomes that emerge from personal experiences, reported experiences of others, and sources of knowledge such as the media. In essence, predicted expectations are what customers think will be realistic given their understanding of your industry. *Normative* expectations, by contrast, are based on what customers believe should or ought to happen; these beliefs are not what customers have come to expect, but what they think is right to expect. Zappos delivers "wow" in numerous ways by exceeding both predicted and normative expectations.

From a predicted perspective, many customers have come to expect that online retailers will make them pay for shipping, and that if a return is needed, that shipping will also be at the customer's expense. Almost from the beginning, Zappos exceeded industry standards on both those fronts. (Some e-retailers have since emulated Zappos, particularly on free shipping to the customer.) Customers have also come to expect that if they need to call the online company as a result of a problem, finding the call-center number on the company's website will be a challenge. Zappos puts "24/7 Customer Service (800) 927-7671" prominently on every page of its site. The choices of Zappos leaders and the actions of Zapponians are geared to consistently exceeding customer expectations, particularly when those expectations are based on the long call wait times, outsourced call-center workers, and scripted customer service interactions offered by other providers.

From a normative perspective, Internet customers believe their items "should" arrive on the date promised at checkout. On this dimension, Zappos often dazzles customers by randomly surprising them with free shipping upgrades or giving them status as VIPs, thus ensuring them free overnight shipping for all future purchases, the ability to call a special call-center number, access to a VIP ordering page, and other exclusive benefits. Anthony Vicars, director of fulfillment, puts it well: "On our website, we say free ground shipping with four to five days delivery. I'd say a little over 70 percent goes out next day air. Customers feel valued when you do more than you say you will. That alone can make the difference between okay and wow service." When customers get more than they believe they should, they are wowed, as evidenced by these representative tweets from customers:

> **@Hyjenrenee**
> wow, @zappos . . . how do you do it? i'm amazed every single time with the next day delivery.

> **@Dsalt**
> If every internet company was like zappos nobody would ever leave their house to shop. I ordered 2 day delivery and was bumped up to next day air free; my order gets here tomorrow.

> **@DrawingInsights**
> zappos I ordered a free culture book 2 days ago, you said it would be here in 6 days. . . . Why's it already here?!?! You guys are the best!

> **@mikestenger**
> Just became a VIP. I felt important already, now they're just making ice cream available WITH the cake!"

The double-edged sword of exceeding customer expectations, whether they are predicted or normative, is that once you deliver extraordinary service, extraordinary can become ordinary and expected. Zappos has created a legion of raving fans that use social media to talk incessantly to their families, friends, colleagues, and neighbors about the service excellence of the brand. That, coupled with significant media attention about service speed at Zappos as well as free upgrades, has produced high expectations for service delivery. Chris Raeburn, a respected customer service blogger, put it this way on his site Service Encounters Onstage: "My experience went off without a hitch through every moment of truth. The registration-through-purchase experience on the site, the in-process updates, and the fulfillment were as expected, and I ended up having a good experience buying a good pair of shoes for a good price. The entire experience was good—pretty much exactly as I had expected. And there's Zappos' problem. Because of considerable build-up, . . . Zappos would have had to absolutely rock my service world in order to be notable. . . . For companies that set high levels of expectations, it is extremely difficult . . . to exceed them. Unless something goes monumentally wrong and is spectacularly recovered, it's unlikely the experience will seem more than adequate. But in a time when many businesses seek to establish and perform to an adequate level of service expectations, Zappos seeks out a higher level of criticism. That in itself says that much of what we read about their culture might actually be true."

Some leaders might see the ever-escalating nature of customer expectations as an exercise in futility. It could be likened to the plight of Sisyphus, the Corinthean king of Greek mythology who was condemned to roll a boulder up a hill each day, only to have it roll back down at night. What's the point of delivering great service if it will soon just become good service? The immediate answer is that if you don't keep reaching, your average service will soon become poor.

In all candor, providing great service is never-ending and, at times, frustrating. Whether you compare yourself to world-class service providers, constantly adjust to customers' increasing expectations, or simply try to be better than you were the day before, service excellence is a dynamic, challenging, and rewarding journey. When your service delivery becomes predictable, it is probably time to recalibrate and look for additional ways to exceed customer expectations. Zappos is always looking for avenues to positively surprise customers and meet the "predictability challenge." For example, it has partnered with companies like The Learning Channel (TLC) and Red Bull to put unexpected objects in customers' delivery boxes. The Red Bull energy drink "surprise" was timed to jump-start a new year and involved the inclusion of cans of Red Bull in 150,000 customer boxes and packages. Tweets about the Red Bull wow (some of which include photo links of the bubble-wrapped can) are exemplified by

> @matrixmagicman
> Zappos you rock! I got a Red Bull enclosed with my order today. How did you know I needed one? Thanks!

> @ressler
> Huzzah! Zappos shipped my order overnight for free *and* tossed in a can of Red Bull. Thanks Zappos team!

The Learning Channel provided 25,000 pairs of red flip-flops that were unexpectedly placed in customers' order packages during a monthlong summer surprise event.

Through strategic partnerships, there is no end to the variety of inserts that customers might find in their Zappos box. In essence, Zappos has found a way to intermittently surprise customers with items that are unexpected. The mere act of delivering something that the customer did not know was coming is a key to widespread wow delivery.

To experience the Zappos ability to deliver surprise, go to zappified.com/flip or direct your mobile QR reader at the image given here.

Zappos diligently looks for effective ways to improve its operational excellence, increase personal service delivery, and go beyond the predictability challenge to exceed expectations and surprise customers. In language used by many Zapponians, Zappos leaders pursue a BHAG, or Big Hairy Audacious Goal (term coined by Jim Collins and Jerry Porras), to "have the best customer service in the world." That goal sits well in a culture that is committed to embracing and driving change.

In many ways, Zappos has accepted the encouragement of American humorist Will Rogers when Rogers suggested, "Why not go out on a limb? That's where the fruit is." Chapter 6 helps you venture out farther onto a limb where you are likely to find the most profitable fruit—a personal connection with your customer.

Chapter 5 *Ideas to Run With*

- Service excellence often comes down to the velocity of service delivery and the knowledge level of staff members.

- Service velocity is important not only in the product delivery process but across every consumer contact point and every channel of contact with a customer.

- While most customers will notice only when service components such as accuracy, ease, or speed are absent, some will consciously test you on those dimensions.

- Customers most often complain about a lack of knowledgeable service staff, which often results in their having to repeatedly seek fulfillment of their needs.

- Learning organizations practice disciplined support of training, irrespective of economic factors that may negatively affect the business.

- Effective service recovery often produces stronger relationships with customers than the business would have enjoyed had it not made a mistake in the first place.

- Leadership plays a significant role in setting a tone for issues such as urgency and service recovery.

- Service leaders innovate policies and processes that exceed industry standards.

- As you set higher service standards, you must accept the challenge of elevated expectations. The fruits of business success exist on those higher branches of excellence.

- Partner with other businesses to positively surprise customers. The possibilities are endless!

Step into the Personal

The companies that survive longest are the ones that work out what they uniquely can give to the world—not just growth or money but their excellence, their respect for others, or their ability to make people happy. Some call those things a soul.

—CHARLES HANDY

Principle 2, "Make It Effortlessly Swift," demonstrates how Zappos delivers wow through service without even having to make customer service personal. But the leadership at Zappos has aspired to a more potent transformational and emotional service outcome, namely, to deliver happiness. While brands can rely on operational excellence in service delivery to garner respect and differentiate themselves from less effective competitors, legendary and beloved companies seek personal, enriched experiences that are easily remembered and readily shared with others. In Chapter 6, "More than a Wallet with Legs," we step into the personal with Zappos by examining how its leaders foster an environment of authentic connections and real relationships with customers. By contrast, Chapter 7, "Connections at All Levels," reveals how the leaders of Zappos openly and consistently provide feedback that helps staff members deliver personalized service to customers, vendors, and even noncustomers. Author Scott Johnson once said, "Caring is a powerful business advantage." So let's get personal with Zappos and understand the advantage the company enjoys through the personal care and connections created by Zapponians.

MORE THAN
A WALLET
WITH LEGS

When I give presentations about service, I often suggest that customers today are tired of being treated like "wallets with legs." Zappos gets what I mean.

The leadership at Zappos understands that business can be about more than discrete transactions or money/product exchanges. Business can be, and increasingly must be, about the development of personal relationships that span a customer's lifetime. While average managers might think a company can thrive simply by selling goods or services to consumers, true leaders understand that all business is personal. In the end, business success relies on one group of people caring for or profiting another. Ordinary brands often take a "one size fits all" approach to service, but legendary companies like Zappos find ways to create individualized experiences that extend beyond their solid service platform.

ZAPPOS IS LEGENDARY?
WHAT DOES THAT MEAN?

In his book *Legendary Brands*, Laurence Vincent notes that leaders in legendary companies "forge deep bonds with consumers through narrative devices. They are storytellers, drawing from a library of timeless narratives . . . to captivate consumers and sustain meaning across cultural borders. It is the narrative of the Legendary Brand that generates and sustains customer affinity."

So, to use Vincent's words, what are the "timeless narratives" at Zappos? At the corporate level, the Zappos epic storyline might include the tale of college roommates who transform their limited resources into a billion-dollar business through persistence, quiet demeanors, entrepreneurial skills, a little weirdness, and a lot of intelligence. Alternatively, it might reflect the journey of maverick leaders who truly placed their team and their culture above everything else and thus secured interpersonal, social, and financial wealth.

While those macro-level themes are important to the Zappos mystique, most legendary service companies have generated a lore surrounding employee interactions with customers. A classic example of such a defining service story is the Nordstrom "snow tire" example, as shared in a *Newsweek* magazine article: "The customer wanted to return a tire. Never mind that the Nordstrom department-store chain sells upscale clothing, not automotive parts. According to company lore, the clerk accepted the tire because that's what the customer wanted."

The myth-busting website snopes.com was unable to con-
firm or refute the existence of the Nordstrom snow tire exchange,
but the site did offer a keen assessment of the story's relevance:
"This is possibly the greatest consumer relations story of modern
times—it's certainly pointed to as such in a multitude of business
articles. In this one simple vignette is captured the essence of
what it takes to build and maintain a loyal client base: The customer is always right . . . even when he's probably wrong." Like
Nordstrom, other service leaders such as The Ritz-Carlton Hotel
Company (which I featured in the book *The New Gold Standard*)
are rich with epic stories of staff members sacrificing themselves
in heroic ways to meet the needs of customers or guests.

So if Zappos is truly a legendary service provider, what are
the stories that form the foundation of the Zappos legend? How
about customer service calls that last seven or eight hours? Lauren Spenser, Customer Loyalty Team member, handled one protracted call that went on for 7 hours and 28 minutes. Lauren
notes that she developed an early rapport with the caller, Alice,
even though Lauren wasn't initially able to meet Alice's need:
"She was such a fun person who contacted me about items she
had seen in a Zappos magazine advertisement at her doctor's office. Surprise, surprise, the magazine was so out of date that we
didn't have any of the items she asked about."

In the hours that followed, Alice talked with Lauren about
"the good old days of service" when Alice enjoyed doctors' house
calls and front-door milk delivery. Alice shared highlights of her
life and events that were significant to her. The call proceeded
unaffected through a series of needed breaks, including the
replacement of a couple of Lauren's battery-depleted headsets.
Lauren shares, "Alice was a delightful older southern woman
much like my grandmothers, and she seemed to just want

someone to listen." Lauren continues, "Honestly, I consider that type of listening to be my job, even if this case was a little to the extreme. I've been asked why I didn't get in trouble for taking such a long call. It's just the way the Zappos CLT works. With no call times and no pressure to end a call, we all work together to make sure that every other call is getting answered swiftly."

Lauren sums up the lesson of this extended phone contact by saying, "I didn't consciously set out to be on a call for 7½ hours, and Alice didn't buy anything. We didn't have the product she wanted. She didn't even have a computer to look at anything; she just remembered the items from the magazine. I served her what I had—my attention and care. If someone needs to talk, that's what I'm here for. I'm not going to say, 'Sorry, I don't do personal.' I'm not hired to sell anything. If I serve well, sales will take care of themselves."

People who genuinely believe that if they "serve well, sales will take care of themselves" tend to build legendary brands. Aaron Magness, senior director of Brand Marketing & Business Development at Zappos, remarks, "It's sad how a little bit of genuine care can make the difference between horrible service and amazing service. If companies thought more about interaction and less about transaction, people would flock to them."

It is this attention to interaction at Zappos that propels people to connect further with the company. One example of a highly engaged connection even involved betrothal and marriage. This legendary event is best shared by the groom, Greg, who reports that the first time he and his girlfriend (now his wife) Tamara visited Zappos Headquarters, they got engaged, "the second time we got married, and the third time—we're expecting her to be pregnant." (Okay, that's probably more information than we needed.)

In a YouTube video captured by Zappos staff, Greg shares that the wedding plans were the result of a call he placed to Pam Cinko, logistics ninja at Zappos Insights. After the couple secured a minister, Pam and team members at Zappos made the wedding possible. Tamara notes, "I didn't want to get married in some place where I'd feel uncomfortable. We wanted a context of love, and we felt love when we first visited Zappos. It was palpable. . . . We walked through, and it felt like we were instant celebrities. We felt like we were somebody special and important. So when he asked me to marry him here, . . . it felt like we were coming home." Wow! A Zappos service culture that was so enveloping that love and engagement were experienced on a tour! From my perspective, those experiences are the ingredients of legend. Robert Richman, Zappos Insights product manager, puts it slightly differently: "People want authentic connections these days. When staff members are not only permitted, but encouraged to bring their humanness to work, memorable—almost magical—things happen with customers and noncustomers alike."

Some people might debate the service merits of 7½-hour calls with prospective customers or weddings at a business office. But the same concerns can be raised about the merits of the legendary Nordstrom example. Is it really good service to accept returns on products that you obviously don't carry? In the end, the content of these types of stories may be less important than the lesson drawn from them, namely, that businesses should place people before profit.

While epic wow service stories capture a great deal of attention, the bulk of what wows or emotionally connects with people tends to involve smaller acts of kindness. In the world of social media, these are the seeds of service lessons carried in tweets that are frequently retweeted on Twitter, and posts that are highly "liked" or readily posted on Facebook walls. These stories are often simple and strike an emotional chord. Typically, they involve comments about a handwritten thank-you note that a customer received from a Zappos staff member after the person placed an order or a Zappos CLT member who helped a cell phone caller with directions when the caller was lost trying to get to a restaurant. As CLT member Shawna Macias puts it, "Our customers know they can call us for anything. They know we are here for them. Not the other way around. Sometimes it's like we are a telephone Google service."

For Zappos, the Internet is abuzz with small Zapponian wows that weave the fabric of the brand's legend. One Zappos service story that has been extensively posted, forwarded, "favorited," and retweeted involves customer Zaz Lamarr. Zaz apparently ordered several pairs of shoes from Zappos for her mother who was dying of cancer. Since her mom had lost considerable weight, Zaz got an assortment of sizes; two fit her mother. Zaz made arrangements to return the other seven pairs of shoes but was unable to follow through on the return in a timely manner. When Zappos contacted Zaz about not receiving her merchandise, she shared her extenuating circumstances: her mother had died, and she would be sending the shoes back as soon as she could. Rather than requiring that Zaz comply with the official return policy, Zaz notes:

> They e-mailed back that they had arranged with UPS to pick up the shoes, so I wouldn't have to take the time to do it myself. I was so touched. Later I received a beautiful arrangement in a basket with white lilies and roses and carnations. Big and lush and fragrant. I opened the

card, and it was from Zappos. I burst into tears. I'm a
sucker for kindness.

While stories like Zaz's gather a sizable following, other posts
simply blend into the rich chatter of social communication. For
example, Jon Ferrara, founder of Nimble Software, tweeted, "My
son wrote Zappos a letter, & they sent him back a book on Company Culture personally signed by the entire management team."
In follow-up contact with Jon, he unpacked the details: "This
customer experience almost brought tears to my eyes. My son,
Ian, had an English class assignment to write a feedback letter
to a company. He chose to write Zappos, since he loved the company." Jon continues, "Zappos then blew me away by sending Ian
the Zappos Culture Book. They then went a step further by having the entire management team personally sign the book, each
writing a short personal message to my son. When he showed
me, I was stunned. I could not put it down. I have rarely had an
experience like this in all my years of business."

TRY THESE ON FOR SIZE

1. What are the small and epic acts that make up your
   service story?

2. What do people remember about the way contact with
   your business made them feel?

3. What are the stories circulating about your company's
   legendary service delivery?

4. How are you capturing and retelling large and small
   wows delivered by your team?

According to Jon, on one of the book's front pages was a modified quote from Maya Angelou "shared by the CEO, Tony Hsieh: 'People may not remember exactly what you did or what you said, but they will always remember how you made them feel.' I will always remember how this experience made me feel. I am a Zappos customer for life!" Now that's a phrase that most business owners can't hear enough of: "I am your customer for life."

AND THE DESTINATION IS?

Educator Lawrence J. Peter once said, "If you don't know where you are going, you will probably end up somewhere else." A large part of a Zapponian's ability to achieve strong and personal connections with customers is the clarity with which the entire organization understands and moves in the direction of a shared service destination.

If you were to wander around Zappos locations in either Nevada or Kentucky and randomly stop Zapponians to ask them, "How should people feel when they have contact with Zappos?" you would get a narrow range of responses. Employees would typically answer "wowed," "happy," or "emotionally connected on a personal level." This collection of responses reflects an almost cultlike alignment, particularly when you appreciate that the three answers really refer to the same outcome. According to Zappos CEO Tony Hsieh, "Most of the phone calls we receive don't result in sales. People might call because it's their first time returning an item, for example. They just want help stepping through a process. But that's our chance to build that personal emotional connection that wows them and leaves them happy."

ZAppIFiED BRAIN BREAK

*T*he term *"Way We Serve Statement"* emerged a number of years ago while I was working to help clients find the essence of the emotional connection that they wish to create with their customers. For example, I define The Ritz-Carlton's Way We Serve Statement as "creating the home of a loving parent," Pike Place Fish Market's as "treating customers like the customers are world famous," and Starbucks as "producing the living room of the community." In each instance, staff members are guided in the direction of a desired emotional outcome on the part of customers. Do you have a Way We Serve Statement for your business? If not, you can access a complimentary tool to guide you in developing one by going to www.zappified.com/wwss or aiming your QR mobile phone bar code reader at the image given here.

Although it may not have been their formal intention, the leaders at Zappos have functionally crafted what I refer to as a "Way We Serve Statement™" that defines and communicates a well-differentiated, branded customer experience. The Zappos Way We Serve Statement goes beyond what staff members need to do to serve well, since that information can usually be found on operational checklists; instead, it addresses what it should feel like to be served at Zappos. Customers should experience personal emotional connections (also referred to as PECs) that are consistent with a Way We Serve Statement declaring that Zapponians "deliver wowful happiness."

Enable Me and Stay Out of My Way

Given that the service destination at Zappos is clearly defined, the company's leaders carefully draft the necessary policies to facilitate staff members' ability to "deliver wowful happiness." In addition, they demonstrate restraint when it comes to policies that might interfere with happiness delivery.

It is easy for supervisors to become so focused on service consistency that they inadvertently restrict their teams' ability to forge personal connections with customers. When a company has procedures in place to handle every situation identically, that company's service will be uniform. In addition, by controlling the customer experience and what employees are allowed to do, a business can reduce the complexity of its offerings. If your people are allowed to offer only "vanilla" service to everyone, your operation is far less complicated than if employees have the discretion to select a vanilla, chocolate, or strawberry option, depending on their assessment of each customer's wants, needs, or desires. Of course, the more the leaders empower staff members to make decisions based on the personal needs of customers, the less consistently service might be delivered and the greater the service complexity.

The ultimate approach to ensuring service consistency is the use of customer service scripts. These scripting strategies can be found in many service sectors, including healthcare, banking, and call-center environments. Some scripts are so restrictive that they give employees no latitude for variation in word use and zero ability to deliver service solutions other than those that are scripted. Many of us have had the traumatic experience of interacting with a call-center staff person who is chained to a service script. The cadence of the service provider's speech sounds eerily robotic, and you know that if a solution to your need isn't written down as part of the call center's "marching orders," you are doomed. Of course, there are risks associated with giving employees "carte blanche" latitude, not least of which is the inability to provide service quality, maintain scalability, or ensure business viability.

Few businesses have sufficient profit margins or pricing opportunities to provide limitless and nonscalable levels of customer personalization. Even when leaders at The Ritz-Carlton suggest that they "will move heaven and earth for a guest as long as it is legal and ethical," they understand when that level of earth moving occurs, additional service charges can be assessed. Overall, most leaders must wrestle with the tension between rigid policies for service consistency and empowered service guidelines that allow for manageable personalized solutions.

This is where Zappos strikes a strategic balance. Its leaders seek to create the policies that are required if the company is to guarantee that all customer needs can be met efficiently and consistently, while at the same time retaining the flexibility to forge personal emotional connections with each individual customer served. Dylan Morris, CLT lead, acknowledges, "We have our share of policies and procedures here at Zappos, but we try not to create guidelines that get in the way of our people. I see us setting up processes or procedures that allow Zappos to run the business smoothly for the good of all and also to create customer experiences at the individual level. Otherwise, we as leaders need to let our people handle situations and make connections with customers through genuine human interaction. For example, in a lot of companies, first-level employees would be required to go through their supervisors or managers to find ways to wow that small percentage of customers who might not be happy. But here at Zappos, every single person is empowered to do what is needed."

An example of a Zappos policy that is designed to drive smooth business operation is a guideline about working with customers who want to speak to a particular CLT representative. Let's say you had a fabulous call with CLT rep Bob on Monday, and you call on Tuesday and ask for Bob. In order for the Zappos call center to perform its function and for you not to become dependent upon one person to meet your needs, Zappos has guidelines that state that CLT members should not seek to transfer a caller to a representative who is asked for by name. This policy exists to avoid the impact such transfers would have on call-center efficiency. In addition, since CLT members can access all prior transactions on their computer screens, and since each team member is capable of producing a personal connection, the customer's stated preference does not rise to the level of a true service need. Every business leader must identify areas where the wishes of a customer can't be accommodated because the impact of that accommodation would reduce quality for all other customers.

Customer service–enriching policy guidelines at Zappos include such things as setting expectations that CLT staff members will follow through on all promises made to a customer and creating expectations that representatives will provide a full order recap before a call is completed. Most noteworthy in the arena of customer experience enrichment policies are those guidelines that do *not* exist. In many important areas, the leadership at Zappos has stayed out of the way of the staff members' ability to build emotional connections with customers. Mary Teitsma, CLT senior representative, notes, "Coming from a world of retail since I was 15, I am used to being told to put the customers first, but, in truth, that was mostly just words. I really don't think I knew what that meant until I came to Zappos. Unlike a normal call center, where policies would limit my customer calls to a minute or 90 seconds each, I am allowed to take the time to connect with customers. I am also given the resources and authority to use my judgment to wow customers. For example, we have blank cards in the CLT area that we use when we want to acknowledge a special event that we learned about during a call. Because people have developed such a sense of trust in our team's desire to genuinely care for them, we have people call us when they don't have Internet access and want to know what movies are playing in their area. So we access the Internet and help them out however we can. Or in the rare cases where we don't have an item they are looking for in our inventory, I'll locate the item at a competitor's site and send the customer to the competition."

Undeniably, putting the customers' needs at the center of your business (up to and including sending them to the competition) is better for the customers. But could it be strangely profitable for your business as well? Steve Downton, Hilbrand Rustema, and Jan Van Veen, writing in their book *Service Economics*, suggest that companies that truly allow staff members to take care of the best interests of customers enjoy, on average, more than 20 percent greater profits than those that operate from a less customer-centric perspective. Treating customers as more than "wallets with legs" ultimately profits those who serve as well as those who are being served.

TRY THESE ON FOR SIZE

1. What is your Way We Serve Statement?

2. If a group of researchers traipsed across your corporate landscape asking your employees how customers should feel after doing business with you, what range of responses would they hear?

3. How would you characterize the balance your business has struck when it comes to service consistency and personalized customization?

4. When you look at your company policies, do they lead to both smoother business operations and enriched customer experiences? If not, which ones might be eliminated or modified?

5. In what ways do your people act to serve customers' needs, even when those needs don't seem to serve the short-term interests of the business? Would you ever send a customer to a competitor if it was in the best interest of the customer?

Personal at Every Turn, with a Generous Mix of Kindness and Gratitude

Even in settings where nothing is for sale, staff members at Zappos understand that they are not in the shoe or merchandise business but rather in the happiness, wow, and PEC business. Zack Davis, Kan-Du enthusiast, who drives a shuttle bus for Zappos, notes, "Just like everyone else in the company, I have a very important job. I am in the relationship and kindness business. My relationships may last only for the time it takes for me to pick someone up at the airport and bring them to our Headquarters for a tour, but if I extend kindness and listen to people, their relationship with Zappos could last a lifetime." When your shuttle bus drivers see themselves as more than transporters and when they are passionate about building brand loyalty through kindness, you are a service organization.

Bestselling author Seth Godin has provided keen insights on kindness, passion, and happiness by noting, "Happiness's best friend is kindness. And passion's best friend is generosity. Going forward, I think it's very hard to be passionate unless you're willing to be generous with people and you're willing to give them the emotional gift of connection and leading them in ways that matter. And I think if you want to be happy, we have to figure out ways to be kind."

Kindness is a key word at Zappos, and it may play an increasingly important role in corporate life worldwide. The international consumer trend organization Trendwatching.com has identified "kindness" and "generosity" as necessary megatrends in the future of business. The organization predicts that people will increasingly seek interactions with companies where they experience generosity and not greed. A *Crucial Consumer Trends* report included, "There's no better way for a brand . . . to put its money where its mouth (or heart) is than engaging in Random Acts of Kindness. . . . Consumers' cravings for realness, for the human touch, ensure that everything from brands randomly picking up the tab to sending a surprise gift will be one of the most effective ways to connect with (potential) customers. . . . A serious (and sincere) Random Acts of Kindness strategy may mean no longer being seen as inflexible and unwieldy but as more compassionate and charismatic instead. Something that is, of course, priceless and actually fun."

By encouraging staff members to practice random acts of kindness and well-considered acts of generosity toward customers, Zappos has created priceless experiences for staff members and customers as well. Ashley Perry, CLT member, notes, "Our Zappos family understands there is a lot more to business than money. One of my trainers, Michael, is a classic example. He received a boot order for a soldier serving in Iraq. A couple of weeks after the order was placed, we were notified that the shipment had not been received. So he tracked it and expedited a replacement order. This happened several more times, and each time new boots were sent at no additional charge. Fortunately, the soldier's boots finally were located—not just one pair of the boots, but all four pairs that had been sent. At many other businesses, three of those pairs would have had to be sent back, but at Zappos, Michael had the authority to say, 'You know what, you're out there serving our country. It took four months for you to get these; just keep all the boots and pass any extra pairs on to some of your fellow soldiers.' For me, that's what makes work and life worthwhile—helping those people, especially those who are helping others."

Derek Carder, CLT supervisor, finds joy in the freedom to deliver memorable service, like that he provided to a caller by the name of Georgina: "She had her heart set on a pair of pumps for her upcoming wedding. Unfortunately, those shoes were out of stock and essentially discontinued." Derek remembers doing everything he could to try to find a different pair that Georgina might like. He looked on the Zappos website and competitors' websites, but Georgina wanted those specific shoes. According to Derek, "I made it my personal mission to find those pumps. When I had breaks in call volume, I'd contact small shoe stores near where Georgina lived." On the fourth day of searching, Derek expanded the area of his quest and located a pair of the pumps in Georgina's size but at a location that was 120 miles from her. Derek notes, "I didn't want her to lose the chance at those shoes, so I gave them my personal credit card to hold the pumps for her. We needed those shoes! So I called her, and she was ecstatic; she was literally screaming for joy. I apologized for the distance she had to travel to pick them up. She said it was no problem at all. The thank-you note I received included an invitation to her wedding. To think, a guy like me working at Zappos in Nevada was invited to her wedding in New York. I love what I get to do here." It's hard to imagine that Georgina would ever consider buying shoes from any other company. Where else would she find call-center employees that not only care *for* her but care that deeply *about* her? Brands become irreplaceable when people make genuine connections. Empowered and engaged staff members build relationships, memories, and loyalty.

More with Less

Leaders at Zappos trust their selection process, training, and culture. As a result, they allow staff members to use their own best judgment to "deliver wow through service," and also to "do more with less." In turn, staff members at Zappos understand the importance of being fiscally prudent. Faby Guido-Romero, CLT lead, notes, "Most of the time a customer wow comes at no cost. I actually think it's best when I don't focus on what I can 'give' customers to wow them but instead on how I must 'be' to wow them. For me, the greatest happiness comes for customers when I fully put myself in their place. It happens when I say and mean, 'I'm here to help you. I'm going to do whatever it takes so that when we hang up, you will feel good,' and when I let them sincerely know that I am grateful for their time and business."

Faby's comments are consistent with those of staff members throughout Zappos. Whether it is a staff member in the Fulfillment Centers who talks about "making sure a shoe box looks perfect when the customer opens up the delivery," a Zappos live-chat member who expresses the importance of "using the written word to make a lasting connection," or website content creators who enjoy thinking of customers smiling when they read a sentence that the creators wrote for the website, like "shoes: now conveniently sold in pairs," employees at Zappos all talk about emotionally connecting with *people*—not with consumers, website users, or shoppers. Staff members at Zappos talk about the people they serve and the gratitude they have for being able to make emotional connections.

In the end, legendary service companies don't happen by accident. They are the result of leaders who have a passion for getting the transaction right and delivering a desired emotional state to the customer. That passion is then shared by empowered staff members who generously and kindly put themselves in the circumstances of those they serve. When high-quality transactions are executed and emotional connections are forged, customer experience stories flow. It is through that confluence of forces that legends thrive!

Chapter 6 *Ideas to Run With*

- Increasingly, business leaders need to think about service experiences that forge lifelong customer relationships.

- Legendary service brands typically have defining service stories that become part of corporate lore.

- In addition to the defining service stories, which tend to be epic in nature, legendary brands weave small acts of service excellence into experiences.

- Great service brands overtly create or happen upon a Way We Serve Statement that informs staff members how customers are to feel while they are being served.

- Success in developing engaging customer experiences comes from staff members who are clear on the desired tangible and emotional outcomes for customers.

- Before business policies are implemented, leaders should consider their possible impact on the emotional connection with customers.

- Forgoing sales to serve the true needs of customers pays off for everyone in the end.

- Your customers are craving random acts of kindness and signs of generosity rather than indications of greed.

- In extraordinary service organizations, all employees understand that they are in an emotional outcome and relationship business.

- Well-selected and well-trained staff members can deliver wow service at minimal cost to the organization.

CONNECTIONS AT ALL LEVELS

It's easy for leaders to encourage staff members to create personal emotional connections with customers. However, it is quite another thing to help them continually grow in service excellence. At Zappos, the process of growing talent in personalized service is tireless and comprehensive.

In the Zappos call center, for example, a Customer Loyalty Team trainee is evaluated on all aspects of service delivery. Through a call review form, a new employee will routinely be rated (with a 1, 2, or 3) on a wide range of quality dimensions, including the degree to which the trainee forms a personal emotional connection with the customer. In the past, the same rating system was used to evaluate the service quality of every CLT staff member. That process of quality measurement, however, was changed in response to staff feedback solicited in an e-mail survey.

According to Zapponian Tami Lemke, "One of the things we want to do is deliver happiness inside and outside of Zappos, and the quality assurance program was creating a little fear in our people and leaving them feeling like they weren't in control. Having a sense of control is linked to happiness, and we wanted to promote growth and not fear, so we made a few changes. To reduce anxiety, we went from performance metrics to pure feedback. We completely did away with scores for full-fledged CLT staff. Supervisors and staff members now just talk about the things the CLTs liked about identified calls and the things they could've done better. Essentially, we are discussing how we can continue to elevate the Zappos Experience while helping CLTs attain their service goals." Tami also notes that in order for employees to have greater control, "We implemented several methods to include the CLTs in picking which of their calls would be reviewed. For example, in our self-assessment process, which we do at least once a month, a CLT lead will pull up a huge list of recent calls. The team member looks at this list and chooses a call, and both the lead and the team member listen to a recording of the phone call. We review that call against key elements of the Zappos Experience, including the strength of the personal emotional connection achieved."

For many leaders, it would take a major "gut check" to move to a true feedback model, essentially letting go of the desire to "grade" performance. Many leaders believe that accountability is linked to numbers and that employee behavior must be quantitatively graded. By contrast, the leaders at Zappos see regular, open, and honest conversations as a key force in elevating performance. At Zappos, the shift from top-down evaluations to partnered conversations makes for happier employees, a less defensive workplace, and an environment of enthusiasm for service growth.

HAPPILY COMMUNICATING CONTINUAL IMPROVEMENT INFORMATION

The revised Zappos assessment tool, without the scoring system, is referred to as the Happiness Form because it has the words "Delivering Happiness One Call at a Time" written boldly across the top. The tool is divided into sections that cover the CLT member's "greeting, personal emotional connection, service, seeking/supplying information, and conclusion." (If you are interested in a detailed look at the call review form or the Happiness Form, you can download both in their entirety as a member of Zappos Insights. The complimentary 30-day membership opportunity for Zappos Insights can be found at the back of the book.) To give an overall sense of the uniqueness of this approach, I will summarize just a few of the service expectations that are set forth by the leadership at Zappos for each of these categories. This sample from the Happiness Form is likely to prove handy across service settings:

> *Greeting.* CLT members are expected to make a genuine offer of assistance and introduce themselves by name. They are asked to present with an upbeat tone and to demonstrate a personal flair or creativity.

> *Personal emotional connection.* Calls from CLT staff members are assessed for such things as helpfulness, patience, sincerity, genuineness, and the degree to which the CLT member engages in conversations about the customer and/or Zappos products.

> *Service.* Evaluations of service look at areas such as a CLT member's ability to provide multiple solutions for each customer's need or inquiry, the degree to which the CLT

member satisfies all the customer's stated needs, whether the CLT member follows through on all customer promises, and the clear and concise documentation of key aspects of the customer's experience.

Seeking and supplying information. Calls are reviewed for dimensions like verification of the customer's full shipping address and the degree to which accurate information is provided by the CLT member.

Conclusion. The final stage of assessment looks at whether the full order was reviewed, whether the CLT member made an effort to wow the customer with an unexpected perk, and whether the CLT member invited the customer into an ongoing relationship with Zappos.

The beauty of the Happiness Form assessment process is that it emphasizes both quality in basic service execution (Principle 2's focus on knowledgeable staff, helping customers get their needs met the first time, and generally providing timely, accurate service) and areas that are geared toward forging the personal emotional connection, delivering wow, and leaving customers feeling happy. By helping Zapponians develop goals across these service areas and providing regular, honest, and nonthreatening feedback, supervisors enable employees to grow in these areas of service excellence and in their ability to offer personal care to customers. Leaders, quality assurance professionals, and CLT members work together for the common goal of "delivering happiness one call at a time." This is a goal that results in reactions on Twitter like that of @davyjoneslock, who tweets, "Zappos is successful because they provide human connections and happiness. More companies need to get this! Business is about people!"

No matter what business you're in, the success, growth, and development of your service talent hinges on the regular and varied feedback mechanisms that your people have at their disposal. At Zappos, in addition to the monthly self-evaluation calls, CLT members also receive full-circle feedback through "service observes," "Sharing Great Calls," and Net Promoter Scores (NPS).

Service observes occur when CLT leads unobtrusively listen in on the calls of their staff members and offer feedback after the live call. Psychologists who specialize in operant conditioning and learning have consistently shown that immediacy is a critical feature in shaping behavior change. By coaching staff members as soon as they complete a call, Zappos leaders create immediate opportunities for growth and reinforce positive service behaviors.

From the standpoint of positive reinforcement and modeling best practices, Sharing Great Calls is a self-nominated review structure described by Christina Colligan. Christina, CLT manager, notes, "The Sharing Great Calls process occurs when CLT members get off the phone and feel they have made a really great connection with a customer. They then send the information about the call to their lead. The lead contacts the customer directly, usually through e-mail, but sometimes also through a telephone call. Typically the lead gets e-mail responses back from those customers, many who share very interesting, detailed, and over-the-top praise for their experience. We get well over a hundred Sharing Great Calls examples every week, and we use them not only for quality feedback but for training purposes as well."

Sharing Great Calls creates an opportunity for the customers' voices to loop back through Zappos so that the culture of service can be reinforced. An example of an e-mail exchange between a Zappos CLT lead and a very happy Zappos customer follows. The CLT lead's e-mail to customer Barbara Friedman asked about a single Zappos call, but Barbara could not resist heaping praise on three Zappos CLT members. The interchange begins with an e-mail introduction from the Zappos lead:

> Our Team Member said what a great time she had talking to you! We have started a special program recently to provide further feedback to our Team Members. We want to give our Team Members an extra pat on the back, so I have a huge favor to ask of you. It will not take much of your time, but it will help us enormously. Please tell us about the service you received and any points of feedback regarding the conversation you had with our Team Member.

Here is Barbara's unedited response:

> Well, I don't know where to start; but my second pair of shoes arrived today in less than 24 hours, and though I never expected to purchase them, your wonderful staff made it irresistible for me to let down my frugal barriers and order another color in the shoes I discovered online Saturday evening. Those shoes arrived magically early Monday morning! Unheard of!!!
>
> When I discovered my last name was missing from my order confirmation Saturday evening, I phoned to correct it, and spoke to CRISTAL, who was warm, concerned, and knowledgeable (I have discovered this is a common thread to all Zappos staff!) and after fixing the address she invited me to be a VIP.ZAPPOS member! The benefits, I learned, are overnight shipping which really is overnight, and a separate website with many goodies! I was very grateful for the honor, thanked Cristal, and expected to receive the shoes by Tuesday or Wednesday. They arrived almost at the crack of dawn Monday morning!

So, I called Zappos once I had recovered from shock, to tell them about my amazement, and there I was befriended by DAWN, who regaled me with her first overnight order and how similar her reaction was to mine. Talk about shock and awe! And I made my second friend at Zappos, as her warmth and welcome were also like returning home to family!

After hanging up the phone, I tried on my shoes which Zappos carries in NARROW, an almost impossible width to find in South Florida, and just wallowed in the comfort for several minutes before deciding to treat myself to the same shoe in another color (even though I owned a similar one in a medium width) and phoned back to Zappos, where KRYSTYN answered my call. Again, that incredible feeling of being part of Zappos special family! She quickly ascertained that the shoe I requested was available, assured me Zappos and its amazing staff were always there for me, 24 hours a day, 7 days a week . . . and I really have the feeling that they would all be there to support me during any crisis that might arrive in my life!!! How does Zappos manage this?

I am so impressed. I have mentioned it to several friends, including my son, who asked "You just discovered Zappos?" . . . and informed me it is my granddaughter's favorite shopping site! So now I have learned how to take care of gifting this special young lady without ever leaving home!

Thank you for giving me the opportunity to share my pleasure received from my new friends at Zappos!

Barbara Friedman, FL

(You can find more Sharing Great Calls transcripts in Appendix A.)

"Her warmth and welcome were like returning home to family" and "I really have the feeling that they would all be there to support me during any crisis that might arrive in my life" are pretty good indicators that the staff members at Zappos made the personal emotional connection that delivered both wow and happiness. To truly build a service culture, customer-facing staff members need to hear about their service successes. What better way could there be to provide that feedback than by having managers solicit comments from customers with whom a positive connection was probably made? Customer service can be difficult, negative interactions are stressful, and customers can fail to show gratitude. Thus, it is extremely important that leaders build morale by looking for ways to share stories of service excellence. Moreover, recordings of these "great" interactions, when accompanied by the customers' praise for how they were served, often result in powerful teaching tools on what it takes to deliver wow through service.

The Zappos leadership does not limit this feedback loop to call-center, live chat, or e-mail support staff members. For example, customer praise regarding delivery speed and other forms of related customer gratitude is regularly shared with members of the distribution staff so that they can appreciate the impact of their efforts. Mary Johnson, tour guide at the Fulfillment Centers, shares, "About 30 percent of our orders are returned to the Fulfillment Centers because customers will order several sizes and send back the ones that didn't fit. With these returns, we receive a lot of things in the boxes that don't belong to us—car keys, remote controls, and even steak knives that were used to open the boxes. We ship back everything we can, and I remember hearing praise from one customer, who let us know that she had blamed her kids for stealing money out of her wallet. She was really upset until she got an envelope back from Zappos with a considerable amount of cash that she had accidentally dropped in the box of a returned item. The customer was thrilled that she got her money back. We were thrilled for her and proud to be recognized for doing the right thing." Leaders at Zappos see that sharing stories of service excellence is an important part of crafting a culture that builds relationships with customers. For that reason, Zappos leadership decided that qualitative feedback mechanisms should be linked to more objective measures, which led them to implement the Net Promoter Score. That linkage is exactly what we will be discussing next.

TRY THESE ON FOR SIZE

1. How are you helping your service staff develop greater "personal emotional connection" skills?

2. Are you assessing your service staff's ability to build rapport and participate in relevant and engaging personal discussions, or do your evaluations focus exclusively on things like "smiling," "eye contact," and "transaction accuracy"?

3. Is your service quality assurance program growth-oriented (goal setting, honest feedback without ratings), or is it designed as a metric of performance?

4. How comprehensive are your service feedback mechanisms? Do employees have input concerning the information solicited? Do you actively ask customers to share their side of what are likely to turn out to be wow stories?

ADDING SCIENCE TO THE MIX

In addition to providing feedback on the impact of great calls, the Zappos leadership gives each CLT member the results from e-mail surveys concerning customer zealotry. One of the results of those surveys is the Net Promoter Score. The NPS reflects the proportion of customers who are likely to demonstrate loyalty and promote your business. Through inquiry, customers are classified into one of three categories: promoters, passives, and detractors. The Net Promoter Score is then calculated by subtracting the percentage of customers who are in the detractor

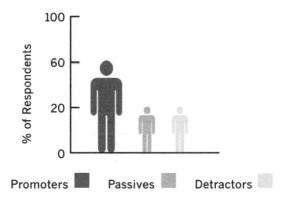

category from the percentage of customers who are in the promoter category. To determine those categories, Fred Reichheld, author of *The Ultimate Question*, recommends that you use a 10-point response scale and ask customers how likely they are to refer your company to a friend or colleague. Respondents who answer 9 or 10 are promoters, those who answer 7 or 8 are passives, and those who answer 6 or below are detractors.

At Zappos, for example, after a customers speaks with a CLT team member and/or after a customer places an order on the site, Zappos sends out an e-mail that guides the calculation of the NPS and collects other helpful information about the customer's view of his experience. Examples of the breadth of questions asked in these surveys include

- On a scale of 0 to 10, 10 being the highest score, how likely are you to recommend Zappos to a friend or a family member?

- If you had to name one thing that we could improve upon, what would that be?"

- During your last interaction with us, you contacted a member of our Customer Loyalty Team. On a scale of 0 to 10, if you had your own company that was focused upon service, how likely would you be to hire this person to work for you?

- Overall, would you describe the service you received from (insert name of customer loyalty rep) as good, bad, or fantastic?

- What exactly stood out as being good or bad about this service?

Each day, Zappos leadership tracks and posts the aggregate results from all Zappos customers who completed surveys. Staff members can then easily view the NPS results, and other information from the surveys, alongside key performance indicators such as call answer time and call volume. NPS scores at Zappos are consistently in the 80 to 90 range; Fred Reichheld describes this range of scores as being "in the stratosphere." Despite that amazing level of engagement, Zappos leaders seek out follow-up conversations with customers in the large promoter group and the small detractor category. In addition, from the perspective of personal feedback, each CLT member is provided with helpful data derived from the e-mails received in response to calls that they specifically handled.

What a vast array of constructive information—feedback from supervisors, input from an identified group of great calls, and unscreened data from the voices of all customers, solicited through scientific metrics. At all levels and across the entire organization, the leadership at Zappos listens, shares, measures, coaches, and encourages growth in service professionalism.

COMMUNICATION FOR ALL

In its classic tagline, the Florida Orange Growers Association proclaimed, "Orange juice is not just for breakfast anymore." Bending that line a bit, at Zappos, "Personal connections aren't just for customers anymore." In fact, leaders at Zappos have a passion for using open communication to foster personal emotional connections, to deliver wow, and to generate happiness for staff members, vendors, and even noncustomers.

Tony Hsieh uses the metaphor of a greenhouse to demonstrate the importance of creating open conversations and fueling growth: "In some organizations, leaders act as though they are the strongest, tallest plants, and all others should look up to them and aspire to be like them. I think of myself more as an architect of the greenhouse. It's my job to enable all plants—our people—to flourish and reach their full potential. As leaders, we need to openly communicate with our teams and do everything we can to produce the right conditions so every individual can grow fully." Principle 4, "S T R E T C H," details the educational opportunities that are offered to Zapponians to fuel their development, and Principle 5, "Play to Win," explores how leaders foster an incredibly cohesive Zappos family. But for now, let's take a moment to explore the bidirectional and transparent communication that serves as the foundation for personal emotional connections with employees and ultimately builds trust.

ZAPPIFIED BRAIN BREAK

*D*id you know that executives at Zappos literally work in a jungle? Tony Hsieh and other Zappos senior leaders, referred to as the monkeys, occupy a group of desks in the center of the Zappos Headquarters. This area features lush green foliage dangling from the ceiling above the cubicles. Thus, the area of desks is aptly referred to as "Monkey Row." Think about the tone set in terms of humility, accessibility, and fun when corporate leaders work in centrally located and playfully decorated cubicles. Leadership at Zappos is well beyond a open door policy. They thrive in a no door environment. Now you know about the jungle and the monkeys . . . so pass it on!

In every organization, leaders and staff members engage in regular, spontaneous, and informal conversations. Most companies go one step further and formalize an annual opportunity to listen to staff members' feedback through an employee survey. By contrast, Zappos has taken staff input to the monthly "Five Second Happiness Survey" level. Every month, the leadership at Zappos essentially conducts an internal survey of the company's employees, giving them the opportunity to complete an assessment in which they assign a quantifiable score and offer comments. While employees can complete the survey anonymously, the leaders personally respond to each comment if the staff member chooses to be identified. All input is posted, with both numeric scores and written comments. Zapponians are also advised of changes that came about as a result of the data collected each month. According to Rebecca Henry Ratner, HR director at Zappos, "Employee participation in the monthly survey varies anywhere between 60 and 85 percent. We trend those results within a week and immediately send them out to departments."

The Five Second Happiness Survey asks staff members to provide numeric answers of 1, definitely; 2, sometimes; or 3, not at all to the following questions:

- I believe that the company genuinely has a higher purpose beyond just profits.

- My role in the Zappos Family has real purpose—it is more than just a job.

- I feel that I am in control of my career path and that I am progressing in my personal and professional development within the Zappos Family.

- I consider my coworkers to be like my family and friends.

- I am very happy in my job.

Forging emotional connections with staff members isn't about what you ask, but that you ask. It involves a willingness to seek input, inquire regularly, personally respond to what is shared, transparently communicate the input received, and take action on suggestions. In addition to the monthly Five Second Happiness Surveys, Zappos has perfected a series of other direct methods of staff communication, including

- Candid leadership blogs

- Daily sales reports

- Messages communicated via video

- An "ask anything" forum

- Open access to Monkey Row

The candor of Tony's blog (blogs.zappos.com/blogs/ceo -and-coo-blog) is reflected in his willingness to speak freely and emotionally on sensitive yet important issues throughout the company's history. These posts have included the rationale for and anguish over layoffs in 2008, the anxieties and uncertainties of the company's purchase by Amazon, discussion of the real growing pains encountered after Amazon's acquisition of the company, a one-year retrospective on predictions that Tony made at the time of the acquisition, and disclosure of preliminary plans for a move of Zappos Headquarters from Henderson, Nevada, to downtown Las Vegas. In each instance, Tony has provided opportunities for public comments on his blog. He and other Zappos leaders are not controlling a leadership message by "top-down" blogging; they are inviting connection and dialogue. Tony also asks for e-mail input and often ends blogs with questions for staff members. These questions address such things as, "What do you want your personal brand and values to be? How can you use Twitter as a tool to help you grow as a person and be happier? How do you inspire people to pay attention to what matters to you?" In addition, Tony's blog often begins discussions that are continued in future Q and A or all-hands meetings.

Beyond the blogging, daily e-mail updates are provided to every Zapponian, based on the view that too much information is better than too little. According to Jamie Naughton, speaker of the house at Zappos, "We want our employees to have lots of information, and maybe even more than they might want. Sharing information allows staff members the opportunity to make decisions that benefit us all. Our approach to communication is to forge partnerships with every single employee, not just have the top 5 percent of the company hold the corporate knowledge while everyone else works in the dark." Jamie explains, "All of our sales numbers are e-mailed every day to our employees so that they know exactly how much we're selling and how much we're not selling."

Jamie adds that information sharing has expanded and improved over time: "For example, one of the things we added was our target goals. That way, staff members can place sales and orders in perspective. This information helps our family see how we're trending, how much we need to generate every day in order to meet our objectives, and it gives projections based on our current performance. By putting all this information in the hands of our staff on a daily basis, we know whether we're going to miss, hit, or exceed our goals, and that helps us make changes and course corrections. There are no unpleasant sales surprises here at Zappos." According to former Zappos CFO Alfred Lin, "The daily sales updates are just another part of full disclosure. That information is very detailed, with more than 1,200 brands reported, and it's sent out to the whole company. You can actually see it on an hourly basis, or even every 15 minutes if you want."

This refreshing approach to honest information exchange between leadership and staff shatters many old paradigms in which corporate communication teams huddle together in closed-door meetings, working on how to give a positive "spin" to sanctioned talking points. From a staff perspective, the communication approach at Zappos leads to reactions like those shared by Sheila Clinard, an employee in the refurbishment area of the Fulfillment Centers: "I feel like I really know what's going on here at Zappos. The leaders don't hide the truth from us. They also don't want us to hide the truth from them or just tell them what they want to hear." Vanessa Lawson, senior trainer at Zappos, echoes Sheila's sentiment by indicating, "This is going to sound strange given the way many people feel about their employers these days, but I trust this company 1,010 percent. I trust that they are giving me the straight facts, that they are listening, and that they genuinely care about the well-being of all of us. That is a great feeling to have. I also appreciate that we are provided financial education at Zappos so we can see where the revenue goes. Most of our employees don't realize how much of our revenue is used to run the business until that education is provided, and training helps us gain a greater appreciation of the numbers we see regularly."

The leaders at Zappos understand that in order for employees to build customer relationships through "open and honest . . . communication," those leaders must embody the same value in their relationships with staff members. David Hinden, Zappos merchandising assistant, may best summarize how open communication builds relationships for Zappos staff members and customers alike: "I think it is true for most people—the way

TRY THESE ON FOR SIZE

1. Are you using some variation of the NPS? Can you isolate data from NPS results and trace it back to individual service providers? Are you sharing the aggregate and individual results of your NPS surveys as a tool to enhance your emotional connections with customers?

2. Can you imagine asking your customers to rate your staff and offer comments in response to the following question: "If you had your own company that was focused upon service, how likely would you be to hire this person to work for you?" What do you suspect the results would look like across your business? Would you also provide those results to your staff members as a tool for enhancing service excellence?

3. Would you be willing to ask your staff members how happy they are at work on a monthly basis? What percentage of your team members do you suspect would respond to the survey each month? What do you think those results would reveal?

4. If you did survey your staff members monthly, would you provide them with all the results of that study, including every comment received?

5. How much do your customers trust your business? How much do your staff members trust your leaders? How do you know?

you are treated often predicts the way you treat others. At Zappos, the communication flows from leaders to staff and staff to leaders. Trust is built by that honest sharing. Trust then gets extended to our customers, who in return trust us." What a great recipe for creating healthy staff relationships and, by extension, personal customer relationships—tell the truth, communicate often, add active and genuine listening, act on the things you hear, enjoy the trust you've earned, and watch that trust move toward customers and back again toward your brand.

WHAT? VENDORS ARE PEOPLE TOO?

As a consultant, trainer, and corporate keynoter, I am a vendor. Speaking from vast experience, I can assure you that there is a great deal of variation in how different corporate clients view and treat their vendors. In some instances, vendors are dealt with as commodities; in others, we are "necessary evils"; and in yet others, vendor/client relationships are personal partnerships. In the early days of Zappos, despite the professional connections of shoe veterans like Fred Mossler, vendors were reluctant to have their products sold through a fledgling online shoe store site. As Tony Hsieh puts it, "From the beginning, we knew we were asking vendors to do business differently. To put their products on our site, vendors had to see and feel us treating them differently. We essentially focused on vendors as real partners—something that was not happening in the shoe industry. We cared about their success, and we wanted our choices to demonstrate our caring."

A Zappos vendor, Butch Hazlett of New Balance, affirms Tony's comment: "Zappos gets it. Clearly it starts with Tony's vision, and then it takes someone like Fred to lead the charge, but the entire Zappos team took time to know our business and to develop mutually beneficial relationships with us and with all their vendors. Zappos shares information in a way that makes them and us more successful. Thanks to the Zappos culture, the care of vendors truly is unlike anything else in the industry, and we end up doing business with friends at Zappos—people who genuinely care about us." Rather than trying to hide sales information from vendors, in the hope that it will give Zappos a competitive advantage when it is negotiating for inventory purchases, Zappos gives its vendors transparent access to real-time sales data. This transparency has helped both Zappos and its vendors work to improve the way products are positioned for sale on the Zappos site and increase overall sales volume.

Vendors consistently talk about the "Zappos difference." Miles Olson, UGG Australia independent sales representative, reflects, "From early on, I would go over to Zappos on Friday afternoons. Fred and I would review our shared business and plan our upcoming work together. We would go have drinks after that, and it became family almost immediately. On many afternoons, we would wrap up our individual work and connect up at a happy hour. Zappos has been treating vendors like people from the outset, and it generated camaraderie. We grasped the Zappos vision, and they grasped ours. Zappos also found ways for us to share common short-, mid-, and long-term goals and allowed us to partner together to achieve shared objectives. They didn't see us as adversaries that they had to prevail over in order to prosper." In essence, Zappos developed a "vendor-centric" collaborative approach. Rather than interfacing with vendors as if those vendors were commodities that could be easily discarded, Zappos sought to serve and wow the vendors with an eye toward long-term relationships.

Tom Austin, a Clarks representative, says, "Zappos staff will go to great lengths to wow vendors through service. In fact, a group from Zappos came out to visit us at our warehouse in Hanover, Pennsylvania, and we were going to be having dinner together. One of the members of the Zappos team called all the restaurants in the area to find out which one had a Clarks reservation, and she then gave the restaurant staff the Zappos credit card to make sure Clarks didn't have to pick up the tab. For me, it's less about who pays and more about the level of care and consideration Zappos extends in all aspects of business and how they take the word *partnership* and run with it." Tom adds, "The Zappos treatment of vendor reps is truly legendary in the industry. I frequently hear other vendors say, 'Don't you wish all our clients were like these guys?'"

Most vendors appreciate the work provided to them and usually strive to offer professional solutions, no matter how they are treated. However, not all customers are equal. Some get that little extra effort. When two clients have a similar profile and both have a special or urgent need, clients like Zappos often get served a little more quickly than those who treat vendors less as partners or with less respect.

EVERYONE IS A CUSTOMER

Okay, so Zappos has personal connections with its customers, staff members, and vendors. Could there be yet another level of brand relationship? How about people who simply have an interest in your company? While many of the people who choose to visit the Zappos Headquarters for a complimentary or upgraded tour are customers of Zappos, some visitors just want to learn more from a business that has garnered positive media attention. Zappos welcomes all comers. From my perspective, it's difficult to imagine that an office and call-center tour could become a highly desired activity for visitors in a city as dynamic as Las Vegas. But, we are talking about Zappos. In fact, it's not unusual for Zappos to accommodate 1,200 tour-goers a month at its Headquarters, and often those tour guests are shuttled to and from the airport and/or their hotel.

To get a sense of what you might experience on a Zappos tour, join me for an inside look by going to www.zappified.com/tour or point your QR reader at the image given here.

So how did Zappos begin running a shuttle service and tours of its Headquarters in the first place? And why would a company commit resources to provide tours for people who may not even be customers?

Let's hear a brief history from the official "Mayor of Zappos," Jerry Tidmore. Jerry recalls, "In the early days, our call center was right next to the airport, and vendors would want to have product meetings with us. They would catch a cab out to us, and we would take them back to the airport. Fred decided we needed a shuttle to take vendors both ways, and we ended up getting a passenger vehicle. About six months later, we purchased a larger passenger vehicle, and about a year later, we needed our first 14-passenger bus to take vendors back and forth. We also conducted a program once a month to teach vendors how to access the data they needed to track the sales of their product on our site. In those days, many vendors were accustomed to selling only to stores like Nordstrom, and therefore, they had an interest in seeing our call center in action. So Fred said, 'Jerry, can you give them a tour?' And that's how the tours started out." Ultimately, the shuttle and tours expanded to anyone who had an interest in Zappos.

Since guests of the tour are given the royal treatment, including a keepsake of their time in the "royal chair," the popularity of the Zappos tour has grown through word of mouth and has spurred priceless publicity for the company. While the Las Vegas Convention and Visitors Authority popularized the advertising tagline, "What happens in Vegas stays in Vegas," the slogan doesn't apply to the Zappos tours. In fact, a Google search of the phrase "Zappos Tour" produces thousands of results, and there are hundreds of YouTube videos chronicling a walk through Zappos.

In addition to tour stories, there are also ample online and offline conversations about the Zappos shuttle service. Roz Searcy, Zappos Kan Du facilitator, shares one such story: "An employee who works in our department went to the airport to pick up a vendor who was running a little behind schedule. Our shuttle driver engaged in a conversation with two ladies who were sitting at the airport waiting for their shuttle. As it turns out, those women had waited for more than two hours to get to their hotel to attend a conference. They also had been treated rudely when they tried to find out what had happened to their shuttle, so our team member just took them to where they needed to go." Roz notes, "The story keeps going. These ladies sent over thank-you gifts to our employee. One of the women even took time out from her convention to come to Zappos and take a tour while she was in town."

What relationships matter to your business? Is it only those with customers? Maybe it's those between your leaders and staff members. Or how about those between staff members and vendors? How much are you investing in creating experiences that personally connect with everyone who has contact with your brand? Many companies spend a great deal on advertising, but they let that advertising down when interactions with the brand fail to demonstrate real caring. At Zappos, as at most great service businesses, authentic relationships are modeled at the seniormost levels of the organization. To last in business today, leaders must understand that people (customers, employees, casually interested parties, and even vendors) have access to instant information and a wide array of choices. As a result, people are unwilling to tolerate being treated like a commodity, an adversary, or a fulfillment object. A brand's equity is often linked to the openness of its leaders' communication and the priority that those leaders place on long-term relationships. By seeking connections on all levels, you will experience the lasting benefits of sales, loyalty, and possibly even fanaticism from customers, employees, vendors, and noncustomers alike.

- Leaders are responsible for helping staff members develop their service talent.

- Staff members are often more willing to embrace service skill development if they are offered elements of control and have performance evaluations removed from the process.

- Wow service stories should be solicited from customers.

- Goal setting and diverse sources of feedback aid in the enhancement of complex skills, such as those that are required if you are to secure customer connection and loyalty.

- The adage "you get what you measure" is also true for the creation of personal emotional connections, wow, and customer happiness.

- Great leaders seek input, seek it regularly, listen, act on what they hear, and loop back what they heard and acted upon.

- It's more likely that you will undercommunicate rather than overcommunicate.

- Vendors and noncustomers are people, too. They also desire authentic relationships.

- Vendors who are treated like true partners form shared goals with clients and give extra effort to realize those goals.

- You can spend money on advertising to create a brand promise and/or spend it to make personal connections through enriched brand experiences.

STRETCH

*If you want to be happy, set a goal
that commands your thoughts,
liberates your energy, and inspires
your hopes.*

—ANDREW CARNEGIE

Maybe the nimble spirit at Zappos reflects the iconoclastic nature of its leadership or the personality of a CEO who was an entrepreneur in grade school. Possibly the unsettled nature of Zappos is the result of naysayers constantly telling its leaders that they couldn't possibly succeed. In any case, the rapid evolution of Zappos is emblematic of what businesses can achieve by being discontented, knowledge seeking, and unwilling to fall in love with the way things are or the way things have always been.

Chapter 8, "Zappos University," focuses on how Zappos stretches staff members to be subject-matter experts, better people, and future organizational leaders. It demonstrates how far a business can go to develop internal talent and actually create the often-talked-about succession or progression plan. The chapter also includes insights into how to achieve both personal and professional development objectives that fuel staff loyalty and engagement. Chapter 9, "Beyond Shoes," looks at how Zappos has stretched its brand elasticity well beyond its original product line into broader merchandising and even corporate leadership training. That chapter will also examine how Zappos innovates processes, technologies, and channels, including the company's thought leadership in social media. It's time to sit back, raise your arms, and S T R E T C H.

ZAPPOS UNIVERSITY

As good as Zappos is at present, staff members and leaders will always tell you that they need to be better. Rebecca Henry Ratner, HR director at Zappos, captures the company's constant sense of striving and restlessness when she says, "Zappos is a place where every day is a stretch. I never know what's coming, but I know I'm going to like it. I'm constantly challenged and placed in situations where I have to live outside my comfort zone. In fact, outside my comfort zone is starting to become my comfort zone. Fortunately, Zappos understands that a key to retaining great people is to keep them challenged and learning, and that's where our Pipeline team comes in."

While I have titled this chapter "Zappos University," there isn't really a university at Zappos. Or is there? While technically the answer to my question would be no, functionally the answer would be yes. Zappos does not have a university per se, but its

Pipeline team framework resembles a university more closely than it resembles a traditional corporate training department. Rather than Zapponians having to face mandatory, often boring, typically predictable, and marginally relevant seminar offerings, the Pipeline team has created a vast catalog of dynamic, interactive courses. This curriculum was developed at Zappos to address two overarching business questions: (1) What are the knowledge sets and behaviors needed to produce strong departments and leaders at Zappos? and (2) What should be offered to grow the culture and increase the happiness of Zapponians? In essence, the Zappos Pipeline serves to facilitate personal, team, leadership, and business growth. Given the breadth of objectives for the Zappos Pipeline program, let's focus our examination of the program's processes and offerings as they relate to essential knowledge, leadership development, and personal growth.

ESSENTIAL KNOWLEDGE

Over the years, organizations like the Conference Board, Corporate Voices for Working Families, the Partnership for 21st Century Skills, and the Society for Human Resource Management have asked employers to rate the knowledge and applied skills of employees whom they have hired straight from high schools, trade schools, and colleges. The findings of these studies, which are often referred to as workforce readiness report cards, often conclude with statements like "significant 'deficiencies' exist among entrants at every educational level" or "workforce readiness is one of the key issues facing the country."

While social debates rage about how to align formal education with the needs of business, the Zappos Pipeline offers its own solutions for short- and long-term objectives at Zappos. Rather than talking about the lack of workforce readiness of its new hires, Zappos has developed a curriculum that ensures workforce success for anyone who is a fit with the Zappos culture and therefore is willing to live the Zappos value of "pursuing growth and learning." Since success is different in various departments at Zappos, the Pipeline team creates department-specific content to aid in career development. For example, Zapponians who interface extensively with vendors, such as merchandise buyers, will have classes on vendor relationships, whereas employees who work in the Zappos Fulfillment Centers will be provided with courses like "Warehouse Optimization." In many ways, these curriculum paths can be viewed as departments within Zappos University. These departments have their own specialized curricula that build on core (general education) offerings provided by the Pipeline team. In fact, the ever-growing catalog of classes offered through Zappos Pipeline is divided into three categories: core, leadership, and elective. All employees who have completed their new hire training can attend core-level and elective classes. Leadership-level classes are provided to any Zapponian who has direct reports, or to those who do not have direct reports but have the approval of their supervisor.

Pipeline team members teach most Pipeline courses, with an occasional class being provided by a department's subject-matter expert. For example, a member of the Zappos finance team typically teaches the "Introduction to Finance" class. Devlyn Torres, supervisor of the Zappos Pipeline team, notes, "Creating our own classes allows us to make them all extremely Zappos family–specific. It also allows us to infuse our core values into each and every class and make sure that the classes help solve real training issues." The unique nature of the Zappos family–specific offerings can be seen in the small sample of class descriptions from the Nevada Pipeline core curriculum given here.

CORE LEVEL 1

Zappos Family History

Length: 8 hours. This is a guided tour through the story of the Zappos Family from our founder's earliest memories to our most current events as told through video by the people who were there. After finishing this class, you will be able to accurately discuss the history of the Zappos companies, as well as incorporate ideas and fundamentals from our foundation into action today.

Communication 1:
Communicating Effectively in Any Situation

Length: 3 hours. This interactive course reviews the basic communication cycle & identifies areas of strength as well as areas for improvement while communicating with co-workers. This is discussion-based and includes activities.

CORE LEVEL 2

Communication 2:
Overcoming Barriers and Resolving Conflict

Length: 2 hours. On each team, there are different personalities and opinions. This class will delve deeper into which barriers may be preventing the best dialogue with your co-workers. Also, we will look at how to encourage "good disputes." Bring your stories of difficult situations to discuss. Prerequisite: Communication 1: Communicating Effectively in Any Situation

The Science of Happiness

Length: 2 hours. The vision of the Zappos companies is to deliver happiness. Did you know happiness isn't about luck, it's about science? Want to know more? Come join us for a discussion about the science of happiness!

Fred Factor and *FISH*:
Go Fishing with the Mailman

Length: 2 hours. Have you ever wanted to go fishing with a mailman? Here's your chance! Reserve your spot on the *Fred Factor* and *FISH!* "Boat of Inspiration"! The goal is to encourage creativity, discover our "FredNESS" and brainstorm ideas to take the FISH! principles to the next level.

CORE LEVEL 2 (continued)
Both books are short and sweet, so please read both by class time. See you aboard!

CORE LEVEL 3
Culture
Length: 5 hours. The Culture class reignites, inspires and challenges you to take your role within the culture to the next level. This class is highly interactive and relies heavily on discussion-based activities. Through these activities and challenges, the culture class is meant to expose you to opportunities where you can make a difference.
Finance 1: Understanding Financial Reports
Length: 3 hours. In this class, we cover the three basic financial reports: the Balance Sheet, the Profit & Loss Statement, and the Cash Flow Statement.

Reprinted with the permission of Zappos.com, Inc.

An examination of this representative sample of class offerings clearly depicts the multiple levels of core classes provided at Zappos, as well as the diversity of the curriculum. Whether it's culture enrichment, basic business education, or increasing personal engagement, the Zappos core curriculum reflects content that has broad value to all Zapponians and that affords general skill development needed across all departments. Mark Sanborn, author of *The Fred Factor*, a book used in the Zappos Core Level 2 course "*Fred Factor* and *FISH*," shares, "It is gratifying to see my work used by Zappos because it shows how an organization with a culture for growth can bring ideas from outside the organization and tailor them for the success of their business. The types of leadership principles I write about have application across time, location, and business setting. Zappos has taken those principles and made them their own to maximize effectiveness. Virtually any business would benefit from taking the same approach." Mark's comments illuminate the key to the ingenuity of Zappos training. Look for what people across your business need to learn. Scour the business and personal literature for the best books, articles, concepts, and technologies. Translate that cutting-edge material into engaging, interactive classes that are relevant to your work setting and to your company's values. You will then enjoy a competitive advantage over companies that do not have that shared foundation of knowledge.

Beyond core classes, the Zappos Pipeline team works with various units, such as merchandising or the Customer Loyalty Team (CLT), to develop department-specific formal training curriculums. Loren Becker, Zappos Pipeline supervisor, suggests, "The success of Pipeline training is the partnership with department leaders to identify the knowledge and behaviors those leaders see as essential in their areas. It is a bit of an odd exercise, but those leaders essentially have to imagine what would happen if all their department leaders were to disappear immediately. Would their department be able to function seamlessly? If not, what are the knowledge sets and behaviors they should be developing, and in what sequence?" Loren notes that the Pipeline team assists department leaders to develop the coursework that helps Zapponians systematically reach the next level in their respective departments. He also emphasizes that completion of coursework alone is not a sufficient basis for advancement at Zappos. As a result, managers work with staff members to create individualized progression plans. Those plans factor in the completion of the formal training and add such things as behaviors and activities that need to be in place for an employee to warrant a promotion.

For those who wish to advance at Zappos, progression plans typically involve a minimum amount of time in a department, completion of required Pipeline classes (both core and department-specific), and a variety of other training, culture, and community elements.

To get a sense of the breadth of department-specific classes that have been and are being built into progression plans, let's look at the merchandising Pipeline. From the position of merchandising assistant, an entry-level job classification, to that of Zappos buyer, an advanced role in merchandising, there are more than 40 department-specific training classes, such as retail math, assortment planning, and forecasting. Progression plans for merchandising assistants also weave in 20 additional non-department-specific Pipeline offerings to assist staff members in their move toward buyer status. Each promotion along a merchandising employee's journey at Zappos is contingent not only upon taking defined Pipeline classes, but also upon demonstrating mastery of that knowledge in the performance of that person's job. Additionally, Zapponians must complete all other aspects of their specific progression plan, such as shadowing other employees, reading additional materials, contributing to the Zappos culture, and performing appropriate volunteer functions. To progress within the company, Zapponians are expected to be actively involved in projects dedicated to strengthening Zappos culture, such as departmentwide or Zappos-wide team-building events. They are also expected to participate in corporate social responsibility projects, such as the Zappos Holiday Gift Drive or LIVESTRONG Day. Alesha Giles, Zappos buyer—Children's Footwear, says, "Pipeline has helped us clearly define what skills, activities, and behaviors we need to see to know when a person is ready for a new level of job responsibility. It also serves as a road map for talent and leadership development."

While many organizations talk about developing talent, Zappos has built an ever-improving training platform to transfer

TRY THESE ON FOR SIZE

1. What would happen if all the leaders in an area of your business left tomorrow? Have you developed other staff members who could seamlessly take over those leadership positions?

2. If you hire new employees straight out of high school, trade school, or college, how workforce-ready are they? What strategies have you developed to supplement any deficits in their workforce readiness in areas of core knowledge for your business?

3. In addition to time on the job and performing well in a current position, what skills, knowledge, and behaviors do entry-level staff members need to possess before they can advance in your organization?

4. Have you developed a map of typical progression pathways in your company, with attendant milestones? Have you identified the skills, knowledge, and behaviors required at each milestone?

5. Do you discuss personalized progression plans with your staff members?

6. Have you developed tool kits, recommended or required reading, on-the-job training activities, or cross-training strategies to assist your staff members' progress?

corporate knowledge and incrementally enhance career-specific growth. In many ways, Zappos is doing what the former chairman and CEO of General Electric, Jack Welch, talked about when he suggested, "An organization's ability to learn, and translate that learning into action rapidly, is the ultimate competitive advantage."

LEADERSHIP TRAINING

Legendary NFL football coach Vince Lombardi once said, "Contrary to the opinion of many, leaders are not born; they are made. And they are made by hard effort." At Zappos, leadership development is taken seriously, and the Pipeline team offers opportunities for leaders to do the hard work needed to bring the best out in their people. Before we look at an example of the activity-based work (okay, they also have fun in the classes) of leadership-level training at Zappos, it is helpful to see a sample of class descriptions. The following list reflects the leadership offerings and the levels of classes provided to staff members with supervisory responsibilities at Zappos.

These examples of the Zappos leadership curriculum demonstrate the active involvement of senior leaders such as Tony Hsieh and Fred Mossler. Both of these leaders personally participate in classes such as manager orientation. The course descriptions also strike a balance between education in "soft skills" (such as interpersonal factors and leadership effectiveness) and in "hard skills" (such as financial planning and performance tracking). More important, the descriptions reflect the interactive and experiential nature of the training environment. To get a better feel for how leadership courses are conducted,

LEADERSHIP LEVEL 1

Manager Orientation

Length: 1 hour. This is a discussion-based introduction to the Zappos Family management philosophy with Tony and Fred. Discussions will be focused on your role as a coach, mentor, and leader to your team members. This will help you understand the big picture and your responsibility as a manager.

Performance Enhancement/Management

Length: 3 hours. Class topics include delivering feedback, coaching, and addressing performance issues with employees.

Leadership Essentials

Length: 3 hours. Tools and tips to help leaders reach their full potential!

LEADERSHIP LEVEL 2

Made to Stick and *Peak*

Length: 2 hours. This is NOT your average book class. This course uses games and activities to teach some of the major themes in the books *Peak* and *Made to Stick*. The goal is to give you practical information that you can use to make your ideas as a manager "stickier" and help your team members reach their peak! Plus, you'll leave class with lots of fun ideas for your next team meeting. While we recommend that you have both books read prior to signing up, we don't require it. As soon as you sign up, we'll email you a Study Guide so you'll know which topics we'll be focusing on!

Finance 2: Understanding the Planning Process

Length: 3 hours. What should we spend money on? How much should we spend? How are we doing? Where are we going? Finance 2 will not only answer these questions, but explain how we answer these questions. The 1st half of the class will help you understand the business cycle and how it relates to financial projections and performance tracking. The 2nd half of class is a game in which you'll get to be CFO of your own company! You'll make projections, spend money, battle against your competition, and answer to the Board of Directors at the end of the year.

LEADERSHIP LEVEL 3—WORKSHOPS
Core Value Workshop: 21 Days of Inspiration

Workshop Length: 3 hours. During this workshop, participants are led down a path which leads to the re-discovery of what it means to live our Core Values. Not only do we take a deep dive into each of the values, but the participants are also provided with information to show how their coworkers perceive their embodiment of the Core Values. If our culture and Core Values are important to you, then you'll be sure to thoroughly enjoy the experience of this journey. This is a 2-day workshop with 21 days between each session.

Reprinted with the permission of Zappos.com, Inc.

imagine that you are attending the Zappos leadership class on the book *Peak,* by Chip Conley. While the book itself focuses on transformation pyramids for employees, customers, and investors, you will be exploring only the employee pyramid and the three levels of that pyramid, namely, money, recognition, and meaning.

As Chip Conley notes in *Peak,* "Companies often misjudge the true motivations of their employees, imagining that compensation is their primary aspiration. . . . Money (or, more broadly the full compensation package) is a base need but also a base motivation for most employees." Chip talks about the middle level of the pyramid as building loyalty and inspiration through recognition of the talents, goals, and dreams of employees and culminates with a discussion of the highest level of the pyramid. "At the top of the pyramid is a concept that few employers talk about or even think about because it is less tangible than the subject of money. Finding meaning in one's work—both in what you do daily and in the company's sense of mission—creates a more inspired employee."

Take some time with Chip Conley as he explores how to help your employees find purpose and calling in their daily work activities by going to zappified.com/chip or by directing your QR reader at the image given here:

Beyond reading *Peak,* a Zappos Pipeline trainer would provide you with worksheets and facilitate discussions between you and other managers from different areas of the company. These discussions would allow you and your colleagues to share your challenges, victories, and best practices for helping all staff members experience peak levels of workplace meaning. You would be afforded insights into the role you play in understanding the talents and goals of your staff, and you would look at how to create a line of sight from your staff members' job functions to your company's overarching purpose and mission. Essentially, you would be doing a lot more than reading a book: you would be actively discussing and developing ways to take the book's knowledge and translate it into immediate leadership action. Leadership training at Zappos requires attendees to work on awareness, strategy, and skills. It does so in a way that results in improved departmental leadership, opportunities for playful connections with peers, and growth on both personal and professional levels.

*I*magine that the final *Jeopardy* theme is playing, and the category is Zappos. You are asked to provide your response to the statement "Something Zappos makes available, for free, to every employee, vendor, and guest." Your time is up, and you reveal your answer, "What are books?" Congratulations, you are the winner!

At Zappos, there are no strings attached to receiving a free book. Well actually, I guess you are expected to read the book you receive (although no one follows you home or quizzes you on it later).

So let's assume you take a complimentary Zappos tour. As that experience ends, you are presented with a leadership book. As an employee, you can grab any book from the library at any time. Employees also have access to a synopsis of all the books in the library so that they can make informed choices about which book they may wish to pick up next.

Even if it's only for your employees, how does a book library or free book program sound for your business?

PERSONAL DEVELOPMENT

So far, in our exploration of the principle "S T R E T C H," we have examined the concept of "Zappos University" as it relates to core curriculum, job-specific skills, and leadership development, but what does Zappos do to help individuals with their personal growth? To answer that question, we will first look at a sample of the Pipeline team's electives; then we will examine how that elective training is linked to both personal and organizational outcomes. Finally, we will examine how Zappos incorporates coaching into personal goal setting.

The list on page 187 furnishes a glimpse of the elective class descriptions geared at professional and personal skills acquisition. In addition to the classes listed, Zappos Pipeline electives include advanced writing skills, multiple classes on creating engaging PowerPoint presentations, time and stress management courses, classes on using spreadsheet software, refresher courses on the CLT orientation training, and much more.

The elective course descriptions exemplify the intersection of personal and professional development resources and offer insights into how to design a curriculum that is a win for the participant and a win for your company. A business writing class produces an important skill for attendees, well beyond the derivable benefits for Zappos. The "WOWing Through Tours" elective provides the requisite knowledge and skills to those staff members who are interested in being scheduled to provide visitor tours. While this tour training is elective, in order to actually be "tour certified," participants must also take a course from the core offerings menu, "Zappos Family History," and pass a certification evaluation. Growth and development occur both in the training necessary to become tour certified and in the experiences that later occur when the person actually conducts those tours.

An offering like "Using Your Superpowers" is provided both as a general class for individuals and as a workshop for existing teams. In both cases, the class is based on the book and technologies outlined in Tom Rath's *StrengthsFinder 2.0*. Upon arriving in class, participants are given the StrengthsFinder book with a code for scoring an online assessment. After completing the Strengths-Finder tool, attendees score their results to find their top 5

GRAMMAR 1: WRITE MORE BETTER!

Length: 3 hours. A lot of people think they have good grammar when it isn't true. So when they send an e-mail to someone they have no idea that the e-mail is making him/her sound unprofessional. This class will teach you some tip's and trick's so you can insure you aren't making a bad impression with you're writing. By the way, the above paragraph is so full of grammatical errors, it would give an English teacher an aneurysm. If you didn't notice any errors, maybe you should sign up today. :) If you did notice a few errors, how can you be sure you noticed them all? This business writing class will teach you some new tricks and remind you of some basics you've probably forgotten. You may not think of writing and grammar as instruments of WOW, but they are! We cover some of the most common mistakes in writing. You'll learn ways to remember some of those exciting grammar rules and how to not be confused by commonly confused words. We also talk about the components of a good e-mail message.

USING YOUR SUPERPOWERS

Length: 3 hours. How often do you think about your strengths? Do you know what your innate talents are? What are the benefits of building up your strengths rather than your weaknesses? How can you do more of what you do best? If you'd like the answers to any of these questions, then this class is for you! PLEASE NOTE: The first 45 minutes of the class are set aside for you to take the online StrengthsFinder 2.0 test. We will provide you with your unique access code as you walk into class. You do not need to read the book prior to class.

WOWING THROUGH TOURS

Length: 4 hours. This course is designed to help you deliver a tour in a fashion that WOWs each tour participant. This course covers significant points of interest that embody the values, beliefs, and attitude of the Zappos Family. Once certified, you will be able to give an inspirational tour with your eyes closed. Note: This is primarily a self-study course. Prerequisite: Completion of Zappos Family History is required before you may become tour certified.

Reprinted with the permission of Zappos.com, Inc.

attributes (out of a possible list of 34). Activities vary somewhat depending upon whether the class is being provided as a workshop for a Zappos team or as a general class for Zapponians from across the company. However, in all cases, interactive learning includes placing individuals in groups and asking them to assess their collective talents to determine what type of business their group would be best equipped to run. The class describes the benefits of knowing and working from a strengths-based team perspective. Participants are asked to reflect upon how many of their strengths are being used at work each day and how they can communicate those personality attributes to their teammates in a way that will allow their teams to play more to them. The culmination of the class is the development of an action plan centered on a specific strength of each participant. In essence, what action will each participant undertake the day after training (both at and away from work) to share that key talent or use it more effectively?

The scope, scale, and exact array of electives offered at Zappos might not work in your company, just as the values at Zappos would not fit in every business setting. What is significant about the Zappos elective offerings is how each course serves both a personal and a business development outcome. If you help your staff members better understand their strengths through the use of a superpowers-type course, you are helping them be better members of their communities, families, and work teams. When you help someone write better e-mails, that training benefits both your business and the individual. As training helps people become more effective in all areas of their lives, employees feel more loyal to the leaders who helped them grow.

COACH ME IN THE DIRECTION OF MY DREAMS

In 2007, Matthew Kelly released a book titled *The Dream Manager*. In it, he told the story of a fictional company that was struggling to combat low morale and high turnover. When traditional approaches like employee rewards and recognition programs failed, the company shifted to a "dream manager" strategy. As dream managers, the company's leaders explored the personal dreams and aspirations of their employees and helped their people realize those personal dreams. The book draws the conclusion that the realization of personal dreams is a greater motivator for people than salary. Now jump with me, if you will, from Matthew Kelly's fictional company to the very real, albeit offbeat, Zappos.

Long before Matthew's book was published, Zappos had its own official dream manager, known at Zappos as "the coach." The coach helped position professional and personal goal setting as part of the mindset of managers throughout the organization. The original coach, Dr. David Vik, was introduced to Tony Hsieh by Zappos founder Nick Swinmurn. During his years at Zappos, Dr. Vik provided an "Introduction to Coaching Workshop," then provided optional one-on-one coaching for staff members; those coaching sessions focused on personal growth and development. Dr. Vik had a large "throne" placed in his office, and, in his words, "People would come in and sit in the throne and let me know their 'deal'—where they were born, information about their family, what happened after high school, and so on. After I got to know them and we created a relationship, members of the Zappos family would declare a 30-day goal for making their lives or the lives of those around them better. It didn't matter if the goal was related to business or personal; most were personal. I have talked with some companies that started goal setting but made it about the company, and it didn't work because if the personal life of the employee isn't right, the company goal doesn't stand a chance." Dr. Vik's throne room was declared "Switzerland," and all conversations were confidential.

Dr. Vik added, "Once a goal was set, I would follow up after 30 days, and there would be a celebration among the person's peers, where a 'Certificate of Achievement' was presented to the staff member for taking life to the 'Next Level.'" When asked how a company could justify paying a "coach," Dr. Vik shared, "Times have changed. In the Industrial Age, the machines were the biggest asset of a company. But in the Information Age, it is the employees. Making sure your employees are doing well and growing in their personal lives creates individual leaders and folks with the right mindset for winning. Those people take that empowerment to their work, and they take the company up with them because it's just how they roll."

Dr. Vik left Zappos in 2010 to "roll" out his dream consulting business, the Culture King. But Zappos continues to invest in a designated coach. Augusta Scott, Zappos coach, suggests, "We are maintaining our commitment to helping our people live the best lives possible at and away from work. When I work with people, I am trying to get at what they are trying to accomplish, what they really want, why they want it, and what they are willing to do to accomplish their goals." At Zappos, leadership understands that when people reach for and achieve goals, they feel the power of personal mastery. Psychologist Albert Bandura refers to this mastery as "self-efficacy." From Dr. Bandura's perspective, efficacy is a fundamental component of self-esteem and forms the basis on which people organize and act in all new situations. By helping people find the power to realize their dreams and ambitions, you essentially help them approach future work challenges with an attitude of confidence and optimism.

While I was touring Zappos early in my research process, Jon Wolske, the lead culture guide at Zappos, shared a personal story of the significance of coaching and goal attainment: "I am a musician, but I was blocked as a songwriter. I did a coaching session with Dr. Vik and decided to set a 30-day goal to write just one song. Once that song was written, the next song came, and the next, and before you know it I had enough new original music to produce a CD, which I completed. I am so grateful for Zappos coaching and for a company that genuinely invests in my growth. I am happy with my songwriting progress, and I bring that happiness with me on this tour today and every day. I guess that's why I needed to tell you." Zappos essentially has blurred the line between personal and work goals. If a person is growing, Zappos sees that growth as being beneficial to the entirety of the individual's life. Where some companies discuss work/life balance, Zappos talks about work/life integration. Personal development classes and coaching support the fundamental human truth that if your people aren't happy and growing, your business will not maintain its success and growth. How firmly have you drawn the line between the personal and business lives of your people?

OWNING GROWTH AND LEARNING

When you combine the Zappos values of pursuing growth and learning and of embracing and driving change, you have a synergy of forces, with individuals being expected to grow personally and to help Zappos change and grow in the process. Excellence and change acceptance are not enough. Individuals must grow, learn, and drive themselves and the business. Rob Siefker, director of the Customer Loyalty Team, notes, "At Zappos, each day, I have to ask myself, what did I do today to make myself better? And what did I do to improve Zappos? But beyond those questions, I also have to accept responsibility for helping my teammates grow and seek learning. Tony says service should not be limited to a single department, and neither should training or growth."

TRY THESE ON FOR SIZE

1. What is the nature of leadership-level training at your workplace? Does it reflect a balance of soft and hard skill development?

2. Do you accept the late coach Lombardi's premise that leaders are not born but made by effort and hard work? If so, what "work" is involved in your leadership skill training program?

3. How do you encourage personal and professional growth in your business?

4. Can you imagine having a "dream manager" or "coach" in your company? Would that position be an unnecessary expense or a justifiable investment?

5. What is your 30-day goal? What are the 30-day goals of your team members? Who will follow up to hold you accountable and celebrate your growth to the "next level"? Who follows up on and celebrates your team members' 30-day goals?

An example of this commitment to facilitating the growth and learning of peers came when an employee approached Tony Hsieh and asked if Zappos had a book club. Tony said no, and shortly thereafter that employee started one. As a result of the Zappos emphasis on learning, the Zappos Book Club is the company's oldest informal group. The club, which is one of the largest clubs at Zappos, has representatives from every Zappos department. Each month the club dives into a new book, alternating between those that are in the Zappos library and fictional works. Like all things Zappos, the book club has a strong social component and mixes learning with fun.

A book club is certainly not unique to Zappos, but its popularity and the broad companywide participation in it are consistent with the priority that the culture places on growth and learning. John Yokoyama, owner of the World Famous Pike Place Fish Market and coauthor of my book *When Fish Fly*, says, "Tell me the results that are showing up in your life, and I will tell you who you are being." Extrapolating Johnny's wisdom in the context of Zappos, when something emerges from the grassroots of a business and generates a dynamic community of lifelong learners (like the Zappos Book Club), it tells you that the company "is being" Zappos University and producing people who stretch.

How much are stretch, growth, and learning showing up in your business? What does that tell you about who you are being as a leader?

Chapter 8 *Ideas to Run With*

- Great leaders are discontented, knowledge seeking, and unwilling to fall in love with the way things are or the way things have always been.

- Rather than focusing on problems with workforce readiness, create solutions to achieve workforce success.

- Evaluate the breadth of your training curriculum in the areas of knowledge, leadership training, and personal and professional development.

- No matter how large or small a business is, its leaders must determine what it takes to ensure the business would run smoothly if its top leadership were depleted.

- Progression planning involves an understanding of the skills, knowledge, activities, and behaviors needed to move forward in an organization.

- Training can be as simple as defining the knowledge needed in your organization, finding and modifying existing resources, and engaging in discussions and action plans based on those resources.

- People are less motivated by compensation and more motivated by recognition, a genuine interest in their aspirations, and meaningful work.

- Think work/life integration, not work/life balance.

- Goal setting and goal accomplishment lead to a sense of self-efficacy that translates into personal and professional benefits.

- Great leaders help their people stretch and make a long-range commitment to growth and learning.

9

BEYOND SHOES

Brand positioning experts understand that consumers give companies "permission" as to how far they can stretch their product and service offerings. For example, in the 1990s, Clorox considered extending its well-established bleach brand in the direction of laundry detergent, dishwashing soap, and other household cleaning applications. Consumer research, however, showed that Clorox was synonymous with bleach in the minds of the buying public and that consumers would be hesitant to purchase any Clorox product that would touch their hands or their dishes. As a result, Clorox focused its brand extension in the direction of toilet bowl cleaners, tub and tile products, and drain openers. Like that of Clorox, the early brand positioning of Zappos put it at risk of being denied permission to grow outside of a shoebox. However, a broad vision of the future, careful listening for customer requests, and an increasing level of consumer trust has allowed the Zappos brand wide opportunities to S T R E T C H.

If you type "www.shoesite.com" into your browser, the Zappos website will appear. Nick Swinmurn secured the address shoesite.com for his online shoe store in 1999, but later that year, the name was changed to Zappos. The company's leaders understood that a made-up name like Zappos would provide a unique, searchable Internet identity and would allow the company to broaden its product offerings if brand extension was ever deemed appropriate. Consistent with the leaders' wisdom in deciding to rebrand the start-up, the Zappos name has allowed the company to stretch outside of its original mission of "becoming the première destination for online shoes" and venture into a broader world of merchandise and services.

BAGS, ACCESSORIES, CLOTHING, HOUSEWARES, BEAUTY, SPORTING GOODS, AND *SO* MUCH MORE

Zappos made its first brand extensions into categories that were closely related to its shoe product line. Like Clorox, Zappos initially moved into areas that were a natural fit with footwear (bags, accessories, and clothing); then product offerings steadily branched out into housewares, beauty supplies, sporting goods, and more. From a pure product perspective, Tony Hsieh attributes this brand expansion to "our success through service. Once we understood that service was our brand, we also realized that all products were just vehicles through which we could deliver service. I hope someday, in the not too distant future, people won't even remember that we started out by selling shoes. We are thinking well beyond e-commerce, and our customers will guide us to where they want to receive Zappos service. Maybe someday we will have a Zappos airline, for example. Additionally, we want to turn downtown Las Vegas into the next Austin, Texas, as a hub of culture, innovation, and community."

Alfred Lin, former Zappos CFO, was quick to laughingly interject, "I've discouraged Tony from jumping into the highly capital-intensive airline business, but suffice it to say that the Zappos current business model is somewhat capital intensive, so who knows. It's clear that the sky is not the limit for Zappos." The breadth of the Zappos brand elasticity is often compared to that of the Virgin Group. Virgin leveraged its edgy appeal and the charisma of its founder, Sir Richard Branson, to create more than 300 Virgin-branded companies worldwide in diverse enterprises involving music, mobile communication, money, and, of course, an airline. In essence, Virgin created an image that people wanted to be associated with, so it was able to extend its brand based on trendiness. By contrast, Zappos is a brand people want to be served by and as such can expand from its service platform.

The initial Zappos forays into clothing sales were a direct result of consumer interest. According to Alfred Lin, "Our customers kept asking us to provide clothing and other accessories to go with their shoe purchases. We went in that direction because of our customers' passion for our service and because of the passion of people in the company. We understood how clothing would augment our customers' purchase experience. We also saw an opportunity, with clothing being a four times larger market than footwear. I hope that Zappos will shift from approximately 80 percent of sales through footwear to something on the order of 20 percent of sales over time."

In this brand extension phase, the leaders at Zappos have sought to capitalize on the infrastructure they developed to dominate online shoe sales, while also learning the nuances of broader merchandising categories. According to Fred Mossler, "just Fred" at Zappos, "We face a very different situation in selling clothes today compared to what we faced when we began selling shoes. Back then, no one was selling shoes on the Internet. We were the leader. We needed to get our selection in place and then add layers of service and personal emotional connection. Fast forward to our current reality, where we are experiencing very fast growth in our clothing category, but also where clothing on the Internet is a $20 billion plus proposition and we have a very small share." Fred explains that many shoe catalog companies learned from Zappos. As a result, they took shoes that were being sold through catalogs and moved them into Internet sales. While Zappos was gaining dominance in the shoe category, well-established clothing providers, both brick-and-mortar and catalog, were making their way onto the Internet as well. Some of these stores were modeling their strategies on what Zappos was doing in the shoe category. Essentially, Zappos is now trying to advance into existing Internet clothing markets, as opposed to innovating and gaining dominance in an emerging category. Fred notes, "This truly has been a stretch for us and a different sort of competitive landscape. We have also had to master a different product presentation. Even our distribution center is slightly more optimized for picking, packing, and shipping a bunch of items in boxes, like shoes, rather than items on hangers or in poly bags. These are the areas we have had to address in making the transition to constantly improve the customer experience for clothing shoppers."

Business success depends on evaluating your key competencies and listening to customer needs. Success also requires a willingness to take calculated risks in the direction of growth. Zappos heard the increasing chorus of customer voices tweeting, writing to the company, and posting blogs asking Zappos to serve them with a broader array of product choices, or to give them the opportunity to buy a complete outfit in the comfort of their home. As Fred puts it, "A lot of times, the biggest gamble you can take, when you have a groundswell of customer interest, is failing to try new ideas and being satisfied with where you are. Clothing, for example, is something we got into in 2007. We saw clothing as a big piece of our business in the future, and it has already grown into an important component for us. We have even made shifts in marketing to include a focus on the three Cs—customer service, culture, and clothing. We want every new customer to think of us as a destination for clothing purchases. While many consumers wanted us to venture into clothing, we still have the challenge of changing the mindset of a large portion of our existing customer base so that they see us as more than shoes."

Fred and other leaders emphasize that, to shift external brand perceptions effectively, the shift must first occur within the business. Galen Hardy, Zappos clothing czar, notes, "We have to focus on internal communication. When your ship has been sailing in a single direction, toward shoes, for seven years, it takes consistent conversations within our walls to remind our people that we are not in the shoe business; we are in the service business. We offer whatever the customers want us to serve to them." Through blogs from Tony and other Zappos leaders, conversations in all-hands meetings, leadership discussions about core values like "delivering wow through service," and emphasizing the business/service opportunity that comes from expanding merchandise categories, Zappos leaders have changed the internal dialogue—away from shoes and in the direction of clothing and service. In addition to the shift in staff perceptions, Zappos has had to develop a new set of vendor relationships and has had to leverage the skills it learned in the early days of courting shoe suppliers.

Jeanne Markel, director of Casual Lifestyle, notes that while many clothing brands have a strong online presence, others are reluctant to let a company like Zappos represent them on the

Internet. According to Jeanne, "Some of these brands prefer the control of a drop-ship model, and most have a strong need to protect their brand presentation. Couture brands, for example, have concerns that often surface through questions such as, 'What if we don't like the way things are presented? What if we don't like the image? How is that going to affect our brand perception?' I think there are fewer of those concerns as our clothing lines progress, but there are still pockets and divisions that are struggling to make peace with online sales."

Clothing experts at Zappos also face vendors who fear Internet purchases will result in their brand being viewed as a commodity. Galen notes, "There are a lot of people thinking that the Internet is purely for discounted products or for coupons or price matching. We have to sell vendors and clothing consumers on our successful service value proposition. They have to understand that our customers are not as price-conscious as they are service- and selection-conscious." Jeanne eloquently summarizes the greatest stretch challenge for Zappos as it moves into other sectors like clothing: "I don't pretend that there's a large part of the consumer population, let alone the Zappos customer base, that says, 'Gosh, I need a blender. Let me go to Zappos.' But that is our challenge: to have people with a want or need automatically run to Zappos to see if we can fill it." Brand positioning and expansion are challenging propositions. The most salient aspects of your brand identity can either propel or restrict you. In the case of Zappos, its strong identification with shoes makes it harder for customers and vendors to think of it when it comes to items in other categories. Conversely, the strength of the service identity at Zappos gives the leaders permission to take that service acumen into other product areas. What are the strongest aspects of your brand identity? How do those strengths help or hamper your brand extension efforts? What are the wants and needs of customers that fit with the brand extensions you are considering?

Customers are certainly letting Zappos know what they want, as evidenced by examples from blogs and tweet streams. Blogger Tim Sanchez shared this observation on his popular Deliver Bliss blog: "While the value delivered by the airlines continues to diminish, Zappos is always striving to incrementally improve itself. As they become increasingly more efficient and refuse to succumb to the good enough syndrome that plagues its competition, Zappos continues to serve as an example for not just a great shoe company, but a great service company. I don't know about you, but I'll be waiting in line to buy my ticket on Zappos Airlines."

Here are some views of the Zappos brand expansion from the Twitter community:

@scheduleflyin
Hey zappos, if you sold health insurance, I'd buy it. Just sayin.

@Jayfromma1
zappos will you get involved in government, then politicians would be more fun

@micahyost
we need zappos to run the custom home building business. They just can't figure out the service after the sale!

@bizshrink
Imagine zappos airline—delivering happiness w/no charge 4 surprise upgrade to 1st class. I'm there. happy flier & early arrival

Name a segment of our economy where service is lacking, and you will probably find disgruntled customers encouraging, if not imploring, Zappos to extend into that marketplace.

ZAPPIFIED BRAIN BREAK

Would you believe that Zappos offered a $50,000 T-shirt that came with one-of-a-kind benefits? The "Cease and Desist" T-shirt was not a spectacular garment. For all practical intents and purposes, it was a fairly traditional cotton T-shirt. But the value-added components were remarkable, playful, and unusual. The limited-time offer targeted the family members of the highest-volume customers at Zappos. The T-shirt was available in five colors, with choices suitable for wife, husband, girlfriend, boyfriend, or "it's complicated." Unique to the shirt was personal hand delivery by a Zappos Customer Loyalty Team member. However, that special delivery was only a small part of what made the deal truly extraordinary. The shirt came with a guarantee by Zappos to permanently disable a significant other's Zappos.com account for life. Jokingly, Tony Hsieh suggested that the shirt was a win for the buyer, a win for Zappos, and a win for the buyer's significant relationship, "We are confident that any buyer of the T-shirt and service will be 100 percent satisfied with the purchase. More important, we will be satisfied with the $50,000 that we receive and the relationships we save." The Cease and Desist T-shirts were advertised in jest; however, the company would have produced them had it received orders. You have to wonder if a few people considered buying a shirt, since top Zappos customers spend well over $10,000 annually.

PRODUCTS YES—BUT CORPORATE TRAINING?

While it's one thing to expand into additional product sectors like clothing, it's an entirely different endeavor to launch a business training service division like Zappos Insights. Some of the most noteworthy ingredients involved in this bold brand extension included Tony Hsieh's desire to promulgate a business revolution or movement, considerable interest in the brand's business practices, and a well-connected community of brand fans who want to understand how Zappos achieved its success.

Over the years, a sizable number of people who requested a Zappos tour did so simply to better understand how this atypical company could become both a survivor of the dot.com crisis and a leader in online product delivery. While those tours offered a glimpse into the Zappos culture and an overview of the company's business practices, many of the tour-goers wanted more. As the company received increased public attention, more business leaders, department heads, associations, and owners of small businesses reached out to see if Zappos could share best practice ideas with them. Zappos was increasingly being defined as a unique thought leader, and something had to be done to address the demand. So, enter the business division Zappos Insights!

The mission of Zappos Insights can be described in both tactical and transcendent terms. Donavan Roberson, Zappos Insights culture evangelist, notes, "We are here to help people at every level of a business. Whether CEO, owner, manager, or front-line employee, people come to us for tools and ideas, and for the opportunity to connect with like-minded individuals. We serve as a resource for those committed to culture building and service excellence." Robert Richman, Zappos Insights product manager, adds the transformational aspect of the Zappos Insights mission: "It is our sincere objective to make the workplace and the world at large a happier place. We want to deliver happiness to those who also want to build happier workplaces. Since people spend so much time at work, we believe happy workers make for happier partners and parents, which make for happier kids. We've seen the power of an engaged workplace here at Zappos, and we want to support that movement, one company at a time."

Like most things Zappos, a trial and improvement approach was used for the Zappos Insights division. Through its various iterations, Zappos Insights primarily offers a service array that is anchored to a reasonably priced monthly membership site. In case you have not started the complimentary 30-day trial membership with Zappos Insights presented at the back of the book, allow me to provide you an overview of the platform through which the following services are easily accessed:

- *Tools.* This section of the site provides regularly updated tool kits, such as the complete downloadable "Zappos Family Core Values Interview Assessment Guide" mentioned in Chapter 2 and the call review form and Happiness Form mentioned in Chapter 7.

- *Culture lab.* In this section, Zappos Insights members are given opportunities to learn from individuals in businesses that have made changes in their company culture or service delivery processes. These video presentations demonstrate the power of the Zappos leadership concepts, particularly as those concepts are adapted to fit the varied needs of other business sectors.

- **Experts.** The Zappos Insight team conducts video interviews with bestselling authors and leadership experts who provide both inspiration and practical advice.

- **Events.** The Zappos Insights team is involved in planning on-site training events, from basic tours, extended visits, and half-day or daylong training to two-day Zappos culture boot camps.

- **Community.** Zappos Insights encourages and develops communities of members who are striving to improve workplace culture and service delivery.

Rachel Cosgrove of Results Fitness in southern California attended the two-day Zappos Insights culture boot camp and notes, "I knew about Zappos culture when I heard Tony speak at a conference I was attending in Las Vegas. After that, I decided I needed to learn more from this company. I felt we had a pretty good culture at our fitness center, but we hadn't dialed in our core values. When Tony talked about leaders' needing to create something bigger than themselves, I was fully plugged in, and I knew I wanted to learn everything I could about and from Zappos. I sent an e-mail to Tony about possible training, and I quickly received a personal e-mail response. The CEO of Zappos responded directly and added a surprise book on top of it. I then joined the Zappos Insights website and received yet another surprise gift. So for me it was like a series of wows right in a row."

Rachel reports that she attended the culture boot camp, and then, "I went back to our gym, had a meeting with our team, and we redid our core values. Everybody started to realize I had been Zapped. I was talking a lot about Zappos, and people in the fitness industry were asking, 'Why are you learning from Zappos?

You run a gym.' But we definitely took a lot from Zappos Insights and have implemented those learnings in our gym, and that has taken our culture to a new level." Rachel and her husband, Alwyn, have incorporated their own core values into the daily conversations of their business. They have made changes in their employee selection processes and their customer service delivery strategies, and they have even invited their staff to create a Culture Book. Rachel sees Zappos Insights as having made a "lasting, long-term, and profound impact on our culture at Results Fitness."

In addition to instilling many aspects of the Zappos culture into his business, Deryl Sweeney, president of DormBuys.com, attended Zappos Insights training and focused on increasing his commitment to the velocity of service delivery: "One of our big takeaways was asking ourselves how committed we are to good customer service. It taught us that we are not going to find a company out there that says it has crappy customer service. We had to look at taking service up to the Zappos level. After we did boot camp, we looked at whether we could offer free overnight shipping, and even though we couldn't, we developed systems to ensure that orders placed by 3:00 eastern time would go out that very same day. By making that change, and given that we are based in Louisville, Kentucky, we are able to have our products to the majority of our customers in one to two days. The Zappos Insights boot camp inspired us to expedite getting our products to our customers' doors. Similarly, we put systems in place to make sure we are answering the phones personally. We came away realizing that people don't want to go through a bunch of robotic prompts—they want to get a person. It may seem basic, but we got a deeper appreciation for taking service to the more urgent and more personal level." Rachel and Deryl's experiences at the boot camp speak to the importance of benchmarking great service businesses. They also identify an approach to maximizing the benefits that come from looking for the best practices of others. After spending time at Zappos, Rachel and Deryl were inspired to enhance their culture and increase their service urgency. Rather than attempting to emulate the Zappos overall service approach, they evaluated what was realistic for their businesses and set service improvement goals that were consistent with their specific circumstances.

Zappos Insights gives a transparent look into what makes Zappos work as a values-based organization. But, ultimately, Zappos is just the beginning. As CEO Tony Hsieh envisions it, "I hope that Zappos can inspire other businesses to adopt happiness as a business model—letting happy customers and happy employees drive long-term profits and growth. Ultimately, it's all about delivering happiness."

This thought naturally explains the creation of Delivering Happiness, the company Tony Hsieh and Jenn Lim cofounded to carry out this vision of applying happiness as a framework not just in businesses but also in organizations and communities around the world. The belief is that Zappos just happens to be the first of many organizations that will incorporate happiness as a business model to positively affect things like productivity, profits, customer service, culture and—as a result—the overall level of happiness in the world. Delivering Happiness emerged as a company to see this vision through.

Jenn Lim, CEO and chief happiness officer of Delivering Happiness, notes, "DH is about spreading and inspiring happiness to companies, in the way Zappos has shown it can be done, as well as to nonbusiness sectors (e.g., education, non-profits) and everyday life (e.g., students and families). It's really been both phenomenal and humbling to hear the feedback from people who have read the book. Taking it all in, we've seen a common thread emerge: regardless of age, background, history or culture, more and more people believe that the science of happiness can tangibly make our world a better place. It's this response that led us to create a company around it and, ultimately, the Delivering Happiness Movement."

Jenn continues, "The unanticipated response comes from wide-ranging places:

- A fledgling bar/lounge in Austin that became the number 1 venue after reading the Culture Book and redirecting its focus on employees

- A CEO of an amusement park in Korea who was reminded of the reason he is in the business (corporate culture and happiness)

- A student from the University of Iowa who dropped the major her parents prescribed to her (premed) because she always wanted to be an art teacher

- A trader on the verge of suicide, who was given some hope after reading about the failures Tony Hsieh had to overcome before his successes

- A mobile marketing entrepreneur in Uzbekistan who was inspired to pursue his passion even though everyone was telling him the "[economic] sky is falling"

- A mom who vowed to be the CMP (chief managing parent) of her household because she knew she was a good parent but realized she could be better

"Even though the response to the book was unexpected," Jenn adds, "it began to make sense after thinking through the research that's been done around it. Following Maslow's hierarchy, once someone's basic needs of food, safety, and shelter are met, people seek to find their higher purpose and happiness in life. You get a sense when you ask people, 'What are your goals in life and why?' Whether the goal is to have children, travel the world, or drive racecars for a living, the 'why' usually comes down to the same things—finding meaning and happiness. We're just talking different paths to get there. An interesting finding highlighted in the book *Delivering Happiness* is that studies show humans are really bad at predicting what will bring sustainable happiness. That's why it was such a revelation. As more and more people told us they were inspired to make a change in their lives—big or small—to be happier, it just made sense to evolve the book into something else. The book seems to have nudged people and companies toward happiness, so our cause is to support and nurture that as best we can. The book also explores other frameworks of happiness that match the subjective nature of 'happiness' to the objective nature of science. As highlighted in the book, research shows that happiness can be described by four fundamental things: perceived control, perceived progress, connectedness (the number and depth of your relationships), and vision/meaning (being part of something bigger than yourself). What's interesting, as Tony Hsieh explains in the narrative, is that these concepts can be applied both to business and in life."

Another framework describes happiness on a chart where the two axes are Time and Level of Happiness. On it, there are three types of happiness: Pleasure, Passion, and Higher Purpose. Tony Hsieh elaborates, "What I find interesting is that many people go through life chasing after the pleasure type of happiness, thinking that once they are able to sustain that, then they will worry about the passion and, if they get around to it, look for their higher purpose. Based on the findings of the research, however, the proper strategy would be to figure out and pursue the higher purpose first (since it is the longest-lasting type of happiness), then layer on top of that the passion, and then add on top of that the pleasure type of happiness."

Similar to other cause-based companies like TOMS Shoes, Delivering Happiness operates as a social enterprise, implementing ways to generate revenue in order to fuel the DH Movement. Some of the avenues to revenue include

- Culture Book creation services (as mentioned in Chapter 3)

- On-site, customized workshops for companies and organizations that want to increase productivity and happiness in the workplace (as a complement to Zappos Insights training)

- The Delivering Happiness Store, which sells inspirational merchandise and, down the road, experiences (as examples, helicopter lessons or group trips to Antarctica) to further instill that the equation of happiness ultimately comes from our collective memories and experiences, not the material goods we buy

- Follow-on books to target the different audiences that have emerged since the first one was launched

Much like Zappos, Delivering Happiness sees revenue as a means to its higher purpose. With "Inspire and Be Inspired" as one of its mottos, if Delivering Happiness continues to be inspired by stories of people's journeys toward happiness, their cause to inspire others will surely go on.

Whether through Zappos Insights or the emergence of Delivering Happiness, Zappos has demonstrated thought leadership in business and social excellence. Often that excellence is fueled by a willingness to provide tools that allow interested individuals an opportunity to learn, adapt, and execute on a few key take-aways gleaned from companies like Zappos.

TRY THESE ON FOR SIZE

1. How elastic is your brand? What are the limits of the product or service offerings you could provide for your customers?

2. If asked, would your customers view you as a provider of such high-quality customer experiences that they would want you to venture into other industries? If so, in what industries might they suggest your involvement? If not, what would you need to do to be considered in that way?

3. Could you imagine offering customer experience or leadership training to other businesses? If so, what is it about your business that is worthy of study?

4. What lessons might you learn from Zappos? Are you actively involved in benchmarking other businesses and/or participating in a community of business leaders who share your interest in service excellence?

LEADING A SOCIAL REVOLUTION

Zappos has stretched its product array, but it has also pushed the boundaries of marketing in the "new media." Inarguably, Zappos has blazed a path in social interactivity that is often talked about but seldom effectively emulated. This top-of-mind positioning led David Meerman Scott, marketing/leadership strategist and writer of the Webink Now blog, to suggest that Zappos may be stifling the growth of social media innovation. Specifically, David notes, "Hundreds of 'social media experts' cite the company in their books, blogs, speeches, Webinars and the like. As a result, the marketing discipline is not moved forward because we don't learn about other companies and their success. . . . My issue is not with [Zappos] but with those who incessantly use this one example as 'proof' new marketing works." David goes on to note that Zappos has definitely earned its reputation as a trendsetter in social media, as evidenced by extraordinary outcomes like company CEO Tony Hsieh having more than "1.75 million followers on Twitter" and its "brilliance in social media . . . cited 5.8 million times on the Web."

As further evidence of this dominance in social media, a customer service chat group on Twitter created a "pseudo-drinking game." Geoff Snyder, a network facilitator and member of that customer service chat group, notes, "We conduct our discussion on Twitter, and Zappos examples come up so often that we decided to make a game out of references to the company. Zappos has set a standard that we look up to. So whenever someone mentions Zappos, we take a sip of our drinks (symbolic or otherwise)." When your name comes up so often that Twitter chat groups salute those references with a real or symbolic toast, you have functionally saturated the social network world. In 2010, when Zappos announced that it was opening an office in San Francisco and that it was hiring 2,000 employees to meet overall employment demand in 2011, each of those messages was retweeted (forwarded, if you will) thousands of times.

So what is it that Zappos does to leverage social media so effectively? In my opinion, the Zappos social networking success can be linked to placing more emphasis on the "social" and less on the "networking." Put simply, Zappos creates authentic connections and delivers enriched content.

Listening to Authentically Connect

Business leaders must always adapt to technology, and this is particularly true when it comes to harnessing the power of the Internet. In the earliest iterations, many companies simply gobbled up Web addresses and developed pages that served as little more than online brochures. To get a sense of the evolution of Internet brand presentation and interactivity, one need only explore the "way back machine" (www.waybackmachine.org), a historical archive of 150 billion Web pages dating back to 1996.

Dial-up connections gave way to broadband, and Web 2.0 opened up the world to applications that enabled a shift from static Web pages to dynamic and shareable content and social networking. While many people knew they "had to" dive into the new media, some companies failed to understand how to benefit from rapidly advancing technology. Not so for Zappos!

Some businesses' foray into social media reflected traditional marketing, advertising, or "selling" approaches. By contrast, Zappos understood that social networking was just one more way (and a rather inexpensive one at that) to build and maintain relationships with customers and noncustomers alike. C. B. Whittemore, chief simplifier of Simple Marketing Now, notes, "Rather than using social media tools to sell products, Zappos deliberately uses them to . . . connect on a more personal level with both employees and customers. . . . Mind you, this is the company that considers the telephone to be the best social media. . . . At Zappos the liberal use of social media facilitates the network that links employees with one another and with the company's customers."

A website that is at the center of the social media phenomenon, Mashable, suggests that "Zappos has set the bar for social media customer service. Its approach focuses on making authentic connections via social networks rather than selling or promoting products. . . . CEO Tony Hsieh recognizes that the Web gives everyone a voice—including Zappos customers—and what customers say on blogs and social networks can reach millions. That's why Zappos treats every interaction as an opportunity . . . to shed positive light on the brand. Staff are encouraged to be transparent in their tweets, which helps make customers feel like they know them and can be comfortable reaching out. The interaction is authentic, leaving the customer satisfied and likely to tell others about the experience." Rather than communicating only through Tony Hsieh's Twitter account (@zappos), the company's personality comes through in the Twitter messages of Zappos employees on their own personal accounts. To see what Zapponians are tweeting about, you can go to http://twitter.zappos.com/employee_tweets.

When someone outside of Zappos tweets about the company (for example, a mention of where Zappos ranks in the *Fortune* Best Places to Work survey), it is common to see a number of Zappos employees spontaneously engage in a discussion about that tweet. If a tweet involves a customer service issue or question, the Zappos leadership has assigned staff members from the CLT resource desk to be available 24 hours a day to respond through the @Zappos_Service Twitter account. CLT members who are on "Twitter duty" address hundreds of customer questions daily. The spontaneous Twitter posts of Zapponians and the immediate personal nature of customer-service Twitter answers and interactions demonstrate how effectively Zappos leverages social media to parallel the personal connections created when customers call the Zappos CLT or engage its customers through live chat.

From a blogging perspective, the Zappos.com home page has a blog link that takes customers to a wide variety of product or Zappos culture blog pages, as well as to the Zappos Facebook page. Videos capturing the Zappos culture are often posted on the Zappos Family blogs and then uploaded to a variety of Zappos YouTube channels.

Graham Kahr, a social engagement scientist at Zappos, explains how Zapponians integrate and engage social media: "If there's a video that my team makes at Zappos and I think it is sincerely funny, I'll put it on my Twitter account, but if it's something that I don't think is going to appeal to my followers, then I won't tweet it. Before I post anything on Twitter, I think about my posts exactly as I think about talking in public. At Zappos, hundreds of our staff members are on Twitter and looking at it in a pretty similar manner. If we wouldn't say it in front of everybody, we probably shouldn't tweet it. When a company treats you well and trusts you to act responsibly, people step up and communicate both honestly and respectfully."

Graham's comments highlight the understanding at Zappos that social media needs to be "raw," authentic, and responsible, without the hype, polish, and extravagance of produced advertisements. Some well-established brands have struggled to appreciate the organic and honest nature of social media and have attempted to control the conversation, and at times, their efforts have backfired. One of the classic examples of this miscalculation was the "Wal-Marting Across America" fake blog (or what is sometimes referred to as a "flog"), which featured the very Wal-Mart-friendly writings of a couple, Jim and Laura, who purportedly crossed the country in an RV. Amid speculation that Jim and Laura weren't real people, BusinessWeek.com provided a series of exposés about the blog. Those articles identified Laura as Laura St. Claire, a freelance writer, and Jim as Jim Thresher, a staff photographer at the *Washington Post*—both of whom had been compensated by Wal-Mart for the blog. Unlike messages delivered through traditional advertising, the social media attract an audience of individuals who are looking for genuine and unpaid opinions. In essence, they are looking for transparency.

Transparency fits well with the Zappos core value of "build open and honest relationships with communication," and the Zappos "fun and weirdness" culture plays well in the context of social media. At Open Mic, the SAS Publishing Blog, Bernie Brennan and Lori Schafer suggest, "Social media is ingrained into the Zappos culture. Zappos believes they don't even need a social media strategy—after the employees constantly post videos, tweet, and blog about their culture—they don't direct sell or market. Visit the Zappos.com Family Blogs, its YouTube channel, or its Facebook page, and you will be entertained for hours watching videos of employees engaging in activities such as the 'Crazy Fat Sandwich Eating Contest,' Halloween at Zappos, as well as more serious Fashion Culture and Cause videos." Social media is definitely personal, and the Zappos penchant for weirdness translates well through short, authentic tweets and highly energized and playful videos.

Delivering Enriched Content

Given the visual nature of the Internet, Zappos has made a sizable commitment to providing enriched video content, not only of its brand in action, but of its products as well. In Chapter 4, we examined how Zappos helps customers make informed

To sample a Zappos Family music video, go to zappified.com/mvid or point your QR reader at the image given here.

choices through rich photographic displays. While this is a more than sufficient approach to product depiction, Zappos seized the opportunities presented in a Web 2.0 environment to integrate videos that showcase products and forge connections with customers. The early adoption of video product depiction at Zappos is a story of S T R E T C H on two levels—how the Zappos staff members innovated video product presentations and how Zappos is changing the future of online product display.

Jason Lee Menard, video production manager at Zappos, highlights the inauspicious start of Zappos product videos: "I worked at the Headquarters in Vegas. I was on the fashion team, writing content for the product descriptions and for brand pages. I'd graduated from college with a communications degree and completed a lot of video classes. About a year into my working here, the manager of the content team asked me to make 10 samples of how I envisioned a product video looking. I was given full creative control. My manager showed the samples to Tony, Alfred, and Fred, and I was told they liked them. In less than two weeks, they gave me the title of lead video content coordinator.

I was a one-man operation, making six videos a month in a little room with no professional lighting, a janky camera, and an improvised sound boom—a microphone attached to a broomstick."

From that makeshift start, the Zappos video team now is located at the Fulfillment Centers in Kentucky, where it is actively involved in shooting short product videos. Essentially, a Zappos. com user who clicks on the site has the opportunity to see a rich array of photos of the products, and on many of the pages, the user can also watch a video hosted by a Zapponian. The Zappos staff member goes over the product description, adds insights beyond the attributes of the product, and usually models the use or wear of the item. Jason notes, "These videos allow the personality of our staff members and our culture to shine through, which was the original concept of the videos. In a minute or less, we want to show the product, make a connection with our staff's personality, and share our culture. The videos should enhance the personal connection with customers through our human presentation of the product."

Given that it takes considerable effort, staff involvement, and money to create product videos, one has to ask, "Are they working? Are they having the desired impact?" According to Jason, "We've gotten a lot of positive feedback. We conducted a user experience test where we brought in professional models to demo the products and compared that to our own staff presentations. For the most part, our users seriously disliked the models because they felt they couldn't relate to them. We got a lot of feedback on our people, noting 'how down to earth' they are or how they 'could be living next door.'" Jason notes that the "realness" of people from Zappos talking about the products parallels what is naturally occurring in social media. "Just look at YouTube. People get a new pair of shoes and share a video about them. People can relate to that because it's the stuff of life." Realness and the compelling nature of the product videos led Zappos to expand Jason's one-man video production efforts, which could create six videos a month, to a team of approximately 20 videographers, video hosts, editors, and other staff members producing more than 50,000 videos a year. This aggressive approach to online streaming content is stretching the e-retail industry. While product video use isn't new, it is still in the formative stages. Acceptance has certainly increased, as business owners appreciate the higher conversion rates they enjoy when shoppers view a product video. But as retail video expert Mark R. Robertson adds, "What has proven most interesting is the fact that even those shoppers who do *not* watch the video are converting at a significantly higher rate than those viewing the same product page without the option for video viewing,"

Zappos is converting product videos into sales while making emotional connections through those videos. Zappos understands that video, like all other content shared on- or offline, must be crafted in a high-quality manner. The material must be well produced but not overly polished. It must also be relevant, engaging, and consistent with overall brand standards. Unlike traditional advertising, the new visual media call for a sense of spontaneity, intimacy, and unabashed candor.

Zappos has achieved maximized returns from its commitment to social media and the production of enriched, high-quality online content. By involving its staff members in genuine conversations through Twitter, blogging, fun Zappos culture videos, and personal product content, Zappos has created a highly benchmarkable social media leadership position that social media expert Jeff Bullas reports delivers the following list of online results:

- "It drives inbound links.

- Its employees create a good deal of internal Web links.

- It raises the Google page rank.

- It enables a customer service forum.

- It accelerates public relations.

- It promotes branding.

- It provides a search engine attraction platform, creating magnets for search engine activity."

Who would not want that set of outcomes from a social media strategy? In the end, as with many other aspects of Zappos, these benefits come less from strategy and more from authentically connecting and enriching human experiences. As Zappos social engagement scientist Graham Kahr notes, "We are just people looking to connect with other people across the range of human experiences. Sometimes those connections involve offering helpful information, and other times it's doing a poll about favorite cartoon characters. That's not a strategy. That's being fully human."

PUSHING THE ENVELOPE IS NOT WITHOUT RISK

Lest you think that Zappos can do no wrong when it comes to its use of technology, some efforts by Zappos to engage customers have met with controversy. For example, the *Wall Street Journal* and other publications have raised questions about a strategy that Zappos and many other online retailers use called "behavioral targeting." Meghan Keane, U.S. editor of *Econsultancy*, notes, "Zappos knows what you did last summer. Or maybe what you did last time you were on the Zappos website. The shoe

TRY THESE ON FOR SIZE

1. How effectively have you leveraged social media in your business?

2. Have you encouraged a large percentage of your workforce to responsibly but actively and authentically communicate through the social media?

3. Is your approach to social media built around conversation and connection?

4. Have you capitalized on the power of videos in blogs and product presentations?

5. Do your online videos and blog content reflect high-quality writing and production? Are your videos converting into sales and building relationships between your customers and your brand?

seller is just one of many companies that tracks customer activity online to serve more relevant advertising. Such tools have the ability to make product searches much easier online. But they also creep some people out. . . . Zappos ads are so smart that they remember past searches and offer similar product images to consumers as they surf the Web. For instance, if you go on Zappos searching for black patent pumps, Zappos will then taunt you on various websites with ads featuring glittering heels you probably shouldn't be purchasing right now (not that I know this from personal experience)." The use of behavioral targeting by Zappos is consistent with a "do more with less" approach to online marketing. According to Darrin Shamo, director of online marketing for Zappos, "We wanted to provide value to consumers given the constraints of the medium and do it in the most efficient way possible. Personalized retargeting was driven from this idea and the feeling that if users are going to be exposed to display advertising, it should be both relevant and easily controlled." Rather than spending money to position advertising in places that it hopes its customers will visit, Zappos took specific items that are of interest to a customer and placed them in the places the customer was actually viewing.

Michael Learmonth, writing in *AdAge*, indicates, "I abandoned [a Zappos] search [for a pair of shorts] and did something else. That's when the weirdness started. In the five days since, those recommendations have been appearing just about everywhere I've been on the Web, including MSNBC, Salon, CNN.com and The Guardian. The ad scrolls through my Zappos recommendations. . . . At this point I've started to actually think I never really have to go back to Zappos to buy the shorts—no need, they're following me."

While other companies use the same technologies, commentators like Meghan caution, "Zappos is testing the limits of targeting with these ads. The company isn't using particularly personal information in these ads. And it has been sending similarly personalized e-mails for a while. . . . A strong argument for behaviorally targeted ads online is that more relevant ads are better for consumers and brands. But what if consumers don't want personalized ads—even when they are relevant?" Twitter posts about this practice suggest mixed results for Zappos. Here are a couple of representative examples:

@grumpymartian
I have to admit the *Zappos* ads that are targeted directly at me relating to what I've looked at on their site previously freak me out a bit.

@shoppinlover

I am so tempted. Sites like Zappos have banner ads with items that I barely resisted buying the first time. What the heck, where's my card?

Clearly not every effort at "stretching" will be well received, and the jury is still out on the acceptability of behavioral targeting among Zappos customers. Based on consumers' initial privacy concerns, Zappos has placed a link on the banner ads that says, "Why are you being shown this banner?" and it offers customers an opt-out option to prevent behaviorally targeted ads. The director of online marketing at Zappos, Darrin Shamo, notes, "We had a rough start, as we quickly learned that some users felt strongly opposed to these ads. Given our user feedback, we realized that we needed to work quickly to either resolve these concerns through optimization or discontinue this particular vehicle altogether. Since these ads are cookie-based and all inventory is purchased in real time, with no data being passed to publishers, our challenge was with a privacy perception issue rather than an actual privacy violation. Unfortunately, this vehicle was so nuanced and new within the industry that our only means of solving this issue was through education."

Great brands continually listen to their customers, educate them, and make course corrections that are consistent with the company's core essence. Those brands understand the limits of the permission that their customers extend and even the areas of need that their customers want them to fill. That permission or brand elasticity is finite. Brands that overstretch or reach beyond what is authentic or honest *break*!

Chapter 9 *Ideas to Run With*

- From the outset, brand positioning should allow ample elasticity of concept, service, and product.

- In addition to broadening product arrays, expertise in business can become a product line in and of itself.

- Brands can stretch their social media effectiveness if they understand that the new media provide an opportunity to maintain and enhance relationships with customers and noncustomers alike.

- Effectiveness in social media depends upon prioritizing communication, connection, and authenticity.

- Overt selling, controlling the message, and poor-quality presentation are trouble zones in new media.

- Businesses that are effective in social media have encouraged their staff members to authentically and responsibly engage their followers in discussions about their company.

- Well-produced product videos can add a personal dimension to item presentation.

- Product videos enhance sales conversion even when they are not viewed.

- If you overstretch your brand, customers will provide feedback when you need to change course.

- If you fail to heed your customers' feedback on overstretching, the elasticity of your brand will snap!

Play to Win

The master in the art of living makes little distinction between his work and his play, his labor and his leisure, his mind and his body, his information and his recreation. . . . He simply pursues his vision of excellence at whatever he does, leaving others to decide whether he is working or playing. To him he's always doing both.

—JAMES MICHENER

In my book *Humor, Play and Laughter*, I suggested that play is a powerful tool for alignment and social cohesion. Unfortunately, many business leaders haven't accepted that premise. If asked, many managers would answer that the opposite of black is white and the opposite of work is play. At Zappos, however, leaders see work and play as being intertwined. Chapter 10, "Play Well," focuses on how Zappos infuses a spirit of play on daily, monthly, and extended timelines throughout the workplace. It places the concept of "play" or "fun" into a broader context of staff pleasure and social bonding. Chapter 11, "R.O.F.L.," looks at how Zappos has transformed fun into a culture that is far from frivolous. "R.O.F.L." further examines the sustained benefits that Zappos enjoys in terms of employee engagement, innovation, and profitability. It's time for fun with a purpose—the rocket fuel of the Zappos Experience.

PLAY WELL

Play and fun have served Zappos well. Undoubtedly, fun holds the rich and highly collaborative Zappos culture together. But let's face it, if Zappos were dedicated only to fun, the company would not be thriving today. The genius of Zappos leaders is the way they blend the fun into the work. The visionary leadership at Zappos understands that work made fun gets done. Moreover, work made fun creates energized, happy, and cohesive teams.

Although I'm saving most of the specific payoffs Zappos enjoys from creating a culture of play and family connectedness until Chapter 11, generally speaking the overarching benefits for Zappos are very consistent with the positive correlations researchers have found. For example, management professor Dr. David Abramis of Cal State Long Beach, among others, has shown that high levels of workplace fun are consistently associated with increased creativity and productivity. Employees who find playful enjoyment in their workplace have more positive relationships with their peers, make better decisions, are tardy or absent less often, and use fewer sick days than employees who aren't having fun. In essence, fun is serious business at Zappos, and in turn, that fun produces serious business results. This chapter is all about how Zappos nurtures a positive and engaging work environment, while the next chapter focuses on how Zappos wins from that nurturance.

Fun at work is not something that can be left to chance or an optional initiative that disappears when things get difficult. Leaders at Zappos have never wavered in their support for a playful culture. The benefits of that approach are supported by research from Hewitt and Associates that shows it pays to invest in a positive work culture, especially during times of business uncertainty. Ted Marusarz, the leader of global engagement and culture at Hewitt, notes, "The extra effort companies put forth in difficult times makes a difference in how successful they are at boosting morale and retaining top talent in a strong economy."

While a Zappos core value expressly mentions fun ("create fun and a little weirdness"), Robert Richman, Zappos Insights product manager, notes that fun is viewed more broadly in the context of joy or employee happiness. According to Robert, "What we're doing is creating short-, medium-, and long-term sources of joy for our employees. Cupcake day, for example, is definitely a short-term comfort. A medium-term source of pleasure might be something like a manager taking a team on a half-day hike. And long-term happiness or purposefulness comes from investing in staff education, helping people achieve their life goals, and feeling the pride of progress with the company." Let's use Robert's structure to examine short-, medium-, and long-term fun and employee engagement at Zappos with an eye to how these approaches might be deployed in your business.

SHORT-TERM JOY

From the moment you arrive at the Zappos Fulfillment Centers or Zappos Headquarters, you realize that you are "not in Kansas anymore." Whether it is the Superhero wall murals and decorations in Kentucky or the pinball machine in the Zappos Headquarters lobby, it's easy to notice that Zappos is different. In fact, one immediately recognizable aspect of playfulness bursts through in the rich and ever-changing visual nature of Zappos buildings. Conference rooms, for example, are not classic boring boardrooms but carry themes like the following:

- *"Elvis,"* which includes a life-sized sculpture of the King of Rock and Roll swinging his hips as he stands at a microphone, along with enlarged depictions of 45-rpm Elvis records hanging on the walls

- *"Betty White,"* complete with a ledge holding a "cherry pie," a picture of her late husband, Allen Ludden, and a corner bookshelf with a plaque that reads, "Betty White is my Home Girl"

- *"Up,"* based on the movie of the same name, with colorful balloons painted on the walls, a mailbox with the names "Carl" and "Ellie," a scout merit badge sash complete with badges, and tennis balls on the bottom of the table and chair legs

- *"James Bond,"* with one wall painted in the British Union Jack flag, pictures of various actors playing Bond, and shadow boxes holding martini glasses and a shaker

Since many staff members spend considerable amounts of time in conference rooms, their daily lives (short-term pleasure, if you will) are affected by the nature of the conference room environment. As a result, Zappos teams are given the money and authority to take control and infuse play and a little weirdness into their surroundings. This casual approach to appointing an office might not be for everyone, but it reflects the Zappos willingness to ask, "Why can't we have fun with this? Why can't we build joy into the way a conference room is designed?" The leaders at Zappos appreciate that every aspect of work is an opportunity to deliver happiness to staff members and that happy staff members, in turn, make happy customers. Steve Hill, vice president of merchandising, suggests, "People make choices about fun and meaningful elements in their environments when they are home. We are a family here, so all of us need to be involved in those choices here as well."

The degree of personalization and playfulness of the meeting spaces at Zappos is carried through to employee cubicles at far greater levels than what you will see in most cubicle cultures. The majority of these cubicles are adorned with toys, games, and constantly changing and playful decorations. While this enriched environment is a source of spontaneous pleasure for Zapponians (for example, one conference room table also functions as a Ping-Pong table, allowing for a blend of play and work), a photographic display of conference room/cubicle color and diversity at Zappos presented at OfficeSnapshots.com (a blog created to show the office space design of primarily Web 2.0 and technology companies) drew the following range of reactions from observers:

- "Whoa! I bet the fire marshal loves that place!"
- "How can anyone work there? It looks like a trash heap."

- "I love it! It's better than a place with no personality. Once again I am struck by the jealousy bug."

And the following reaction from a Zapponian:

- "I love working amongst so many displays of individualism. The office is exactly what you make it, and it gives those of us who have not done so on previous jobs a chance to get to know ourselves through the atmosphere we create in order to work. Some folks go the distance with decorating while others are more Spartan. Either way, it's you/yours."

For an opportunity to take a peek at some of the Zappos conference rooms, go to zappified.com /meet or point the QR reader on your mobile device at the code given here.

Much of the freedom Zappos staff members are given to take control of their work environment, decorate their areas playfully, and continually change their setting adds up to a vibrant, dynamic, and innovative workplace. Malcolm Gladwell, author of *The Tipping Point*, captures the wisdom behind the Zappos communal design when he suggests, "The office used to be imagined as a place where employees punch clocks and bosses roam the halls like high-school principals, looking for miscreants. But when employees sit chained to their desks, quietly and industriously going about their business, an office is not functioning as it should. That's because innovation—the heart of the knowledge economy—is fundamentally social. Ideas arise as much out of casual conversations as they do out of formal meetings. More precisely, as one study after another has demonstrated, the best ideas in any workplace arise out of casual contacts among different groups within the same company."

Not only does the Zappos leadership facilitate this casual contact through design and through encouraging personalized workspaces, but many Zappos interdepartmental challenges bring people together in pursuit of team-building goals. Jennifer Van Orman, Zappos software engineer, gives a sense of the *friendly* interdepartmental contact by sharing, "The big thing in my department is Nerf gun wars. I don't know how the ritual began, but on the day you start in Software Engineering, you're handed a Nerf gun. The other day we did a little attack on Finance. We were tactical as we descended upon their building, bombarding them with Nerf rounds. Don't you think that's a great way to engage a department you don't often have contact with? It's our way of saying, 'Hey, we are Software Engineering; long time no see.' In that situation, other departments not only remember you, but plot ways to get back at you, or should I say, get to know you better."

Mark Madej, Zappos software engineer, adds, "We had a meeting to plan this attack. We mapped out the whole finance area; I bought 16 packs of 35 Nerf darts, and we brought strobe lights. Our basic plan was to go over to Finance at a time that would be least disruptive to its workflow, turn off the overhead lights, turn on the strobes, and launch our assault through the back door. Our blog team videotaped our planning meeting and our preparation. I gave a motivational speech, in keeping with the one delivered by Mel Gibson in the movie *Braveheart*. The entire event was amazingly fun, and we are ready for their counterattack." When leaders share control of the physical work environment and encourage work groups to playfully band together (attending, of course, to how and when the work must get done), companies benefit. These organizations affect individual employee enjoyment, foster team collaboration, and break down organizational silos. One can imagine the solidarity forged among Mark's teammates as they listened to his *Braveheart*-style speech. Additionally, it is easy to see the culture-building benefits of two seldom-interacting business units engaging each other (with or without Nerf guns).

To step inside an epic Nerf battle at Zappos, visit zappified.com/nerf or point your mobile device here.

ZAPPIFIED BRAIN BREAK

Can any mundane task be made fun? At Zappos, routine experiences such as fire drills often have a playful twist. Leah Morris, safety and risk manager at the Zappos Fulfillment Centers, shares, "When it comes time to do evacuation drills, we try to make them fun. One year we rented snow cone machines, and after the evacuation drill, we all got to eat snow cones outside. Another year we purchased 800 water guns, and after everyone was accounted for and the building was safe, we had a water gun fight in our parking lot." Similarly, while some businesses might have a fairly tame party following a merger or acquisition, when Amazon acquired Zappos, Zapponians threw a wedding bash. As one Zapponian puts it, "We were encouraged to dress up as if we were going to a wedding or as if we were getting married. So I told my wife we should dress in our wedding attire! She asked me if I was crazy. Persuasively, I asked her when in her life would she ever be able to wear her wedding dress again. So we wore our wedding clothes to a company party. I think that is what makes the Zappos Experience—doing things you know you will never do again at any other company." Why not make a list of ordinary tasks at your workplace? How might you add snow cones, squirt guns, or a wedding to liven up those tasks or events?

Reducing Barriers and Increasing Connections

Often the greatest benefit of play at work is that it lets people actually get to know one another. If, like Zappos, you seek to form personal connections with your customers, and if you believe that effective customer service is a team sport, you have to find ways for staff members to form personal relationships with one another in order to create a customer service team. An example of how Zappos facilitates personal connections between staff members is the "face game." In essence, the game begins each time an employee logs into the Zappos intranet. Upon login, before an employee can get to work, he is presented with a picture of a random fellow Zapponian. The individual is then provided with four employee names and a "don't know" option. After the employee chooses a name, the screen indicates whether that choice was correct, and then the full bio of the actual individual is shown. (For an opportunity to experience the face game, go to zappified.com/face. No QR code is provided because the game has interactive functions that may not be supported on your mobile device.)

Noel Cusimano, a buyer for Zappos.com's sister site, 6pm .com, which focuses on discounts, shares how the biographical information in the face game has additional value: "People can click on you and see your journey in the company. It gives them something to relate to or to talk to you about. You can also select things like, 'I'd love to have people job shadow me' or 'I'm really interested in this topic,' so that you can search for people in the company with interests similar to yours. That idea came from our speaker of the house, who wished for a database where she could tag people and could pull up everyone, for example, who loves doing face paintings or who is an artist."

The face game has been taken to yet another level thanks to a final project completed by participants in a Zappos culture class. That class developed the "you got faced" project in support of the Zappos value of building a positive team and family spirit.

According to Rachael Brown, Zappos Pipeline manager, "You got faced encourages Zapponians to send an e-mail to someone whose face popped up on their screens but whom they didn't know well enough to name correctly. The class suggested the e-mail carry the subject line 'you got faced' and that the e-mail include an invitation for lunch or to do something to get to know one another. That culture class came up with the you got faced campaign, splashed it everywhere, and marketed it throughout the company. That's an example of how we are always looking for opportunities to build the Zappos family connection."

This type of enthusiasm for knowing one another fosters an environment in which people are consistently greeted, doors are held open for peers, and staff members call one another by name. Roz Searcy, Zappos Kan Du team facilitator, suggests, "It really is different here compared to anywhere else I have worked. In some places, people might occasionally talk to individuals outside their work groups, but here it is rare if they don't. It's common for me to sit at the front desk and be greeted by name by everyone—all day! Of course that makes me love my days at work."

Zapponians experience that fully engaged and interactive work setting by design. In fact, much of the short-term play at Zappos is there to set a tone for daily task alignment. At the Fulfillment Center, for example, Dan Campbell, photo supervisor, notes, "We take a few minutes at the start of our shift to just have some fun and also to bring business messages to life. One of the most popular activities in the morning warm-up in our department came from a team member as a modification of the TV show *Minute to Win It*. That's a game where participants have a minute to complete some type of challenge. Our activities have proven to be fantastic, and we've made these challenges a regular weekly feature. One challenge, for example, has a team member place three Oreos on another team member's forehead. The person with the cookies on their forehead has to get the cookies into their mouth and eat them within 60 seconds. We take volunteers because some team members enjoy watching more than participating, but everyone gets involved, even if it is only through cheering." Dan's comment addresses the misconception that everyone at Zappos is extroverted and loud. Tony Hsieh acknowledges that he would not be a fit at Zappos if extroversion were a selection criterion. Diversity in the ways in which people engage and support a playful yet weird culture is welcomed. Leaders like Dan are aware of the importance of that diversity, and they structure playful activities accordingly.

Daily fun events at Zappos turn out to be not only quick, as is the case with the modified *Minute to Win It* activity, but also inexpensive. Cody Britton, Zappos STAT advocate, notes, "We have *Zappos Idol* karaoke going on in our break room on a regular basis. For Mardi Gras one year, each department was given a big cardboard box and $25 and was asked to make a float. We were given some time off work to have fun with one another and make our masterpiece. We borrowed German beer girl outfits from our training department, which puts on our yearly Oktoberfest parade, and one of our team members bought a dollar's worth of leopard fabric and made a vest. We completely reenacted *Ferris Bueller's Day Off*, and our float proudly came in well under budget at $1.26. I love this company. I really appreciate that fun is not complicated and that it is immediate and always present."

The spontaneity and immediacy of fun at Zappos is further exemplified by Shawna Macias, Customer Loyalty Team member, who comments, "In training, we did our parades. We'd dress up and go through the call center making a bunch of noise. We'd have happy hours where we actually enjoyed being with coworkers outside of work. We recently had a cupcake contest for National Junk Food Day. The person I sit next to and I entered and made sushi-looking cupcakes." Shawna adds, "There is always something quick and fun happening here. We did a CLT horror prom where we all dressed up in the worst prom dresses we could find, and we captured those fun memories in photos from the event. We had a tailgate party at work, with various teams decorating their areas and conducting a floorwide potluck. We went from station to station to grab food. Leadership inspires a lot of fun here to keep the spirits up. You never get bored. Often it feels like I'm going in for eight hours of work/fun."

Shawna's conclusion that Zappos is a place where staff members "never get bored" fits well with a leadership rationale for workplace fun. Zappos leadership understands that boredom is at the heart of decreased workplace productivity. William Balzer, Patricia Smith, and Jennifer Burnfield, writing in the *Encyclopedia of Applied Psychology*, suggest, "The consequences of boredom for businesses and organizations include higher employment costs, . . . performance problems, . . . and reduced organizational effectiveness. . . . Boredom at work may also have consequences for society as a whole including lost productivity, reduced quality of life, and reduced consumer safety." These authors also note that boredom is rampant in work environments where employees are "unhappy" and where company policies restrict breaks and social interaction. The leaders at Zappos are continually stirring up the workplace to keep it lively. In addition, they encourage every employee to take responsibility for a dynamic culture of fun. Are you creating days that your people would describe as "never boring" or "eight hours of work/fun"?

"Old school" managers are probably balking at the Zappos focus on short-term, daily fun. Some might even say, "I am a manager, not an activity director. Staff members can worry about fun on their own time." Increasingly, scientists, inspirational leaders, and staff members agree: in order for people to create

TRY THESE ON FOR SIZE

1. How genuinely committed are you to the joy and fun of your work environment?

2. Has your commitment to workplace positivity been sustained through the ups and downs of the economy, with the result that you have created "an environment focused on key human capital elements"?

3. How innovative and interactive is your work environment? Do you accept Malcolm Gladwell's view that "the best ideas in any workplace arise out of casual contacts among different groups within the same company"? If so, how are you encouraging that casual contact?

4. Are you thinking about workplace fun in the context of short-, medium-, and long-term employee joy and happiness?

5. How do you encourage employees to playfully get to know people beyond their immediate work team? Do you have a process that rivals the face game?

6. Do you have daily ritualized and brief activities (like the *Minute to Win It* example) that energize employees to engage in their work more enthusiastically?

and produce, they must be given space and opportunities to re-create, reenergize, and find enjoyment in the very setting where they spend the largest percentage of their waking hours.

MEDIUM-TERM FUN AND ENJOYMENT

Much of the fun at Zappos occurs in celebration of mid-range accomplishments. Chad Boehne, process manager at the Zappos Fulfillment Centers exemplifies this by noting, "Our team set a performance goal, and since I manage the team, I asked them what they would want to have happen if we reached the goal. So, I have to dress up like a garden gnome on Monday." According to Chad, his garden gnome payoff reflects a reward for positive team effort that created a 20 percent increase in total unit count. He explains how the garden gnome incentive came to be: "I'm not the tallest guy in the world and I've got a beard, so one of our team members suggested that if they reached the goal, I should dress up like a garden gnome. Why not? Will I be embarrassed? Probably. Will it make my team laugh, put a smile on their faces, and provide them with the reward of their choice? Absolutely. So why wouldn't I do it? Now the entire management team knows I'm going to be wearing this garden gnome outfit, so I will have to go around to every department in Zappos and make my presence known. I can guarantee you that our photographer will be following me. Rewarding people with a $20 gas card or in some monetary way honestly isn't as motivating to my team as reaching a goal and having me dress silly. So I'm all about unconventional team-driven incentives." Chad's use of the word *silly* is a wise one, as "silly" derives from the Old English word *saelig*, which means to be happy and blessed. Creating silly fun for achieving goals delivers happiness to Zapponians and is a blessing to any business. How are you engaging your staff to produce silly, social, and powerful incentives?

Much medium-term joy at Zappos comes from peer awards and recognition. One example of intermittent recognition is the COW award, which is provided to select CLT members. COW stands for Cultivators of Wow, and it is bestowed on CLT staff members who have been chosen by their peers as being the ultimate embodiment of the Zappos culture. Pamela Griggs, a three-time COW winner, notes, "Being a COW is a really big deal. We have a lot of people nominate coworkers who have wowed them. For example, a recipient like Jenn Pike wows us all regularly through bubbles. She is constantly filling the air with bubbles by means of a bubble gun or just waving a bubble wand. She is spreading joy daily. We COWs are proud of our award, and we enjoy mooing. An awards group delivers a certificate, a pin, and a bundt cake. When the winner is off of customer calls, the group surrounds that person and yells, "Hey everybody in CLT, we want to let you know that Crystal is a COW!"

Although the opportunity to be a COW is limited to CLT members, other similar awards are open to everyone at Zappos. One such example is the Master of WOW parking award. Mark Madej, Zappos software engineer, explains, "You can nominate anyone for the Master of WOW if they've wowed you. The VIP parking is a nice perk, as is the free car wash, but the e-mail blast announcing the winner includes your picture and a significant description of what you did to earn the award. That alone is an honor!" Master of WOW awards have been given for everything from small acts that wowed a peer, such as checking in on a fellow Zapponian when the person was out sick, up to large-scale initiatives to help a fellow Zapponian achieve a time-sensitive goal. According to Aaron Magness, senior director, Brand Marketing & Business Development, "Zappos is an environment of recognition. That means we have every Zapponian involved in saying thank you . . . you did a great thing today. One of our not-so-secret success tools is that all of us at Zappos are a source of positive reinforcement and acknowledgment."

It may be common to develop an award that celebrates individuals within a team or that typically solicits recommendations about teammates, but it is particularly unusual to create playful recognitions like the Happy Hooter award. That award, which of course is a stuffed owl, was intentionally created to transcend team boundaries. According to Rafael Mojica, senior user experience architect, "The technology happiness team was the first to bestow the Happy Hooter, and from there each recipient selects the next recipient. The only stipulation on the award is that the person to whom you give it has to be from a different department. I was fortunate to get it, and in order to pass it on, I had to write and say, 'I bestow this award because . . . ,' and then the award is officially presented by the happiness team." Rafael notes, "These fun awards make a difference and keep morale high. We are always on the lookout for peers who are extraordinary at delivering happiness or living our values and finding small but significant ways to intermittently recognize one another."

It's been said that what you track, you become. Some organizations have found ways to track gossip and complaining—yielding ample harvests of both. At Zappos, leadership has developed ways to maximally track positive recognition and expand it beyond the supervisor-to-employee level. In essence, the leadership has created mechanisms by which staff members across the organization can playfully catch one another in acts that fully demonstrate the culture and reflect peer-directed kindness.

The concept of peer recognition is given a monetary twist through the Zappos employee bonus program. Each month, all Zappos employees are given the opportunity to select a peer to receive a $50 bonus in recognition for the employee's outstanding contribution to Zappos. Zapponians fully embrace this peer recognition opportunity. In fact, in 2010, more than 2,800 bonuses were given, for a total amount of $140,100. Bryce Murry, Zappos software engineer, notes, "When you select someone for the employee bonus, you have to say why you chose them. Even bigger than the money is the leadership's announcement of the winners. The peer selection and public recognition is every bit as powerful as the money."

I can imagine some leaders saying, "What a nightmare to police such a program against abuse. Won't this result in friends giving friends the $50 each month?" Bryce's response to that is simply, "One of our values is to do more with less. Therefore, I don't give out the bonus unless it's earned. This is money we don't have to spend. The money is there for situations where people should be acknowledged. For example, the programming and development that our team does can affect other front-end programmers. Sometimes those programmers work weekends or come in early to get things done in order to make our jobs easier. As a result, I've given bonuses to front-end guys because I'm asking a lot of them, they're not on my team, and they have their own projects to work on. I'm disrupting what they're doing." Leaders in companies that lack a value-based culture and a foundation of trust in their employees often create complex policies that restrict 99 percent of the workforce because of the abuses of 1 percent. Zappos is light on policy and long on trust and accountability. Rather than not allowing employees to reward one another monetarily because there will be abuses, the leaders at

Zappos believe in treating employees well, encouraging them to be good stewards of company resources, and asking them to do the right thing for the company and their peers. Abuses can be handled if and when they arise.

Pam Cinko, Zappos Insights logistical ninja, indicates the value of allowing staff members to tangibly reward their peers by sharing, "I used to be in charge of ordering and stocking the Zappos library and all the books you see in the lobby. Those books were kept in lockers far away from where the books were actually needed. I would regularly take this huge book cart and maneuver it through narrow hallways. One day, I noticed a more convenient storage option, so I approached Dave Myers, the facilities manager, and said, 'Hey, Dave, is it possible for us to move these lockers to the other side of the building and put them in this hallway near the lobby instead?' Without hesitation, he said, 'No, we're planning something else for that hallway.' I accepted that my idea wouldn't work and didn't think about it until a week later, when Dave's team and some of the Kan Du team members walked into our lounge and said, 'We just wanted to tell you we moved all your book lockers to the hallway where you wanted them.' My jaw dropped; I couldn't believe it. One, it wasn't just Dave who came in to tell us, it was his team; and two, the people who executed it did so as a surprise for me." Pam notes that she later asked Dave how this large-scale move was conducted without her being aware of it, and she was told, "'We used the emergency exit doors and did it in the back so that you wouldn't see us.' Talk about a wow! He made me think it couldn't be done, and—boom—it happened. Dave told me that Bill, a member of Dave's team, did the bulk of the work, so I gave Bill a $50 bonus. Hauling those heavy lockers to the other side of the building was such a Zappos thing, such an act of kindness; it felt terrific to offer a small token of gratitude to an individual who demonstrated what is great about my company." Pam was gratified by being entrusted with the ability to recognize the greatness happening around her. In turn, Bill was rewarded for the type of effort that builds coworker morale, goes well beyond job requirements, and makes the workplace more enjoyable.

Wow and caring are celebrated at Zappos, whether they are delivered to customers or to members of the internal Zappos family. Recognition comes from leaders, managers, and peers alike. The more that wow and caring are seen and acknowledged, the more joy will be experienced by all stakeholders.

TRY THESE ON FOR SIZE

1. Are your managers willing to be silly to provide incentives for employee performance? How often are your performance goals linked to playful outcomes?

2. Do you have reward and recognition programs in place that involve employees tracking the value-based behaviors of their peers? Do those programs recognize extraordinary things done to wow colleagues, or are they developed only to recognize extraordinary efforts directed toward customers?

3. What recognition programs do you have that require staff members to acknowledge people outside of their work groups?

4. Would you consider allowing your staff members to provide financial bonuses to peers at their own discretion? Why or why not?

LONG-TERM JOY

As implied in prior chapters, much of the sustained enthusiasm that comes from working at Zappos is the result of the leadership's fastidious commitment to core values. At Zappos, leaders understand that people don't keep coming back to the same place of employment simply to receive a paycheck. Employees need to be passionately connected to a higher purpose and to feel a sense of belonging. In addition, employees need to know that they are growing and developing through opportunities and training.

Rachael Brown, Pipeline manager for the company, notes, "Managers at Zappos understand that we are not just responsible for the success of our departments, but we have to consider what's best for all of the Zappos family. For example, I often think about how an opportunity in another department might bring happiness to a team member of mine, and I encourage them to seek out that type of opportunity." Merchandising assistant David Hinden contributes, "I think the leadership understands that if you do what is best for your people, your company will prosper. I have always felt that the leadership has my interest at heart and has encouraged me to grow in the direction of my passions, as opposed to trying to have me fit into a preset expectation for my career."

In essence, by directing staff members to seek opportunities that are consistent with their existing interests, Zappos capitalizes on the positive psychology concept of "flow" championed by Mihály Csíkszentmihályi, professor and former chairman of the Department of Psychology, University of Chicago. By "flow," Mihály is referring to a state of being completely involved in an activity for its own sake, with people being so positively emotionally engaged that they learn and perform seamlessly. Zappos leaders realize that a great deal of pleasure comes simply from being allowed to follow one's passion and not necessarily being forced to move from a desired position or in the direction of management.

According to Rachael Brown, "We are trying to give our colleagues the skills to be whatever they want to be at Zappos. Everyone is responsible for being a culture leader and for being passionate, but no one has to go into an area like management if it is not where she finds purpose." All too often, individuals feel pressured to leave positions that they enjoy in order to "advance" in a company. Sometimes leaders inadvertently push people into positions for which those individuals have less interest, passion, or talent. Ultimately, leaders must take the time to understand the unique values and interests of their people and help them find the career and calling that suits them.

Even the day-to-day work policies at Zappos reflect an attention to individual needs. Like other companies, Zappos requires employee attendance and has a point system whereby a pattern of tardiness or taking leave without preapproval can ultimately be grounds for dismissal. But unlike the supervisors at some businesses, the Zappos leaders deeply appreciate the importance of helping staff members address personal circumstances and develop in areas of interest that fall outside of work. As a result, these leaders have the discretion to go above and beyond to accommodate employees as those staff members attend to critical personal needs and/or pursue personal fulfillment and passion. Rather than placing limits on employees based on the strict adherence to language in an employee handbook, leaders at Zappos look for ways to treat each employee's circumstances with discretion and respect.

According to Rebecca Henry Ratner, HR director at Zappos, "Fair and equal are not the same thing to us. A hard policy of a specified amount of time is something we try to stay away from, since that treats everyone equally but really isn't fair. Should a great employee with long tenure get no more consideration than a new employee who is not yet performing strongly? Instead, we like to consider these requests on a case-by-case basis and do what's fair for that particular employee at that particular time. That said, we do have some general guidelines, like an up-to-six-week personal leave policy, but it's just that, a guideline, and if that's not the fair thing for an employee, exceptions can certainly be made." Because Zappos leadership focuses on fairness, employees reciprocate with loyalty to their leaders and to Zappos. Specifically, Zappos managers are looking for reasonable accommodations that balance the needs of the employee and the needs of the company, even if that takes the form of staff members being given a leave of absence from Zappos. Often such departures are only temporary, as was the case for Jesse Cabaniss, CLT lead, and Alicia "AJ" Jackson, CLT member.

Jesse shares, "I had an opportunity to go on tour with my band, and I was blown away by the support of leadership in not only allowing me to take time away, but encouraging me to do so. Before I left, they threw a huge party in my honor, and every single person was wearing rock shirts with drums on them. We even had pizza and games. I'm not one to get emotional, but I got a little teary-eyed. I couldn't have imagined that so many people, at various levels of the organization, would go to so much trouble and send secret e-mails among themselves to get everything planned and organized. We're family here, but it's the amount of genuine caring that is astounding. I have friends that I have known for 10 years that don't treat me as well."

The situation that required AJ to take a leave from work was far less pleasant and occurred very early in her employment. AJ notes, "I left a horrible job in a very different industry where I didn't really matter to my employer. So I came to Zappos looking for happiness and sanity. Right after my first 90 days at Zappos, I got a message at work saying that my biological father, whom I had not seen since I was very little, was looking for me. As it turned out, he had brain cancer, was dying, and had a last wish to see me after all these years. I was at my desk crying, and people immediately reached out. My lead, Jim, was at a meeting, and three people went to bring him to me. Jim pulled me into a room, and I told him the story. Without hesitation, he said, 'Just go.' To which I said, 'I have to talk to Scheduling. I have to see if I can get this approved.' He calmly reiterated, 'Just go; I'll take care of everything. Log out of your phone. Turn off your computer. Go home.' That took a second to process. I had never been treated with that level of compassion before in my work history."

AJ's reference to compassion offers a key lesson for creating employee engagement. In order for employees to feel "passionate" about your business, they must first feel that you are "compassionate" toward them.

Sometimes the compassion provided at Zappos actually results in staff members realizing that their life purposes fall outside of Zappos. Augusta Scott, Zappos coach, emphasizes, "Leaders at Zappos really do want staff members to be happy, even if that means leaving Zappos permanently. If your passion is somewhere other than at Zappos, we'd rather you be doing what you really want to do than be here and feel like you're stuck in a job." Augusta's predecessor, Dr. Vik, notes, "It was tough for me to leave Zappos, but it was time to take my coaching message out to other audiences. What I appreciate most is how well I have been supported by my friends at Zappos through my transition and how it feels like home when I come back to visit."

Whether it is encouraging staff members to grow in the direction of their interests, supporting their other ambitions, or helping them move to the employment opportunities that best suit them, Zappos understands the value of creating and fostering purposeful and pleasurable work. In the end, Zappos tactically maximizes fun to inspire, enliven, and meld its workforce. Leaders demonstrate that business relationships do not need to be different from family relationships. People in both types of social units can and do stay together in pursuit of a common goal, especially when they are encouraged to laugh, recreate, and go beyond superficial tasks.

Any company can develop a unified and dynamic workforce. Doing so starts with an understanding that employees who play together stay together, and they also work hard together! But, as evidenced by Zappos, that understanding must extend to compassionate, encouraging, and playful actions that fuel short-, medium-, and long-term fun and enjoyment.

- Individuals who have fun on the job tend to be more creative and productive.

- Workplace fun can be conceptualized as short-, medium-, and long-term employee pleasure.

- People who are having an enjoyable time on the job tend to have more positive relationships with their peers, make better decisions, are tardy or absent less often, and use fewer sick days.

- Innovation emerges from casual contact between diverse work groups.

- Brief bursts of workplace fun can be an inexpensive, energizing force that increases team alignment, solidarity, and productivity.

- Social motivation is a powerful performance incentive. Allowing team members to choose rewards that may include acts of leadership silliness often produces impressive results.

- Opportunities exist for creating recognition programs in which staff members acknowledge wow moments delivered to one another.

- Play and fun can be infused into, and are often most needed for, routine tasks such as evacuation drills.

- Employees find workplace happiness when they are allowed to do what they enjoy, even if that means they do not choose management positions but instead function as culture leaders.

- Long-term enjoyment comes from helping staff members grow in the direction of their passions.

R.O.F.L.

As an Internet acronym, R.O.F.L. stands for "rolling on the floor laughing." For the purposes of this chapter, I suggest that it should stand for "Return On Fun Lasts." In fact, Zappos may be the best example of an often-underappreciated truth: a small investment in workplace fun will produce tangible and profound benefits for your staff members, your customers, and your brand's equity. As an offer of proof, let's look at how the nominal but consistent investment in workplace fun produces lasting returns for Zappos as it relates to

- Improvements in the quality of life of Zappos employees

- Extra-mile effort by staff members

- Exceptional outcomes on key performance goals

- Impassioned employee and customer evangelism

QUALITY OF WORK LIFE MATTERS

A great deal of research shows that purposeful work has a positive impact on health and that emotionally negative workplaces erode employee well-being. The book *Unhealthy Work: Causes, Consequences, and Cures*, edited by Peter Schnall, Marnie Dobson, and Ellen Rosskam, notes that "the ways in which work is organized—its pace and intensity, degree of control over the work process, sense of justice, and employment security, among other things—can be as toxic to the health of workers as the chemicals in the air. These work characteristics can be detrimental not only to mental well-being but to physical health. Scientists refer to these features of work as 'hazards' of the 'psychosocial' work environment. One key pathway from the work environment to illness is through the mechanism of stress; thus we speak of 'stressors' in the work environment, or 'work stress.' This is in contrast to the popular psychological understandings of 'stress,' which locate many of the problems with the individual rather than the environment." In the context of this definition of "work stress," the approach taken by Zappos leaders on behalf of employee happiness essentially mitigates the toxicity of the psychosocial work environment, removes emotional hazards, modulates the pace and intensity of work, establishes a sense of "justice," and increases employees' sense of control.

Donavan Roberson, Zappos Insights culture evangelist, shares how employees perceive "work stress," or the absence thereof, at Zappos: "We sat down with our team and asked, 'How has Zappos changed your life?' Every single one of us talked about the impact of Zappos on our overall quality of *life*, not just our time on the job. One of our team members, Jon, whose wife also works here, said, 'When I go home at night, I'm not stressed and she's not stressed; we go home and laugh about the day.' Personally, the way I feel as a result of working at Zappos makes me wonder why more businesses don't get the value of fun, family, and flexibility. I think that's how our team at Zappos Insights delivers happiness—we help business leaders build healthier cultures that lower work stress and help employees engage, create, and relax at work and beyond." Zappos leaders commit to stress reduction and happiness enhancement because they understand how the impact of that commitment is felt both within and outside the walls of their business.

David Tyler, Zappos facilities/Kan Du manager, suggests that reduced work stress and the overall culture of Zappos have had an impact even on strangers: "When you take the leap of faith that you will profit in untold ways from taking care of people, your life changes. I used to be the type of person who wouldn't let you get in front of me on the freeway; I had to be first. There was nothing more important than what I had to do. As a result of my time here at Zappos, I'll let you in. I'll wave at people and actually try to deliver happiness to other drivers. The way I am treated at Zappos has really changed my life." Often, if you as a leader take the "leap of faith that you will profit in untold ways from taking care of people," your staff members will do the same.

Lisanna Lawson, solutions coordinator at the Zappos Fulfillment Centers, indicates that in order to reduce workplace stress, leaders may have to rely on science, not tradition. Lisanna notes, "What other warehouse settings have a nap room? Our CEO, Tony Hsieh, talks about research showing that a 20-minute power nap makes employees more productive. As a result, we have a nap room, referred to as the Zen Den, that we can take advantage of during our work breaks." Zappos is not the only workplace environment in which napping is supported. For example, Google has napping pods, and Nike has "quiet rooms."

However, Angela Haupt, writing for Yahoo! Health, notes, "For now, workplace naps remain the exception, rather than the rule." Often business leaders are not driven by evidence but rather by a "way things have always been done" mentality. Since napping has been shown to increase productivity and improve employee retention while decreasing absenteeism, why wouldn't you consider a trial napping program in your company?

When leaders create a dynamic and vital work environment guided by evidence-based innovations, employees often experience great enthusiasm for their work. In fact, a common theme echoed throughout conversations with Zapponians was their overall eagerness to bound into Zappos! This prompted me to contemplate an unscientific gauge of work stress and employee engagement that I have come to call the "alarm clock test." Do your employees wake up and *want* to go to work? Do your people feel eager and privileged to be able to contribute as a part of your company? Passing the alarm clock test is epitomized by spontaneous comments from Zapponians like Sarah Johnson of the Zappos Fulfillment Centers, who shares, "You know the feeling you have when your alarm clock goes off and you want to sleep for two more hours? Well, at Zappos, I realize we're having a costume contest or our peak star-a-rama, and I jump out of bed to be there with my team. That even extends to community events that happen on my day off. We have substantial numbers of volunteers throughout the company who rise to their alarms on their free days to make a difference in our communities."

Customer Loyalty Team supervisor Jeff Lewis notes, "For a lot of us, this is a career that we've been fortunate enough to have landed after having had a couple of prior jobs that we didn't like. It's really difficult to grow as a person when you're stuck in a role where you're pretending to be somebody else every day. I can honestly say, after being here for four years, that I wake up eager to go in to work each morning, and there's not that sense of dread I've had in prior experiences. I think my enthusiasm is linked to the sense of family and support I feel here at Zappos. Anything we need is already provided for us, whether it's benefits, fun, a sense of belonging, respect, or just making our lives better."

The P.E.A.C.E. (Programs, Events, Activities, Charity, Engagement) team and the Kan Du teams at Zappos are dedicated to fostering employee engagement and expressly easing the complexity of Zapponians' lives. Jamie Naughton, who has been actively involved in creating employee engagement events at Zappos, explains, "We simply focus on employees' needs. For the most part, that occurs through events, incentives, employee programs, internal communications, and organizing employee efforts to give back to the surrounding community." Employee engagement teams oversee the Five Second Happiness Survey discussed in Chapter 7 and submit applications for awards such as *Fortune* magazine's designation as a Best Place to Work. Jamie notes, "Like any major company, we have a few large events each year, like Bald and Blue, where our employees get together and shave each other's heads or put blue dye in their hair. We also have quarterly and monthly events to keep the level of fun high. Of course, we have countless mini and departmental events happening continuously throughout the day every day here at Zappos. If an employee says, 'I want to have a cupcake-eating competition,' they just do it. They don't have to ask. This is a workplace marked by lots of seemingly random craziness that sparks a culture of crazy results and social good."

Some social giving at Zappos takes place via corporate sponsorships, but the P.E.A.C.E. team helps employees give back directly to their communities. As Jamie notes, "When people see that they can make a positive difference through their lives, they find personal power that also shows up at work. So a lot of what we

Bald and Blue

do here is help employees match their passions with face-time volunteering. There are about 10 'cause walks' each month in which our people can participate, but we try to focus on areas of even more direct involvement—true personal connection opportunities. For instance, here at Headquarters, the Nevada Childhood Cancer Foundation is one of our top charities. There is a cancer unit at Sunrise Children's Hospital here in the area, so once a month we throw a party for the kids on the unit. Employees go to the Cancer floor; bring pizza, cake, and all the good stuff; and facilitate crafts and games. That's just one of many causes where our people are directly delivering happiness and receiving it in return." When asked about the goal of the staff and community involvement efforts at Zappos, Jamie simply shares, "It is to contribute to an environment where staff members know that the people here really care about them and really support them. They need to know that no matter what's going on in their lives, they have a thousand people who have their backs. That's the way I feel about being here. I can't imagine a world without Zappos."

David, a member of the Zappos Kan Du team, explains the essence of his team's support function: "We at Kan Du are willing to do anything, any time, and whatever it takes to improve the quality of life for Zapponians. You can come and ask us for anything; we will look for ways to say yes and put systems in place to make it happen." Roz Searcy, Kan Du facilitator, concurs: "There's actually no limit to what we will do as long as it's not going to hurt any of us, and it's not immoral or illegal. For example, not only does our shuttle service pick up guests and bring them to Zappos, but we are happy to give our employees a ride. We have a travel team that takes care of all the arrangements for our employees as they journey the world to attend trade shows and conduct other business. We also work to bring services into our company based on what our employees tell us they need. For example, we screen and arrange discount services that employees can take advantage of onsite; they can bring in dry cleaning, get their clothes tailored, have their car washed, or get a massage. We are always asking our employees what we can arrange for them while they are here at work so they don't have to worry about those types of errands or tasks on their weekends or time off."

Unlike other major businesses that spend a lot of money on capital-intensive employee perks (for example, Google's swim-in-place swimming pools, complete with lifeguards, and/or its onsite physicians), Zappos is always looking to "do more with less." As Roz puts it, "The strength of our employee care programs is based on how much we strive to listen to our employees' needs and find cost-effective ways to meet those needs. It's classic Zappos: build relationships that deliver wow to everyone. That's why we select only service providers (dry cleaners, massage therapists, etc.) who are as committed to service as we Zapponians are." Leaders at Zappos warrant emulation because they assess their employees' broad needs and find cost-effective partnerships to get those needs met. In the process, Zappos reaps the benefits that emerge from an engaged workforce. Ultimately, the Zappos competitive advantage is strongly linked to employees enjoying a low-stress environment and feeling relaxed, alert, and eager to come to work or volunteer with peers in the community.

TRY THESE ON FOR SIZE

1. How would you and your staff members assess the level of work stress in your environment?

2. What is being done at your organization to mitigate the toxicity of the psychosocial work environment, remove emotional hazards, modulate the pace and intensity of work, and increase your employees' sense of control?

3. What is the impact of your workplace on the families and acquaintances of your staff members?

4. Do you have, or would you consider, a nap zone or quiet area in your workplace? Why or why not? How do you use research on workplace productivity to guide decisions like initiating a trial "power nap" initiative?

5. Do you think your workplace is passing the alarm clock test, or is work less attractive than the snooze button?

6. Assuming that your resources are limited, how are you partnering with outside service providers to offer discounted services to make the lives of your staff members easier (dry cleaning pickup or chair massage, for example)?

7. How are you mobilizing your workforce to make "face time" contributions in your community?

TAKING IT THE EXTRA MILE

By now, you have had to wonder whether Zappos is more like a "party van" or "cruise ship," where the employees are having a grand time, but little work is getting done. In essence, does dedicated investment in staff happiness and fun really return dividends? Or is all this fun and frivolity an unnecessary workplace indulgence?

Equity theorists suggest that most humans have a sense of fairness or justice that drives their overall performance. For example, if people feel extremely overcompensated or extremely undercompensated, they do not exert their maximum effort. Optimal performance typically occurs when people feel they have been treated slightly better than they deserve, and thus put forth extra effort to remedy the mild inequity.

The extraordinary business growth at Zappos is probably, in part, a result of employees feeling that they are being treated so well that they can't let Zappos down. Nicole Smith, Zappos buyer, shares, "As buyers, we use our own money to get chocolates and cards to send out to Zappos vendors. Those cards or token gifts say thank you on behalf of our overall company and us as individuals. You'll hear it from everybody, and it's sincere— Zappos gives us so much that $5 of our own money is not a big deal. One of my coworkers wanted specific color-coded files, and even though she knew Zappos would buy them upon her request, she bought them on her own because, like me, she doesn't want to take advantage of Zappos. That would be like taking advantage of a family member. Zappos takes care of us, and we take care of Zappos. Heck, we *are* Zappos." Wow—investing in employees helps them appreciate that the company is *not* something separate from them but that the business *is* them.

Before and after the Amazon merger, Tony Hsieh has drawn a salary of $36,000 per year for his role as Zappos CEO. Some might argue that this is a symbolic gesture for a man who has more than ample means and net worth. However, I would counter that most leaders who receive multimillion-dollar salaries also have substantial existing wealth, and it does not stop them from negotiating lucrative compensation plans. While I am not arguing that corporate executives should lower their salaries to Tony's level, I am suggesting that leaders should consider how their salaries affect the perceptions of fairness and equity held by the people they lead. At Zappos, most staff members know their compensation is fair relative to Tony's salary, and in many cases, they know they make more than the company's CEO. Angie Holt, Zappos Fulfillment Centers process manager, notes, "When you see the top leaders in your organization getting compensated less than they deserve and putting out massive generosity for all of us, it comes back around. In fact, most top performers around here give 110 percent every day and don't ask for anything special in return." Laura Slaughter, senior photograph manager, suggests that peers play a significant role in encouraging employees to work harder and focus on team goals in response to the support they all receive from the leadership: "A big part of giving back to Zappos falls to coworker relationships. I definitely feel like people I work with here have made me a better person, so that makes me work harder. I am responsible to leaders who treat me well, plus I don't want to let my peers down. I am proud of those who have exerted so much effort for me, and I have to live up to those efforts on behalf of my team."

Dr. Robert "Bob" Cialdini, author of the book *Influence*, describes the notion of people giving back what they are given as the "principle of reciprocity." According to Bob, "The tendency among humans is that we want to give back to those who have given to us. . . . There's not a single human society that does not teach its children the rule of reciprocity—the idea that you must not take without then giving in return." From a leadership perspective, Bob's view of influential management is consistent with the positive and playful effort extended on behalf of staff members at Zappos. He notes, "As leaders, we were taught to ask ourselves, 'Who can help me here?' But the first question you should really ask is, 'Whom can I help here?'. . . If what you give to somebody is meaningful, tailored and unexpected, that's really the best you can do. . . . All the evidence shows you will be repaid."

Beyond employees reaching into their own pockets for incidentals, where is the Zappos leadership seeing reciprocal returns? In essence, through extraordinary staff efforts that allow the company to achieve exceptional outcomes on key performance targets.

Exceptional Outcomes on Key Performance Targets

Sales growth is often one of the most salient financial indicators associated with the vitality of a workforce. As demonstrated in the timeline provided in Chapter 1, Zappos has created a remarkable growth trend in a fairly short time window. Key revenue growth markers show Zappos as having virtually no sales in 1999 and topping the $1 billion gross sales mark by 2008, with consistent breakthrough numbers thereafter. Since product sales represent such a multifactorial outcome variable, let's focus on the smaller but significant goal attainment that is most easily traced to leadership's investment in employee pleasure and workplace fun.

One such example is the achievement of safety goals at the Zappos Fulfillment Centers. Leah Morris, safety and risk manager, shares, "We have worked hard to achieve several very important safety awards, including the OSHA SHARP (Safety and Health Achievement Recognition Program) award and the governor's safety and health award. I am convinced these objectives were met because we made safety fun, we take care of our people well, and we instill in them a responsibility for taking care of one another in the context of our Zappos culture. These awards were achieved because we set them as goals and because we include our family in creating the solutions to achieve the goals. We also emphasized awareness of the goal and celebrated the goal's attainment as a family." Leah explains this family celebration by noting, "When we achieved one of these awards, we were given two options—we could have it presented at the Fulfillment Center, or it could be given at the Governor's Safety and Health Conference. We chose to have it presented here because we wanted to touch everyone who made this safety achievement possible. You would have been amazed at the turnout at our humongous safety award party. We ordered T-shirts for everyone. It was phenomenal and so much fun."

The extra effort that Zapponians put in is also reflected not only in how they set and meet the BHAGs (Big Hairy Audacious Goals) referred to in Chapter 5 but also how far they exceed those goals. Jason Menard, video production manager, notes, "We do some crazy things when it comes to goal setting and even crazier things when it comes to exceeding them. A classic example is how we have set goals on product videos. One year our team heard that there would likely be about 50,000 new products in footwear, bags, and the like coming into Zappos. I'm not sure how accurate that number was, but it helped us with establishing a goal. The prior year, we had set a goal of 7,000 videos and actually ended up doing 10,000. When it came to setting a goal for that year, we didn't choose something, say,

15 percent greater than the 10,000 the year before; we instead went for 50,000 videos to match the number of products we expected to have flowing in. You have to admit that's crazy goal setting, but our culture is tight, we are treated amazingly well, and we gave it our all, so we smashed the 50,000 video goal and topped out above the 60,000 mark that year. Better yet, we had fun and felt great about achieving the goal." Not only was that goal attainment a "fun" accomplishment for Jason's team, but it turns out to have been a rather profitable one for Zappos as well, since the company reported a range of 6 to 30 percent increases in conversions to sale on product pages that had a video.

To experience one of the more than 60,000 product videos, go to www.zappified.com/gear or point your QR reader here.

Caring about and for employees produces breakthrough results. Often these breakthroughs come as a result of the staff members' enthusiastic response to workplace challenges. One classic example of the eagerness of Zapponians comes when various departments need help during peak workflow periods. In Chapter 3, we discussed the investment Zappos makes in putting all staff members through call-center orientation, ensuring that every employee at Zappos Headquarters has experience handling customer calls. Since Zapponians who typically work outside the call-center environment feel a strong sense of commitment to the business's success, they are more than willing to jump in on the phones during high-volume periods. Rebecca Henry Ratner, HR director at Zappos, shares, "The call center is the absolute heart of Zappos. During the holiday season, you will see people from every level of the company helping out. And they do so enthusiastically and gratefully. With all those Zapponians pitching in, we do record business and provide outstanding levels of customer engagement. Of course, we also celebrate those record sales days with T-shirts that have slogans like 'My company sold $8 million merchandise on one day and all I got was this lousy T-shirt.'" Easily and successfully mobilizing divergent parts of the Zappos enterprise to provide lateral service in crunch times also results in some pretty significant, spontaneous celebrations in the Zappos family, as evidenced by a tweet from Zapponian Andrew Kovacs thanking Tony Hsieh by writing, "Holy Cyber Celebration, Batman! Open bar-hopping downtown tonight with all Vegas employees, for a record-breaking day. Thanks <Tony>."

An additional targeted outcome of Zappos leadership's effort to create a pleasurable workplace culture is ease of recruitment. Robert Richman, product manager at Zappos Insights, reflects, "Zappos set a goal early on—we wanted to be on *Fortune* magazine's Best Companies to Work For list, and we wanted to do that within 10 years. Why did we set that goal? It wasn't so much that we wanted to be on a list, but we did want to benchmark our culture against the best. We wanted to see our efforts to produce happy employees in context and further attract those who believe they might fit our culture." As with most things at Zappos, the company made *Fortune*'s list by its 10-year goal and did not skim in at position 100. In fact, it was the highest-ranked newcomer that year, entering the list at position 23. It subsequently improved its position to 15, and then to 6 in 2011! No matter how hard a job category is to fill, like the call center and the warehouse, by being a recognized leader in the care and treatment of its staff, Zappos has become an employer of choice.

While awards and recognition have their advantages, Zappos leaders provide care and playfulness simply because they are the *right* things to do. As with most business decisions, when leaders choose the *right* path (not necessarily the most expedient one or the one that is most lucrative in the short term), the *right* results typically are sustained.

ZAPPIFIED BRAIN BREAK

*T*o help you consolidate what you have learned from Zappos, I'd encourage you to take a moment to write down a concept, idea, or "aha" that is applicable to your business. In the spirit of the Zappos commitment to build open and honest relationships through communication, I encourage you to share that message with those you influence. If you are a social media user, you may want to take a moment to share it on Twitter, Facebook, or your blog. If social media isn't for you, call someone and share your story. Heck, knock on your neighbors' door and tell them. Service revolutions and leadership movements happen one shared story at a time!

EMPLOYEE AND CUSTOMER EVANGELISM

Ben McConnell and Jackie Huba have literally written the book on customer evangelism. It is titled *Creating Customer Evangelists*. In their popular blog site *Church of the Customer*, Ben eloquently defines how companies like Zappos generate customer zealotry through "purpose-driven" cultures and fastidious adherence to values: "Companies with great word of mouth tend to operate by a simple, yet inspiring purpose and well-defined values. They have created a cultural constitution, and every employee is sworn to abide by it, so help them God and the HR department. They understand that a purpose-driven company helps clarify decision-making while inspiring longer-term unity. They know that abiding by community-driven values compels employees to think of customers first, company second. They see the benefits of inspired, evangelistic customers and how company culture is the feeder river for streams of word of mouth."

Ben hits on a theme that is often overlooked in discussions of customer loyalty. In order to get customers to refer you to their friends, you need to have employees who are deeply loyal and who themselves are evangelists for your brand. Erica Weil, lead buyer at Zappos, typifies the level of zealotry within Zappos: "I love my company, and I know they love me. There will always be a place for me here, and quite honestly, I don't care what my title is or will be. I just care about the company, and I care about doing a great job and making it better for whoever comes in next."

Similarly, Linda Utley, who was brought into Zappos as a seasonal recruiter at the Fulfillment Centers, shared, "This job may have been a temporary position, but I'm not leaving. I'm staying. If I can't recruit, I will take any job they have. I won't work anywhere else again. Ever." While these remarks reflect the intense passion that staff members have for Zappos, maybe the best example of true employee evangelism comes from a comment by Jesse Cabaniss, CLT lead, when she shares, "I really can't resist telling everybody I know about how great it is to work here. I'm sure my non-Zappos friends and family are getting tired of hearing how great this place is, but what can I say—it just is."

When employees draw a positive sense of identity from being a part of your business, that positivity is infectious. When your employees are sharing the greatness of your workplace in their tweets, blogs, and casual conversations with acquaintances, friends, and family members, you are well on your way to achieving a sustainable workplace culture, customer loyalty, and a strong "word-of-mouth" following. For example, employee evangelism pays significant benefits for Zappos recruitment efforts, as it receives approximately 60 résumés for each open position and hires approximately 1.5 percent of all applicants. Rebecca Henry Ratner, HR director, notes, "Most of our hiring, especially for the call center, comes from employee referrals. If you go to our website, there are lots of jobs posted, but call-center positions are almost never there, even though we hire between 30 and 40 people each month. Those new hires come from employee referrals, and a large number of applicants are family members of current Zappos employees. They have heard so much positive from our employees that they clamor to join us."

Brand watchers and customers also notice how business owners and leaders treat their employees. For example, it is common for people to extol the virtues of Zappos in the social media partly based on the commitment Zappos has to its staff and the playful culture that has been created throughout the company. The following comments are representative of how brand evangelists, customers and noncustomers alike, share positive word of mouth based on the Zappos commitment to employees:

> Zappos is different because employees believe in a service mission But how do you get your staff members to embrace the vision? From the beginning, Tony Hsieh demonstrated his care and a desire to have his employees be happy.

Zappos employees "drink the company kool-aid." While that may seem funny, it's important that every employee in any business has a connection with the employer. If employees don't have a connection, then leaders don't have buy-in to accomplish their business strategies.

I call Zappos.com and I hear warmth in human voices. It is clear to me that employees love what they do, and it takes great leadership to foster that level of enthusiasm. I sense those employees feel engaged, and they certainly engage me.

Leaders at Zappos get that to deliver a great customer experience, you must first deliver a great employee experience.

Fun and family culture are monetizable! Through its culture, Zappos has reduced workplace stress, increased productivity, exceeded its performance goals, and grown sales in enviable ways. In the process, its leaders have secured the loyalty of their employees and their customers. Additionally, investments made to achieve the cohesive culture have been more than offset by the need for only minimal marketing and advertising budgets, relying instead on word-of-mouth referrals. When people share their positive views of your brand, whether in the context of the way they are served as customers or the way they perceive you playfully treating your staff, there is an intangible marketing benefit. No amount of advertising has the power and credibility of unpaid brand advocacy born from the genuine respect and care of your people. That brand equity is the ultimate proof that *return on fun lasts*.

TRY THESE ON FOR SIZE

1. On a continuum from extremely undercompensated to extremely overcompensated, factoring in all elements of how employees are treated (not just pay and perks), where do you think most of your employees would rate your company?

2. What low-cost ways (for example, small acts of recognition or appreciation) could you use to increase the likelihood that your staff members will see your business as more than equitable?

3. Do you believe in the principle of reciprocity, or are you concerned that too many staff members will take without giving back? How does your perspective affect the way you lead?

4. Do your teams set audacious performance goals? Is performance against those goals consistent with your level of investment in your culture?

5. Are your employees evangelists for your brand? How can you tell?

6. How many of your job applicants are referred to you by your existing employees? Are your customers and other observers talking about the way you care for them and for your people?

Chapter 11 *Ideas to Run With*

- Purposeful employment enhances employees' self-esteem and well-being.

- Conversely, stress adversely affects their health.

- Mitigating work stress involves modulating the pace and intensity of work, providing an environment of fairness and increasing employees' sense of control.

- Healthier work environments lower work stress and help employees engage, create, and relax.

- Power napping at work has been shown to increase productivity and improve employee retention.

- Workplace engagement needs to be groomed, monitored, and facilitated, often by departments that are given the task of creating emotionally compelling activities and community opportunities.

- Equity theory predicts maximum performance when people feel slightly overvalued.

- Reciprocity predicts that people typically repay in kind.

- Often what leaders see in their team's performance reflects the leaders' level of investment in their people.

- Supporting employee fun and staff pleasure often results in sales growth and exceptional performance on key performance objectives.

- Employee evangelism is integral to customer evangelism.

- Your customers and other observers notice and will talk about the way you treat your staff members, as well as the way they themselves are treated.

CONCLUSION: ENDINGS, BEGINNINGS, AND YOU

In just a few pages, this exploration of Zappos will come to a close. While that appears to be an ending, it truly represents a new beginning on your journey to fire up a service movement in partnership with your staff and customers. Before we examine ways for you to personalize the application of the unconventional wisdom of Zappos in your setting, let's first look at the opportunities and challenges Zappos itself faces into the foreseeable future.

In the span of a decade, Zappos leadership has taken a fledgling idea and parlayed it into a billion-dollar business known for service, culture, and delivering happiness. While this rapid success is noteworthy, in the overall context of business longevity, the company is relatively youthful. When I think about the accomplishments of Zappos, the words of Winston Churchill come to mind, as he suggested that failure is not fatal or success final. The leaders at Zappos have managed small failures well, but many questions remain on how well they will manage their runaway success.

Tony Hsieh, Zappos CEO, notes, "We have been fortunate enough to make a number of sound choices on behalf of our staff, our customers, and our overall business, but we have a lot more to learn." Much of the immediate "learning" at Zappos is likely to be from reciprocal opportunities that will occur as a result of its relationship with Amazon. While each company is likely to learn from the other, both Amazon and Zappos will also have to maintain their uniquely different, albeit aligned, cultures. In fact, Amazon CEO Jeff Bezos notes, "The culture and the Zappos brand are such assets. . . . There is a lot of growth ahead of us with Zappos, and I am totally excited about what can be accomplished over time."

Maybe the greatest challenge Zappos leaders face is the adjustment required when going from a charming business outlier to an expanding, mature business benchmark. While many people root for you in your start-up phase, some will become tired of hearing about your thought leadership, or they will become suspicious, critical, and envious as you gain size and prowess. Moreover, as leaders and staff members take pride in the very successes that lead to business growth, everyone can be lulled into a false sense of security.

In his book *How the Mighty Fall*, bestselling author and business consultant Jim Collins outlines his research on the stages of business meltdown. The first of Jim's stages, "Hubris Born of Success," focuses on corporate pride, which often emerges before a fall. Jim suggests that yesterday's success, in many ways, can be one of the biggest hurdles for tomorrow's accomplishments.

While Zappos is certainly not immune to failure, the company is well positioned to circumvent significant pitfalls simply by adhering to one of its most crucial and unusual values: "be humble." Jennifer Van Orman, Zappos software engineer, reflects, "My favorite value is 'be humble.' I have never worked in a department with so many geniuses. Really smart people surround me, and none of them are divas. No one is ever too busy to help anyone else out. There are no egos around here. That's refreshing."

Unlike other successful businesses, where pomposity and vanity have been an Achilles heel, Zappos is likely to sustain its success as long as people like Tony Hsieh continue to demonstrate the curiosity, humility, and service described by a Zappos senior user experience architect: "I was working in Kansas City for another company, and I met Tony Hsieh following his presentation at a conference I was attending. The day after Tony spoke, the conference was coming to an end. As I looked out the window getting ready to leave the conference venue, I noticed that it was raining and resigned myself to getting wet. To my surprise, at the door of the conference center was Tony Hsieh, the CEO of Zappos, giving out ponchos. As he handed one to me, I thought, 'Wow—they *anticipated* the weather and my need.' That's something I have never seen from senior leaders at any other business, and I wanted to work for and be a customer of Zappos."

ZAPPOS PLUS YOU

Since we constantly synthesize information as we acquire it, I suspect you have been thinking about how to bring the best of the Zappos Experience to your life or your business. But how do you translate that thinking into an action plan? In keeping with Confucius's observation that "a journey of a thousand miles begins with a single step," how do you decide on the step that is best for you?

While I can't hand you a poncho in anticipation of a rainstorm, I did anticipate that you and other leaders in your organization might benefit from a comprehensive assessment and action-planning tool to help you evaluate and drive change in areas such as

- Values viability

- Culture strength

- Operational excellence in service

- Brand elasticity

- Work stress reduction/employee pleasure enhancement

- Other areas related to lessons from *The Zappos Experience*

You will find your Action Assessment Toolkit titled How Zapponian Are You? at zappified.com/action or via the QR link given here.

Whether you elect to use the assessment and action-planning tool, decide to sign up for Zappos Insights (using the complimentary membership provided at the back of the book or joining directly by going to www.ZapposInsights.com), or dive directly into an area of obvious need, allow me to offer overall guidance about benefiting from the Zappos lessons.

1. ***Refine it to meet your need.*** Anything from Zappos that you might wish to incorporate into your business must be filtered through the lens of what will make it work for you. It is important that you conduct some level of self-assessment and do not simply mimic Zappos. For example, rather than adopting the Zappos 10 core values as your own, it would probably be better for you to emulate the process that Zappos used for uncovering and formalizing values that are already operating in your culture.

2. ***Think about the unconventional.*** While I certainly hope the preceding pages gave you ideas for ways to make incremental improvements in your business, I want to make sure that the underlying message of "big idea focus" is not missed. *The Zappos Experience* is a story of leaders who did not set out to follow a cookie-cutter template on how other online retailers were achieving short-term success. Instead, it is a lesson about leaders who passionately pursued goals that had a long-term timeline and resulted in a transformational legacy.

WHAT'S YOUR LEADERSHIP LEGACY?

Zappos is no longer in the shoe business; it is in the happiness business! Its leaders became passionate about a goal that transcended products or processes. Those leaders shifted their attention from business success to transformative objectives and, in the end, elevated their significance and their legacy. Columnist and author Irving Kristol once suggested that leaders need to define that "one big thing and stick with it. Leaders who had one very big idea and one big commitment are the ones who leave a legacy."

I am an advocate of taking the time to think of that "one big thing" that you want to accomplish as a leader and forging your own "leadership legacy statement." Leadership guru John Maxwell suggests, "People will summarize your life in one sentence. Pick it now."

When asked about a Zappos legacy statement, Tony Hsieh said, "I hope that Zappos can inspire other businesses to adopt happiness as a business model—letting happy customers and happy employees drive long-term profits and growth. Ultimately, it's all about delivering happiness."

So what's your leadership legacy statement? Go ahead and write it down—but, more important, live it! If you do, you truly will understand the transformational power of *The Zappos Experience*.

NOTES

Acknowledgments

p. xi "[E]ach book is a journey, an adventure, a hunt, a detective case, an experience, like setting foot in another continent in which you've never traveled. That's the joy of it.": David McCollough as quoted by Scott R. Lloyd, "A Celebration of Family History," *Church News*, May 8, 2010; http://www.lds churchnews.com/articles/59322/A-celebration-of-family-history.html.

Chapter 1

p. 4 "Cultures are maps of meaning through which the world is intelligible.": Peter Jackson, *Maps of Meaning: An Introduction to Cultural Geography* (Routledge, 1989).

p. 15 "The quality of customer service has been on a serious decline for years. Research from TARP Worldwide and the American Customer Satisfaction Index both agree.": Sherrie Mersdorf, *Whose Responsibility Is Customer Service?* (2010); http://survey.Cvent.com/blog/cvent-web-surveys-blog/whos -responsibility-is-customer-service.

p. 17 "[A] commitment to someone else's growth and development.": Peter Senge, *The Fifth Discipline* (New York, NY: Currency Doubleday, 1990).

Chapter 3

p. 53 "[T]he process of *acquiring, accommodating, assimilating* and *accelerating* new team members, whether they come from outside or inside the organization.": George Bradt and Mary Vonnegut, *Onboarding: How to Get Your New Employees Up to Speed in Half the Time* (New York, NY: John Wiley, 2009).

p. 60 "[O]ne of the best things about differentiation is that people in the bottom 10 percent . . . very often go on to successful careers at companies and in pursuits where they truly belong and where they can excel.": Jack Welch and Suzy Welch, The Welch Way (website), based on material from *Winning* (New York, NY: HarperCollins, 2005); www.welchway.com/Principles/Differentiation.aspx.

p. 63 "What gets measured gets done; what gets measured and fed back gets done well; what gets rewarded gets repeated.": John E. Jones, Ph.D., and William E. Bearley, Ed.D., *360° Feedback: Strategies, Tactics, and Techniques for Developing Leaders* (HRD Press, 1996).

p. 70   Information about eliminating annual performance reviews obtained from a study by the business publication *Workforce Management*; www.workforce .com.

Chapter 4

p. 81   "Conventional wisdom holds that to increase loyalty, companies must 'delight' customers by exceeding service expectations . . .": Matthew Dixon, Karen Freeman, and Nicholas Toman, "Stop Trying to Delight Your Customers," *Harvard Business Review* (2010); http://hbr.org/2010/07/stop-trying-to-delight-your -customers/ar/1.

p. 82   "[D]elivering wow through service.": Tony Hsieh, "How I Did It: Zappos's CEO on Going to Extremes for Customers," *Harvard Business Review* (2010); http://hbr.org/2010/07/how-i-did-it-zapposs-ceo-on-going-to-extremes-for -customers/ar/1.

Chapter 5

p. 104   "Zappos customer experience is seamless and integrated. Amazon would never upgrade shipping to overnight, for example . . .": Jason Busch of *Spend-Matters*, as quoted by Marshall Kirkpatrick, "Getting the Goods: The New Amazon/Zappos Supply Chain Story," *ReadWriteWeb* (July 22, 2009); http:// www.readwriteweb.com/archives/getting_the_goods_the_new_amazonzappos _supply_chai.php.

p. 104   "Amazon is a master of the supply chain. It's got so much capacity, . . . and Zappos is no slouch at rushing goods to your house . . .": Marshall Kirkpatrick, loc. cit.

p. 107   "If an eCommerce site is slow in loading a page, they are risking losing a potential sale. In an age where consumers have more and more options . . .": Joseph Yi, *Turn Your eCommerce Site Page Load Speeds into Speed Racer* (2010); http:// viralogy.com/blog/ecommerce/turn-your-ecommerce-site-page-load-speeds-into-speed-racer/.

p. 110   "[M]oments of truth": Jan Carlzon, *Moments of Truth* (New York, NY: Harper Collins, 1989).

p. 110   "[W]here people continually expand their capacity to create the results they truly desire, where new and expansive patterns of thinking are nurtured, where collective aspiration is set free.": Peter Senge, op. cit.

p. 114   Research on service breakdowns: Amy K. Smith and Ruth N. Bolton, "An Experimental Investigation of Service Failure and Recovery: Paradox or Peril?" *Journal of Service Research*, 1 (1), 1998, pp. 65-81.

p. 116   "Last week I ordered 2 pairs of black cargo shorts by Jag for the summer that's finally coming to Michigan. I've ordered from Zappos before . . .": "My Uncomplaint against Zappos," Karen, Midlife's a Trip (blog), May 26, 2009; www.midlifesatrip.com/my-un-complaint-against-zappos/.

p. 121   "My experience went off without a hitch through every moment of truth. The registration-through-purchase experience on the site, the in-process updates . . .": Chris Raeburn, "Zappos Is Just Okay, Service Encounters Onstage" (blog), July 10, 2010; www.servicemarketer.blogspot.com/2010/07/zappos-is-just-okay.html.

p. 123   "In language used by many Zapponians . . .": "Building Your Company's Vision," *Harvard Business Review,* 1996.

Chapter 6

p. 128   "Legendary brands forge deep bonds with consumers through narrative devices. They are storytellers, drawing from a library of timeless narratives . . .": Laurence Vincent, *Legendary Brands: Unleashing the Power of Storytelling to Create a Winning Market Strategy* (Chicago, IL: Dearborn Trade, 2002).

p. 128   "The customer wanted to return a tire. Never mind that the Nordstrom department-store chain sells upscale clothing, not automotive parts. According to company lore, the clerk accepted the tire because that's what the customer wanted.": Pamela Abramson, "Nordstrom's High Style," *Newsweek,* January 5, 1987, p. 43.

p. 129   "This is possibly the greatest consumer relations story of modern times— it's certainly pointed to as such in a multitude of business articles . . .": "Snopes.com Rumor Has It," www.snopes.com/business/consumer/nordstrom.asp.

p. 130   "[T]he second time we got married, and the third time—we're expecting her to be pregnant.": Greg and Tamara, YouTube video, www.youtube.com/watch?v=-Rrc4c-wLZg.

p. 132   "They e-mailed me back that they had. . . . I am a sucker for kindness.": Lamarr Zaz as quoted by Meg Marco, The Consumerist (blog), October 16, 2007; www.consumerist.com/2007/10/zappos-sends-you-flowers.html.

p. 134   "If you don't know where you are going, you will probably end up somewhere else.": Lawrence J. Peter and Raymond Hull, *The Peter Principle* (New York: William Morrow, 1969).

p. 139   Information about allowing staff to take care of the best interest of customers: Steve Downton, Hilbrand Rustema, and Jan Van Veen, *Service Economics: Profitable Growth with a Brand Driven Service Strategy* (Seattle, WA: On-Demand Publishing, 2010).

p. 141 "Happiness's best friend is kindness. And passion's best friend is generosity. Going forward, I think it's very hard to be passionate unless you're willing to be generous . . .": Seth Godin, YouTube video on Delivering Happiness page, *Happiness' Best Friend is Kindness*, 2010; www.delivering happinessbook.com/seth-godin-happiness-best-friend-is-kindness.

p. 141 "There's no better way for a brand . . . to put its money where its mouth (or heart) is than engaging in Random Acts of Kindness . . .": Alejandro Saavedra, *11 Crucial Consumer Trends for 2011*, December 19, 2010; www .alesaavedra.com/11-crucial-consumer-trends-for-2011.

Chapter 7

p. 155 "[R]ecommends that you use a 10-point response scale and ask customers how likely they are to refer your company to a friend or colleague.": Fred Reichheld, *The Ultimate Question: Driving Good Profits and True Growth* (Boston, MA: Harvard Business School, 2006).

Chapter 8

p. 181 "An organization's ability to learn, and translate that learning into action rapidly, is the ultimate competitive advantage.": Jack Welch, as quoted on multiple Internet sites, including www.brainyquote.com/quotes/quotes/j /jackwelch173305.html.

p. 181 "Contrary to the opinion of many, leaders are not born; they are made . . .": Vince Lombardi, *What It Takes to Be #1: Vince Lombardi on Leadership* (New York, NY: R.R. Donnelly, 2001).

p. 183 "Companies often misjudge the true motivations of their employees, imagining that compensation is their primary aspiration . . .": Chip Conley, *Peak: How Great Companies Get Their Mojo from Maslow* (San Francisco, CA: Jossey-Bass, 2007).

p. 186 Tom Rath, *StrengthsFinder 2.0* (New York, NY: Gallup Press, 2007).

p. 189 Matthew Kelly, *The Dream Manager* (New York, NY: Beacon, 2007).

p. 190 "self-efficacy": A. Bandura, "Self-Efficacy: Toward a Unifying Theory of Behavioral Change," *Psychological Review*, 84, 1977, pp. 191-215; www .psychology.about.com/od/theoriesofpersonality/a/self_efficacy.htm.

Chapter 9

p. 201   "While the value delivered by the airlines continues to diminish, Zappos is always striving to incrementally improve itself . . .": Tim Sanchez, "Zappos Airlines: A First Class Ticket to Customer Experience," Deliver Bliss: The Business of Customer Experience (blog), 2010; www.deliverbliss.com/2010/11/zappos-airlines-a-first-class-ticket-to-customer-experience.

p. 212   "Hundreds of 'social media experts' cite the company in their books, blogs, speeches, Webinars and the like . . .": David Meerman Scott, "The Trouble with Zappos," Web Ink Now (blog), 2010; www.webinknow.com/2010/12/the-trouble-with-zappos.html.

p. 213   "Rather than using social media tools to sell products, Zappos deliberately uses them to . . . connect on a more personal level with both employees and customers . . .": C. B. Whittemore, "Zappos Uses Social to Share Culture," Flooring the Customer (blog), 2010; www.flooringtheconsumer.blogspot.com/2010/11/zappos-uses-social-to-share-culture.html?utm_source=feedburner&utm_medium=feed&utm_campaign=Feed%3A+Flooring TheConsumer+%28Flooring+The+Consumer%29.

p. 214   "Zappos has set the bar for social media customer service. Its approach focuses on making authentic connections via social networks rather than selling or promoting products. . . .": Meghan Peters, "3 Examples of Stellar Social Media Customer Service [MASHABLE AWARDS]," Mashable (blog), November 23, 2010; www.mashable.com/2010/11/23/customer-service-award.

p. 215   "'Wal-Marting Across America' fake blog . . .": Pallavi Gogoi, "Wal-Mart's Jim and Laura: The Real Story," *Bloomberg BusinessWeek*, October 9, 2006; www.businessweek.com/bwdaily/dnflash/content/oct2006/db20061009_579137.htm.

p. 216   "Social media is ingrained into the Zappos culture. Zappos believes they don't even need a social media strategy—after the employees constantly post videos, tweet, and blog about their culture—they don't direct sell or market. . .": Bernie Brennan and Lori Schafer, "Putting the 'Zap' into Zocial Media," Open Mic: The SAS Publishing Blog, December 2, 2010; www.blogs.sas.com/publishing/index.php?/plugin/tag/bernie+brennan.

p. 219   "What has proven most interesting is the fact that even those shoppers who do *not* watch the video are converting . . .": Mark R. Robertson, "Videos Sell Products—Even If Users Don't Actually Watch Them," ReelSEO (blog), 2010; www.deliverbliss.com/2010/11/zappos-airlines-a-first-class-ticket-to-customer-experience.

p. 220 "Zappos knows what you did last summer. Or maybe what you did last time you were on the Zappos website . . .": Meghan Keane, "Behavioral Targeters Need to Find a Balance between Helpful and Creepy," Econsultancy: Digital Marketers United (blog), August 3, 2010; www.econsultancy .com/us/blog/6372-behavioral-targeting-needs-to-find-a-happy-medium -between-helpful-and-creepy.

p. 222 "I abandoned [a Zappos] search [for a pair of shorts] and did something else. . . .": Michael Learmonth, "The Pants That Stalked Me on the Web," Ad Age Digital (blog), August 2, 2010; www.adage.com/digitalnext /post?article_id=145204.

Chapter 10

p. 227 Information about Dr. David Abramis and others in regard to workplace fun: Mary Rau-Foster, "Humor and Fun in the Workplace," workplaceissues.com (blog), 2000; www.workplaceissues.com/arhumor.htm.

p. 228 "The extra effort companies put forth in difficult times makes a difference in how successful they are at boosting morale and retaining top talent in a strong economy.": Ted Marusarz, as quoted in "Hewitt Analysis Shows Steady Decline in Global Employee Engagement Levels," Hewitt online, July 29, 2010; http://origin-www.hewittassociates.com/Intl/NA/en-US /AboutHewitt/Newsroom/PressReleaseDetail.aspx?cid=8775.

p. 230 "Whoa! I bet the fire marshal loves that place!": Stephen Searer, "Office Snapshots Tours Zappos HQ," OfficeSnapshots.com, April 4, 2008; www.office snapshots.com/2008/04/04/office-snapshots-tours-zappos-hq.

p. 232 "The office used to be imagined as a place where employees punch clocks and bosses roam the halls like high-school principals, looking for miscreants. . . .": Malcolm Gladwell, "Designs for Working: Articles from The New Yorker, December 11, 2000"; www.gladwell.com/2000/2000_12_11_a_working.html.

p. 238 "The consequences of boredom for businesses and organizations include higher employment costs, . . . performance problems, . . . and reduced organizational effectiveness. . . .": Information contributed by William Bazler, Patricia Smith, and Jennifer Burnfield in Charles Spielberger, ed., Encyclopedia of Applied Psychology (Philadelphia, PA: Elsevier, 2004).

p. 246 "flow": Mihály Csíkszentmihályi, Flow: The Psychology of Optimal Experience (New York, NY: Harper & Row, 1990).

Chapter 11

p. 253 "[T]he ways in which work is organized—its pace and intensity, degree of control over the work process, sense of justice, and employment security, among other things—can be as toxic to the health of workers as the chemicals in the air. . . .": Peter Schnall, Marnie Dobson, and Ellen Rosskam, eds., *Unhealthy Work: Causes, Consequences, Cures (Critical Approaches in the Health, Social Sciences)* (Amityville, NY: Baywood Publishing, 2009).

p. 255   "For now, workplace naps remain the exception, rather than the rule.": Angela Haupt, "Why Power Naps at Work are Catching On," *Yahoo! Health* (Internet site), November 15, 2010;   www.health.yahoo.net/articles/sleep /why-power-naps-work-are-catching.

p. 261   "The tendency among humans is that we want to give back to those who have given to us. . . .": Robert Cialdini, *Influence: The Psychology of Persuasion* (New York, NY: William Morrow, 1993).

p. 267   "Companies with great word of mouth tend to operate by a simple, yet inspiring purpose and well-defined values. . . ."; Ben McConnell, "The Roots of Word of Mouth," Church of the Customer.com, June 10, 2009; www .churchofthecustomer.com/blog/word_of_mouth/page/3/.

Conclusion

p. 273   "The culture and the Zappos brand are such assets. . . ." : Jeff Bezos, "Video from Jeff Bezos about Amazon and Zappos," YouTube video, July 22, 2009; www. youtube.com/watch?v=-hxX_Q5CnaA.

p. 273   "Hubris Born of Success": Jim Collins, *How the Mighty Fall: And Why Some Companies Never Give In* (New York, NY: Harper Business, 2009).

p. 277   "[O]ne big thing and stick with it. Leaders who had one very big idea and one big commitment are the ones who leave a legacy.": Irving Kristol, as quoted on multiple Internet sites, including www.brainyquote.com/quotes /authors/i/irving_kristol.html.

p. 277   "People will summarize your life in one sentence. Pick it now.": John C. Maxwell, *Go for Gold: Inspiration to Increase Your Leadership Impact* (Nashville, TN: Thomas Nelson, 2008).

Much of the content of this book emerged from face-to-face meetings, telephone interviews, and other forms of support from Zappos employees and other stakeholders. These include, but are not limited to:

Aaron Magness, Abbie Morris, Alesha Giles, Alfred Lin, Alicia Jackson (AJ), Andi Root, Andrew Kovacs, Angie Holt, Annette M. Smith, Anthony Vicars, Ashley Perry, Augusta Scott, Austin Blair, Brandis Paden, Bridget Dorsey, Bryce Murry, Butch Hazlett, Chad A. Boehne, Chris Judd, Chris Nielsen, Chris Peake, Chris Winfield, Christa Foley, Christina Colligan, Christina Kim, Christina Mulholland, Cody Britton, Courtney Bareman, Craig Adkins, Crystal Reid, Dan

Campbell, Daniel Muskat, Dave Brautigan, David Hinden, David Tyler, Denise Reynolds, Dennis Wegenast, Derek Carder, Deryl Sweeney, Devlyn Torres, Donavan Roberson, Doug Meenach, Dylan Morris, Eileen Tetreault, Erica Weil, Erin Ryan, Faby Guido, Fred Mossler, Galen Hardy, Grace Kee, Graham Kahr, Greg Bowen, Greg Richards, Jamie Naughton, Jason Lee Menard, Jason Whittle, Jeanne Markel, Jeff Lewis, Jenn Lim, Jennifer Van Orman, Jerald Tidmore, Jesse Cabaniss, Jim Rowland, Jon Wolske, Josh Schlekewy, Josie Del Rio, Justin Williams, Karen Sue Miller, Kaycee Crow, Kayla Cline, Keith Glynn, Kristen Kaelin, Lacy Goodlett, Laura A. Miller, Laura Slaughter, Lauren Spenser, Leah Morris, Lianna Shen, Linda Utley, Lindsay Roberts, Lisanna Lawson, Liz Gregersen, Loren Becker, Mark Madej, Mary Falter, Mary Johnson, Mary Teitsma, Matt Wong, Matthew Dunaway, Miles Olson, Nicole Smith, Noel Cusimano, Pamela Cinko, Pamela Griggs, Phillip So, Rachael Brown, Rachel Cosgrove, Rafael Mojica, Rebecca Henry, Rhonda Ford, Rob Siefker, Robert Avila, Robert Richman, Roz Searcy, Sarah House, Sarah Johnson, Shannon Roy, Shawna Macias, Sheila Clinard, Sidnee Shaefer, Stacey Eddy, Stefanie Walls, Steve Hill, Steven Trentham, Sue Maurer, Susan Disbrow, Tami Lemke, Tammy Johns, Thomas Knoll, Timothy Clemons, Sr., Tom Austin, Tony Hsieh, Vanessa Lawson, Zack Davis

APPENDIX A:
SHARING GREAT CALLS

As outlined in Chapter 7, the Sharing Great Calls program at Zappos begins with the CLT member identifying a great customer call and sharing the call information with the CLT supervisor. The CLT supervisor then writes an e-mail to the customer, asking for feedback and the customer's input into the service that was received.

The following are examples of feedback received. The first example includes the e-mail sent to the customer from the CLT supervisor, but to avoid repetition, the remaining examples include only the customer response.

CUSTOMER: Melissa Holt
Hi Melissa! I'm Alexa, and I am the Lead for Tamara here at Zappos CLT, Inc. Our Team Member said what a great time she had talking to you! We have started a special program recently to provide further feedback to our Team Members. We want to give our Team Members an extra pat on the back, so I have a huge favor to ask of you. It will not take much of your time, but it will help us enormously. Please tell us about the service you received and any points of feedback regarding the conversation you had with our Team Member.

CUSTOMER FEEDBACK: Melissa Holt
First, I love Zappos! I have never had a negative experience with any of your customer service sales people, but Tamara was so helpful and went way above and beyond what any sales person has ever done for me in the past. I order a

lot, I mean a lot, online and through catalogs and have never met someone so nice and caring. By trying to find the right glove and size for my daughter, she made me feel like I really mattered and she cared to get my daughter the right pair. If you had more people like her, you wouldn't ever lose a customer. Thank you so much for having such a wonderful and helpful employee. I hope next time I call, I get her again. She also sent me a card, which made my day and put a HUGE smile on my face.

Thank you!!

CUSTOMER: Bruce Fisher
Outstanding service!!!! The best! Please take care of your employees because they are what make you different from the other websites. I can buy stuff from a number of websites, but employees like Michael S. make the difference in my buying decision-making process. . . . I have actually found products on other sites at a cheaper price, but I always come to Zappos because of employees like Michael S. that I know will give great service at a great price. In today's world it is very refreshing to deal with a company like Zappos that takes service to the customer very seriously, and that is the very reason for my shopping with Zappos. The employees handling your shipping are also the best—the product always arrives in great condition, unlike my experience at other online retailers. Keep doing what you're doing and take care of all your people because a great company operates from the ground up and your employees are the foundation that the entire company resting on, which is a fact that I think they forget to teach in business school these days.

CUSTOMER: Darleen Foreman
I am happy to talk about my experience with Lauren and to say what a great one it was indeed. She sounded so warm and pleasant, and she was also willing to be patient with me and to provide me with all of the information that I needed and to offer additional information to make my purchases as pleasing as could be. It felt as though I was shopping with a friend. It is always a wonderful thing when one can get a Sales Associate so willing to take a moment and truly be of assistance. Shopping online is fairly new to me; in fact my first purchase was from Zappos a few months ago. That person was also helpful and patient; however, the whole experience was different because of the circumstances (this time I wanted to make a purchase for my daughter who lives in Colorado and to have it shipped directly to her). Lauren walked me through the entire process—again, very patiently. I am grateful for her and for my new shoes that arrived in time for me to wear them job hunting. They are terrific,

my feet are thanking me, and I am thanking you. All of the accolades, gifts, money, etc. that you are allowed to give Lauren, she so deserves.

CUSTOMER: Julie Redinger

Hi Dana, Kim was OUTSTANDING!!! I had placed an order and didn't immediately realize that the card I had on file had been replaced and the numbers were not the same. It didn't dawn on me until the next day, and I dreaded the call as I knew it would be time consuming and probably involve my having to re-order online. I called Kim, and she quickly deleted the order and replaced it for me using the new number. It didn't delay my shoes arriving, which when you are only home 2 days a week is huge. If my order had been delayed, I would have had them sitting on my porch for 5 days, or I would have had to find someone to go to my house and pick them up. I need to add that Kim did this without my feeling like an idiot for using the wrong card or that this was any kind of inconvenience for her. She totally understood, and I felt like I was talking to a good friend, not just a voice on the other end. Believe it or not Kim made my day better. Traveling weekly is stressful, and having one thing go right can free up precious time at home. Kim gave me that time. Please thank her for me. Kim is the face (voice) of Zappos to your customers, and she speaks volumes about how important customer service is to your organization. So many other companies could learn a valuable lesson from you guys.

CUSTOMER: Matt Dobski

This was my first experience ordering a gift through Zappos. Aside from electronics, my experience ordering clothing online was less than perfect. Either the material was not what was expected, or the fit was inaccurate. As a result, what may have been an impulse buy turned out to be a hassle. Customer service, both online and in the retail stores, is terrible these days so my expectations were low. Having ordered the wrong dress size for my wife (I need some help there), I steeled myself for a lengthy interrogation about why I was exchanging the merchandise and then a long delay through the return mail and exchange process. Given that it was the holiday season, I expected, or have been conditioned to expect, that the person in customer service would give an attitude and really just wanted to be somewhere else. I could not have been more surprised.

From the start of the call, Dan answered with a positive, "I am here to help you" attitude. Honestly, I was caught off guard. Not only was he courteous, friendly, and professional, he was engaging in conversation. I was blown away. Here was someone who really got it and seemed to be enjoying his job. Clearly this was a part of culture that is missing in most companies today. So not only was the exchange so simple with the return labels sent via e-mail, but the customer service exceeded my expectations so much that I walked out of my office and asked if anyone else had ever bought anything online from Zappos. Those that hadn't, I shared my experience with and told them they had to try it. It is amazing. I can honestly say that you have converted a jaded consumer, and with service like I experienced with your team, you will have raving fans everywhere. Thank you for your refreshing approach to business and true customer service.

CUSTOMER: Veronica Fischer
Monday is NOT my favorite weekday, particularly after a long Thanksgiving weekend. However, if I could start every Monday talking with Heather and ordering from Zappos, it would be a wonderful start to Monday and the week! Heather was a gem. She was enthusiastic, knowledgeable, and totally engaging. She is a wonderful asset to your Zappos team. Good customer service can be elusive these days. If all your employees are "Heathers," you are fortunate, indeed! Thank you, Jean, for the truly great experience, and please convey to Heather my sincere thank you for the fun and great service. Additionally, "Merry Christmas"!

CUSTOMER: Lucy U. Vasquez
Thank you Zappos for a positive experience. It is uncommon today, whether offline or online shopping, to experience sincere and caring customer service representatives. It is apparent that the Zappos culture starts with the founder. The founder's "why" is the cornerstone for Zappos success. Zappos hires people who share in his "why," therefore, creating a happy environment for all their employees. The minute that Debbie answered my call, she made me feel special, like I was the only person in the universe that mattered to her at the time. When I could not find exactly what I was looking for, she volunteered to go online to help me look elsewhere. What a concept, Zappos *really* cares about their customers' needs! After creating a relationship with me, Debbie had me hook, line and sinker. I purchased my items from Zappos, not caring whether or not I had found the right color of sweatshirts for my grandsons. She also upgraded me to a VIP customer. I am now a loyal customer of Zappos, not interested in what Zappos sells but "why" Zappos sells what they sell. Debbie deserves a "pat on the back" and much more for sincerely projecting the Zappos culture to her customers.

CUSTOMER: Bonnie Greer

. . . I enjoyed speaking with Shannon and was hoping for a way I could compliment her service, and what a nice surprise to be able to do just that! My good friend Judy had been raving about Zappos forever, so I thought, why not? I am beyond thrilled that I finally listened. As I told Shannon, I suffer from fibromyalgia and experience pain every day. I try not to let it limit me (laughter is the best medicine!), but walking and the pain in my feet can be a real challenge sometimes. Finding a pair of shoes that don't add to that pain can also be a challenge! I'm hard to fit, and the salespeople at local comfort-shoe stores just don't seem to have the patience to help me find a comfortable shoe (can't say I blame them, nothing seems to be ok for me, and it must be very frustrating dragging out all those boxes or seeing me return what they've finally found me:)). And this is where your Shannon shines! I called with a particular shoe in mind (the Asics Gel Cumulus 12), and Shannon very enthusiastically confirmed I had made a good choice. I had tried the shoe on in a local sporting goods store but did not find the correct size. Not only was Shannon friendly and patient, but her cheerful attitude really reflected her genuine concern and compassion for my situation. She even suggested some other shoes I could try that she thought might help me find relief, and she very gently steered me away from a brand she thought might not fit my needs (this particularly impressed me; I love an honest salesperson!). I'd like to say that I ended up purchasing two other pairs of shoes on her advice . . . now *that's* a great salesperson! The entire transaction was so pleasant and easy, and Shannon was helpful and fun throughout. I really felt as if I was speaking with a new friend . . . a very knowledgeable friend! She's an asset to your company, and I'm very, very impressed. I'm looking forward to my new shoes and to being a Zappos customer for many years to come. Thanks for the opportunity to give you feedback, and thanks again for such great service.

APPENDIX B:
EXCERPTS FROM ZAPPOS
CULTURE BOOKS

Zappos culture to me is fantastic. To be a company that sells service, not just merchandise, is unknown by most people. And a company that not only wants to WOW their customers, but also WOW their employees, is very much unknown. Free lunches and free medical are both very hard to come by in a company. The Zappos culture of WOWing the customer and their employees is absolutely awesome. In the time I have been at Zappos, I have been WOWed myself by the managers and leads; that does not happen at other companies. I love Zappos culture.   —Darlene J., CLT

Zappos has a caring, nurturing environment. I have no doubt that I am a valued team member and my team (everyone at Zappos) wants me to succeed. We are empowered to make decisions on what we think will best serve our customers. We are all about giving our customers the best service they have ever received. That is made easy because that is how each individual at Zappos is treated! It is a happy place to be, and that makes one want to work all the harder to give the best they have!   —Donna M., CLT

Given that we are speaking of Zappos as a company I work for, I would like to say that the company, and how it is labeled, has changed for me over the years. It is no longer just my employer. Zappos is my family. I can see this sense of family when I hear anything involving the Zappos name or explain our culture to someone new. This is evident when I refer to Zappos as "us" or "we" and not "the company I work for" or "my job." My time here at Zappos is one of very few occasions in my life where I feel a sense of belonging and kinship. Being a part of this company has changed my life and its direction because I am beginning to experience, more and more, a sense of belonging with the friends I've made within the company and in other situations in my life. It feels as if Zappos was the actual reason for blessings in my life.   —Linda H., CLT

The culture at Zappos is absolutely amazing! It is awesome that each department can rely on other departments (something I have never experienced before). I love the fact that outside companies want to emulate what we have perfected.   —Andrea W., Help Desk

In the two years that I have been here, I have had the great pleasure of not only seeing some amazing changes, but also having a small hand in some of them. I have had a significant change in my role here at Zappos. My thoughts and way of thinking about our company culture have grown leaps and bounds. In many ways, I feel that our culture is even more defined. It's even more talked about. People have quality discussions about it. I think that in many ways, it's become very much like the "WOW" we give our customers. It's something you can see and touch.   **—Jacob P., Human Resources**

I have been part of the Zappos family for four years now. I have seen the company grow and change to what it is today. As we have matured as a company, our culture has been untouched. Zappos' culture is still the same as my first day in July 2001. I am WOWed just thinking about our growth and accomplishments. Our culture comes in many forms and expressions. We truly care about our partnerships with employees, customers and vendors. I have not worked for another company that treats everyone with respect.

—Ethel F., Corporate

I enjoy working at Zappos more, not less, as the company is growing. To me it is amazing as I've seen such transitions before, and in my previous experience(s) the bigger the company got, the more impersonal my work relationship became, and I would fill less and less significant as an employee. Not at Zappos; somehow we've managed to keep that cozy feeling of a small start-up company that is over one thousand employees big.

—Alex R., Tech Support

The most remarkable thing about Zappos Culture is camaraderie. In San Francisco, we were always very friendly with one another; in Las Vegas, we have truly become friends. The amazing thing is that this creates a feedback loop that helps us both as a company and as individuals. For me, as I've gotten to know people outside of work, I'm able to better understand them and know their strengths and abilities as they (I hope) are able to know and understand me and trust mine. Because we're better able to communicate with each other and work together, there's a wonderful shared sense of achievement upon achievement, which feeds back into the friendship. There's a small price, of course. I would be remiss to not mention that, like all relationships, friendships within the company can ebb and flow over time (hopefully more flow than ebb!). This can be a temporary stress. But on balance, the ability to be with new and exciting people outside of work makes work itself a much more congenial and sociable place.   **—Eric W., Development**

Perhaps the single most important factor that makes the Zappos culture so successful is respect. Zappos respects its employees! If it's important to the employees, it's important to Zappos. When I first came to Zappos, it was really mind altering . . . a company that goes out of its way to keep its employees happy?! And in turn we all contribute 110% towards the success of not only the company, but the Zappos family?! What a concept!

Norbinn R., Development

People come to Zappos from many different professional backgrounds. Frequently, they are impressed by the perks. However, the perks are really a by-product of the company's vision. The leadership seems very committed in making sure that people are not only comfortable in their work environment, but actually enjoy coming to work. I believe Zappos' goal is to provide everyone an environment that they love to thrive in. The Zappos workplace has a youthful zeal that is pervasive throughout each department. I can honestly say that I think Zappos is one of the best places on the planet to work. The people are unique, the culture is vibrant and the environment is uplifting. I am a very particular person and I honestly can't think of a place I would rather be.

—Richard B., System Administrator

Zappos.com culture may be many things to many people, but to me it's about creating change. It is about creating new processes, policies, strategies and goals to move forward. Contributing to the changes first-hand is what makes Zappos Culture different from other companies. We each have the ability to contribute to the change in a positive way. Zappos is an innovative company, and it is exciting to be a part of its change and its growth.

—Lisa M., Legal

This will be my second entry for the Culture Book. It got me thinking about what impresses me this year versus last year. Everything was so new last year. The impact was pretty big on me. Everything was new and powerful. Now, with a full year under my belt, I find that Zappos still WOWs me. As a company, Zappos still loves to evolve and not stay with the status quo. I love to be challenged and yet I also love to do what I am currently doing in my job with accounts payable. The WOW factor at Zappos gives me the option of learning new things by taking the classes that are now offered internally and still staying in my position. So while I continue to learn and expand my horizons, I can do my job and be ready for the day my inner drive says it is time to try the next challenging job Zappos has to offer. I LOVE THIS PLACE!! **—Debra J., Finance**

To me, Zappos Culture is about an entire company of individuals, who are not only allowed, but also encouraged to be themselves, working together to make the group stronger as a whole. When you have a company that is so honest and open about everything that goes on, whether it is in good or difficult times, it makes everyone feel as though they are truly part of a great organization— unlike most others. Because our culture brings us so close, we have an entire company of people who love being here, and who would do anything they can to help make the company successful. **—Jason C., Marketing**

The Zappos Culture to me is like a guideline to life and hope to live that life at Zappos. I think it gives you guidelines to the way you should act and respond to different happenings at Zappos. Also, the culture of Zappos teaches you to be yourself and not to change for anyone. How many places can you work and wear your style of clothing, piercing, hair, and tattoos any way you like; no- where, except for Zappos. The best advice I can give to you about working at Zappos is to be yourself, don't let anyone change you, live one day at a time and enjoy being here . . . this is your home away from home.

—Jenny H., KY Warehouse

The best way to sum up how I feel about Zappos is pride. I am so proud that our company is in the top 25 of the best places to work in Kentucky and the top 25 of the best places to work in the nation. I am so proud that the HR team works so hard to drive the culture at the FC in Kentucky and does such a great job. I am so proud that our employees get involved in the community, whether they are jumping in the Ohio River in February to support Special Olympics, or bowling to raise money for Big Brothers/Big Sisters or bed-racing during the Kentucky Derby Festival or walking to raise awareness for cancer or making sure local children have clothes and toys for the holidays. I am so proud that when I am out and meet new people and tell them I work at Zappos, they rave about how much they love us. I am so proud of Zappos.

—Andi P., KY Warehouse

Today, my job consisted of scaling a 40-foot-high ladder onto the roof of the old Zappos warehouse to shoot a group photo. Yesterday, I was photographing protein candy bars and then go to eat them. Tomorrow . . . well, tomorrow I'll probably get back to shooting adult apparel, children's apparel, footwear, elec- tronics or housewares. My point is that you never know what each day is go- ing to bring at Zappos. To be successful, you really have to embrace and drive change, and we do! I have been working here just over one year, and while my first year has zipped right by, I feel like I've known everybody in our depart- ment for years. Through so much change, we have been able to stick together as a team, all the while maintaining a positive atmosphere.

—Jimmy M., KY Warehouse

Working at Zappos makes me feel like I have my own business, but even better. Everyone you come across, from co-workers to vendors, wants you to succeed. With help from other departments, your ideas could come true in just a matter of a few minutes. There are no roadblocks, and you can go as crazy as you want, as long as you can learn from your mistakes. And the end result is rewarding—you are happy to be part of the family.

—Angela C., Merchandising

I love Zappos more than Chai Lattes and yoga and as much as lounging on the beach. Thank you, Uncle Zappos, for letting me be a buyer, teaching me and challenging me every day, and thank you for allowing me to work with my best friends.

Catie F., Merchandising

Zappos is like no other, and I love that. It's so refreshing to wake up every morning wanting to come to work. Wanting to actually see and interact with all your co-workers. Because this isn't just a job, and they're not just co-workers; they're all great friends. And when you get to go to work every day and work with all your friends and do what you love, it isn't work at all. They say time flies when you're having fun, and this last year has FLOWN by!

—Michelle F., Merchandising

So my first full year at Zappos has passed, and it is time to again write about what the culture means to me. Here is what I know: I know that this past year has gone by faster than any other I can remember. I know I have grown personally and professionally the most this past year. And this past year has been filled with the hardest work and the most fun I have ever had at a job. I think all of these contributed to the culture here at Zappos. Without them, none of what I accomplished this past year would have been possible. The culture here is priceless in that it allows us, as individuals, to be ourselves and grow and learn to better ourselves, and in turn, the company. I can only imagine what the next year(s) have in store, but because of the culture, I am thankful to be here and I am excited to experience it all!

—Dena M., Product Info

There is no question that Zappos has turned the brick and mortar business upside-down with their excellent customer service. However, the most impressive part of the Zappos stories is the professional manner in which the buyers interact with wholesalers. Calls are returned. Appointments are easily obtained. Follow-on meetings and orders are totally hassle-free. The buying group dresses and conducts themselves with professionalism on a full-time basis. Zappos has embraced the shoe industry by supporting shows and trade events, and senior management is very visible and approachable (clearly raising, if not destroying, the bar compared to the competition). Zappos employees are candid and open regarding the direction, methodology and mistakes of their business. Zappos has set a new standard that all retailers could learn from. The Zappos success is no fluke and is well deserved.

—**Bob L., Partner**

To me, Zappos Culture means revolution. The shoe business has become a sedentary, unchanging world, where the same old thing had become the daily grind. Zappos came along and turned the shoe industry upside down! It lit a collective fire under retailers and wholesalers alike, and breathed life into an otherwise comatose community. Many people doubted that your business model would survive, nonetheless flourish into what it's become. Zappos is now a household name, and should be in the dictionary. We are all proud to be a part of what you have accomplished. —**Daniel L., Partner**

I have been a business partner with Zappos since the days when the company was headquartered on Van Ness Street in San Francisco. Over the years, I have experienced the Zappos Culture as it relates to the concept of partnership. Zappos has taken the concept to an unprecedented level where personal and business relationships are of mutual benefit. Many retailers talk about relationships of mutual benefit; some pursue it in a cavalier way, but few achieve the desired goal. Zappos is in a league of its own. Zappos has distinguished itself from the rest of the retail community, which is most commendable. The Zappos Culture reinforces the values of good working relationships based on trust and integrity. As vendors, we are made to feel important and appreciated. Our contributions to your sales and earnings are valued, which makes us feel like members of the Zappos team. We are vendors, but Zappos Culture makes us feel like associates. Thanks for this association, and for the opportunity to be a part of this exciting on-going retail adventure. —**Lewis G., Partner**

Zappos lives in this world of high expectation. It used to be that the measure of service was Nordstrom, but no longer. Next day delivery, huge selection, easy returns . . . all of the components of the business pale to what Zappos really gives: old fashioned service. Zappos combines the best of what technology has to offer with an emphasis on the basics—treating the customer with respect. What is the culture of Zappos? To me it is a combination of technology, old school service, and the ability to laugh. I find myself lucky to be part of the process. —**Dominique S., Partner**

INDEX

ABOUT THE AUTHOR

Dr. Joseph Michelli is a sought after keynote speaker, workshop presenter, organizational consultant, and the Chief Experience Officer of The Michelli Experience.

He has dedicated his career to helping leaders create compelling customer experiences and dynamic workplace cultures. In addition to *The Zappos Experience*, Dr. Michelli is a *New York Times* bestselling author who has written books such as

- *The Starbucks Experience: 5 Principles for Turning Ordinary into Extraordinary*

- *Prescription for Excellence: Leadership Lessons for Creating a World Class Customer Experience from UCLA Health System*

- *The New Gold Standard: 5 Leadership Principles for Creating a Legendary Customer Experience Courtesy of The Ritz-Carlton Hotel Company*

Additionally, Dr. Michelli and John Yokoyama, the owner of the World Famous Pike Place Fish Market in Seattle, Washington, coauthored *When Fish Fly: Lessons for Creating a Vital and Energized Workplace*.

Dr. Michelli transfers his knowledge of exceptional business practices through keynotes and workshops. These informative and entertaining presentations focus on the skills necessary to

- Create meaningful customer experiences

- Drive employee and customer engagement

- Enhance a commitment to service excellence

- Create quality improvement processes

- Increase employee morale

In addition to dynamic and relevant international keynote presentations, The Michelli Experience offers

- Consultation on the development of optimal customer and employee experiences
- Service excellence training
- Enhancement of staff empowerment
- Leadership team development services
- Group facilitation and team-building strategies
- Creation of customer and employee engagement measurement processes
- Customized management and frontline training programs

For more information on how Dr. Michelli can present at your event, provide training resources, or consult with you, please visit www.josephmichelli.com.

Dr. Michelli is eager to help you achieve a Zappos Experience. He can be reached through his website, by e-mail at josephm@ josephmichelli.com, or by calling either (734) 697-5078 or (888) 711-4900 (toll free within the United States). Follow him on Twitter: twitter.com/josephmichelli.

DELIVERING Happiness

First a book, then a bus tour, and now... a company with a cause: to grow a movement that inspires happiness at work, home and the world at large.

Delivering Happiness exists to nurture the **global community** that's sprung up around this movement and to spread happiness, one at a time. How? Some of the ways...

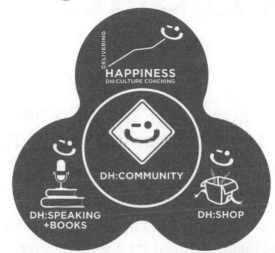

DH:SHOP
a hand-picked selection of inspirational gear and goods to deliver happiness to yourself and others

DH:SPEAKING +BOOKS
books and talks given by the DH Team, Tony Hsieh (CEO, Zappos.com) and Jenn Lim (CEO and Chief Happiness Officer, DH)

DH:CULTURE COACHING
helping companies apply happiness as a business model while strengthening their individual company culture

Take the first step to nudging our world towards a happier place.

Are you ready to **Inspire and be Inspired?**
For more info: **info@DeliveringHappiness.com**
Join the movement at: **www.DeliveringHappiness.com**
f facebook.com/DeliveringHappiness
t @DHMovement

insights Z ™

FOR A FREE 30-DAY TRIAL OF ZAPPOS INSIGHTS, GO TO ZAPPIFIED.COM/CODE.

As a member, you will have access to tools and templates to create a strong culture, networking with other professionals who are driving culture, and best practices from cutting-edge authors and experts in the fields of customer service, engagement, and growth. Come be a part of the Zappos family!

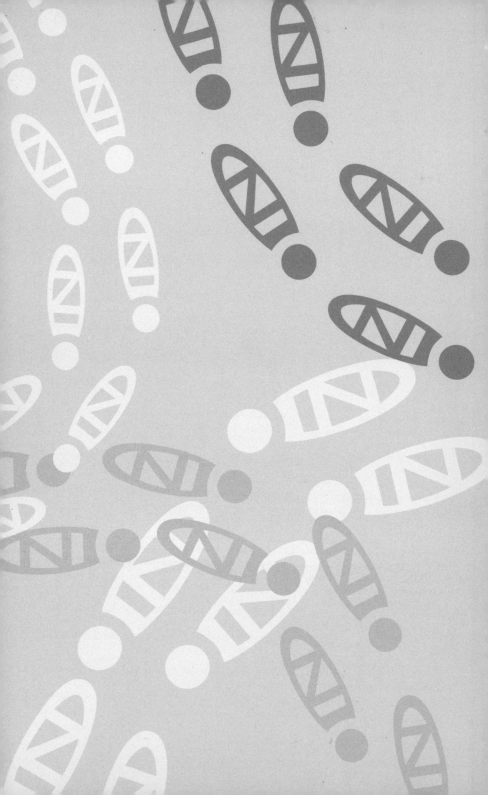